# OUR HOLY FAITH

# OUR HOLY FAITH

BOOK EIGHT

# ALPHA AND OMEGA

TAN Books

Gastonia, North Carolina

Originally published in 1960 as *Our Holy Faith Book VIII: To Live Is Christ* by Bruce Publishing Company and reprinted in 1998 by The Neumann Press.

Nihil Obstat:
John F. Murphy, S.T.D.
Censor Librorum

Imprimatur:
William E. Cousins
Archbishop of Milwaukee
October 6, 1959

This TAN Books edition has been re-typeset and enhanced with additional content and revisions, including modernized language and updates to the practices of the Catholic Church. Catechism questions and answers have been replaced with the TAN edition of *The Third Council of Baltimore: Baltimore Catechism 1–4*.

Excerpts from the English translation of the Catechism of the Catholic Church for use in the United States of America © 1994, United States Catholic Conference, Inc.—Libreria Editrice Vaticana. Used with permission.

Scripture quotes are from the Douay-Rheims 1899 American Edition and are in the public domain.

Content revisions and updates by Elisa Torres

Interior design by Caroline Green and David Ferris
Cover design by www.davidferrisdesign.com

ISBN: 978-1-5051-1927-5

Published in the United States by
TAN Books
PO Box 269
Gastonia, NC 28053
www.TANBooks.com

Printed in the United States of America

# Contents

# Publisher's Note

The original editions of the Our Holy Faith series textbooks were published between 1959 and 1964. They were compiled by many different authors over the course of several years. Consequently, the texts varied in their organization from year to year, with similar sections appearing with different names throughout the series and often in varying sequences.

For greater ease of use and consistency, we have reorganized each book so that the Catechism lessons, tests, and other exercises are placed at the end of each relevant chapter or lesson. We have also included answer keys for your convenience in the back of each book.

While the teachings in the original editions remain relevant due to the enduring truths of our Faith, it was necessary to update other aspects in order to more accurately reflect the Church today. These new editions have been revised to incorporate some of the changes to the practices of the Catholic Church.

To the extent possible, we have adapted the text to reflect both the ordinary and extraordinary forms of the Mass and liturgical calendars. In addition to these updates, we have inserted, where relevant to the text, traditional prayers and quotes from the Bible, the Catechism, and the saints.

This new Our Holy Faith series is faithful to the work of the original authors. It honors the fundamental and unchanging truths of the Catholic Church and is heavily influenced by tradition. We believe it is the catechesis you can trust with your children's faith.

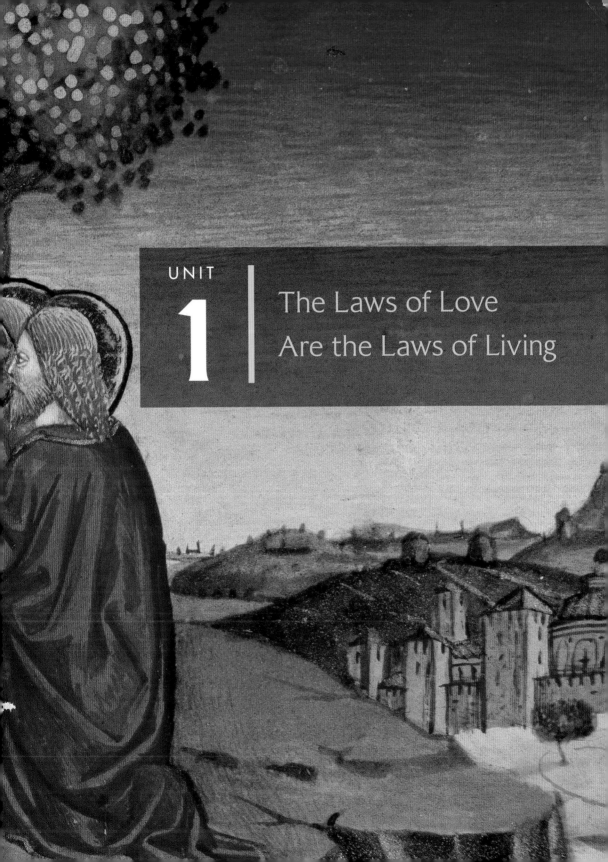

# The Laws of Love
# Are the Laws of Living

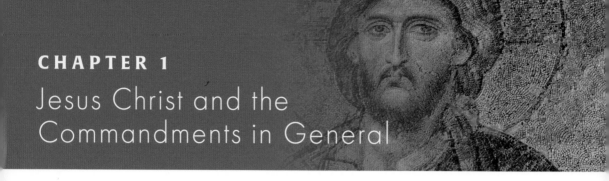

# CHAPTER 1

# Jesus Christ and the Commandments in General

### LESSON 1

# The Two Great Commandments

In this section we shall review the commandments in general and see how their observance helps us to lead a true Christian life. Second, we shall see how the law of charity (love), the first great commandment, is at the very heart of all Christ's teaching. Only when we practice charity can we serve Christ as He wishes us to serve Him.

Volunteering at a homeless shelter is one way which we can practice charity.

> *"You see that a person is justified by works and not be faith alone. … For just as the body without the spirit is dead, so faith without works is also dead."*
>
> —*James 2:24, 26*

### Faith Without Good Works Is Dead

We are fortunate to be members of the Catholic Church, which teaches the truths needed for salvation. Is believing in the truth of the Church and its teachings enough for our salvation? Will faith alone save us? The New Testament is clear on this point: "You see that a person is justified by works and not by faith alone" (James 2:24). *Besides believing what God has revealed, we must also act in accordance*, if we wish to be saved. We must believe the doctrines which God has revealed and practice the moral directives He gave us in the commandments. Just because a person is a Catholic, a member of Christ's Church, does not mean he will automatically be saved. To be saved, he must lead a good life and serve God by keeping His commandments. However, we must be careful to understand that the Church, while recognizing the true role of "works" in salvation, does *not* teach that our own actions (when apart from the grace won for us by Christ) are capable of meriting and attaining salvation. Both the letter of James and St. Paul teach that there is a necessary relationship between faith and works for the Christian. For James, faith and works must be united to each other the way a body and a soul are united in a living being: "For just as the body without the spirit is dead, so faith without works is also dead" (James 2:26). In his letter to the Galatians, St. Paul spoke of "faith working through love" (Gal. 5:6). Thus, we must understand that neither faith nor works *in and of themselves* lead to righteousness. Rather, our faith is made alive through works, and our good works flow from the love of Christ, the Savior, in Whom we put all our faith.

Thus, we see that it is not enough for us to belong to the Church and to hear and believe the Word of God; we must keep it. In the Sermon on the Mount, Christ also taught the importance of "doing" when He said: "Not everyone who says to me, 'Lord, Lord,' shall enter the kingdom of heaven; but he who does the will of my Father in heaven shall enter the kingdom of heaven" (Mt. 7:21). St. James preached the same truth: "Be doers of the word," he said, "and not hearers only" (James 1:22). What did he mean by this? He meant that besides believing what God has revealed, we must do as God teaches us if we wish to be saved.

## The Law of God Is the Law of Love

One day a Jewish doctor of the law thought he could make Jesus look foolish. He asked Him which was the first commandment of all. Jesus replied, "Thou shalt love the Lord thy God with thy whole heart, and with thy whole soul, and with thy whole mind, and with thy whole strength. This is the first commandment. And the second is like it: Thou shalt love thy neighbor as thyself." By quoting these words from the book of Deuteronomy, our Lord summed up the Ten Commandments in the two commandments of love of God and love of neighbor.

Like the good Samaritan, you must love your neighbor as yourself, practicing charity especially when it seems difficult.

Why did Christ declare that the commandment of love is the most important? Why do we say that these two commandments contain all the commandments? Because, if we love a person, we will serve that person. So if we love God we will adore Him; we will not take His name in vain; and we will attend Mass. If we love our neighbor, we will respect his life, his property, and his reputation.

St. Augustine clearly explains that as we need two feet to walk, so we must have the love of God and love of neighbor if we wish to enter heaven. As the bird needs two wings to fly, so we must be borne aloft upon these two commandments if we would soar up to heaven.

In order to comply with our Lord's expressed wish *to love God, our neighbor, and ourselves we must keep the commandments of God and of the Church, and perform the spiritual and corporal works of mercy*. Before studying the commandments, we shall discuss the works of mercy, as they put emphasis on what we should *do*, whereas the commandments are more concerned with what we should avoid.

**The Corporal Works of Mercy Relieve the Physical Needs of Our Neighbor's Body**

The works of mercy are a check list of positive practices of love of neighbor. Christ is our example and model in practicing them. There are numerous instances in the Bible which illustrate Christ's charity toward His fellow men. Can you relate any? Which works of mercy did Christ perform in these examples: Mk. 6:34–44; Lk. 10:30–37; Lk. 15:11–32?

As our divine Saviour devoted Himself to caring for man's spiritual and corporal (bodily) needs, so we should also follow His example and prove our love for neighbor by our works of mercy. *The chief corporal works of mercy are seven*:

1. *To feed the hungry.*
2. *To give drink to the thirsty.*
3. *To clothe the naked.*
4. *To visit the imprisoned.*
5. *To shelter the homeless.*
6. *To visit the sick.*
7. *To bury the dead.*

Christ regards these deeds of charity done to others as done to Himself, for He said that at the last judgment He would say to those on His right hand: "I was hungry and you gave me to eat; I was thirsty and you gave me to drink; I was a stranger and you took me in; naked and you covered me; sick and you visited me; I was in prison and you came to me." And if, at the last judgment, they ask Him when they did these things, He will tell them, "Amen I say to you, as long as you did it for one of these, the least of my brethren, you did it for me" (Mt. 25:35 ff.). What a glorious opportunity is ours—to serve Christ in our fellow men!

If we perform the corporal works of mercy, we shall receive the promised reward: "Blessed are the merciful, for they shall obtain mercy."

**The Spiritual Works of Mercy Relieve the Spiritual Needs of Our Neighbor's Soul**

Christ also commanded us to practice the seven *chief spiritual works of mercy*:

1. *To admonish the sinner.*

2. *To instruct the ignorant.*

3. *To counsel the doubtful.*

4. *To comfort the sorrowful.*

5. *To bear wrongs patiently.*

6. *To forgive all injuries.*

7. *To pray for the living and the dead.*

The spiritual works of mercy are deeds of love performed to help guard our neighbor from spiritual harm and to lead him to grace and salvation. They are greater than the corporal works of mercy, as we know from the words of Christ (Mt. 10:28).

If we have true charity, we shall love people we might not naturally like, especially if they are poor, or destitute, or are people who offend us. They are all children of God. How sublime is the example of our divine Saviour who prayed for and forgave those who crucified Him!

Have you read about Father Damien, who devoted his life to the service of the lepers and became a leper himself? Do you know about St. Peter Claver, a Jesuit priest? In Cartagena, Colombia, he labored forty years among the slaves and became a slave of the slaves. Do you realize that

The works of mercy are charitable actions by which we come to the aid of our neighbor in his spiritual and bodily necessities. Instructing, advising, consoling, comforting are spiritual works of mercy, as are forgiving and bearing wrongs patiently. The corporal works of mercy consist especially in feeding the hungry, sheltering the homeless, clothing the naked, visiting the sick and imprisoned, and burying the dead. Among all these, giving alms to the poor is one of the chief witnesses to fraternal charity: it is also a work of justice pleasing to God.

—*Catechism of the Catholic Church, 2447*

> *"The bread you store up belongs to the hungry; the cloak that lies in your chest belongs to the naked; the gold you have hidden in the ground belongs to the poor."*
>
> —*St. Basil the Great*

priests, sisters, brothers, and lay teachers spend their lives in Catholic schools instructing youth in religion and other subjects? For this they "shall shine as stars for all eternity" (Dan. 12:3). There are numerous examples of saints who practiced the spiritual works of mercy. Can you mention any examples of spiritual works of mercy which can be practiced right in the family?

You have many opportunities to show your charity in a spiritual way. The missionaries in faraway lands, as well as the priests of your parish, need active helpers in gaining souls for God. You can share in the missionaries' work of instructing those who have not heard the Gospel by praying and by making sacrifices for them. Your kind words or good deeds to those who are in sorrow or are suffering may comfort and cheer them. Being a true Christian, you can imitate Christ by suffering wrongs patiently and forgiving injuries. Would you be performing a work of mercy if you included in your night prayers the needs of our Holy Father? How are you bringing others closer to Christ? Are you a real Apostle for Christ and His Church?

As you read this paragraph call to mind a building you know. Recall how one stone supports another and thus keeps the whole structure strong and intact. We can think of the Church as a *spiritual* edifice. One member must aid and sustain another. Charity is the cement that binds us to our neighbor and keeps us all firm.

We should accustom ourselves to the daily practice of the works of mercy. It entails so little labor, but brings so great a heavenly reward. The works of mercy are the proof of our faith, the testimony of our love for God, the citizenship papers for God's kingdom. For only if we perform them can we hope to hear Christ, our future Judge, say: "Come blessed of my Father, take possession of the kingdom . . . for I was hungry and you gave me to eat . . . Amen I say to you, as long as you did it for one of these the least of my brethren, you did it for me" (Mt. 25:34–40).

### The Works of Mercy are an Obligation

The works of mercy put an obligation on us, for we read in the catechism that *everyone is obliged to perform the works of mercy, according to his own ability and the need of his neighbor.* This obligation varies with our condition in life, our vocation, and also with the degree of the neighbor's needs. For instance, it is obvious that a millionaire has a greater obligation to help the poor and the needy of his city than does a wage earner with a large family. Would the obligations of a bishop of a diocese and that of a layman be the same? Why not?

If it is difficult for us to perform corporal works, we can always offer spiritual help, such as prayer. What really counts before God is not the *amount* we give, but the good *intention* with which we give what we can. St. Paul makes it clear in one of his letters. He says: "If I distribute all my goods to feed the poor, . . . and yet do not have charity, it profits me nothing" (1 Cor. 13:3).

Besides the chief corporal and spiritual works of mercy there are other true works of mercy. Can you think of any? We read in

**TERMS TO KNOW**

- voluntary
- poverty
- spiritual
- neighbor
- commandments
- law
- counsel
- observance
- corporal
- goods ability
- chastity
- satisfied
- recommend
- perpetual
- obedience

the catechism that *all the ordinary deeds done every day to relieve the corporal or spiritual needs of others are true works of mercy, if done in the name of Christ*. Hence it is wise to begin the day by consecrating our deeds to God and by resolving to do everything during the day for the love of Him.

As the works of mercy give us a list of positive practices which show our love of God and our love of neighbor, so the Ten Commandments present a list of things we should *not* do if we love God and our neighbor. We must observe them faithfully because through our observance of them we prove our love for God, at least in a minimum way.

*We should not be satisfied merely to keep the commandments of God, but should always be ready to do good deeds, even when they are not commanded*. Children who really love their parents do not wait to be commanded to do things to please them. They do more than is expected of them. If God is our closest friend and greatest benefactor, and we say that we love Him, we will not only want to obey His commandments but we will also be willing to do extra things, to make sacrifices to prove our love for Him.

Thus far we have seen that the commandments state the minimum requirements for our salvation. Here we might recall the words of Christ: "If you love me, keep my commandments" (Jn. 14:16).

## Christ Invites Man to the Life of Perfection

Keeping the commandments is the beginning of love. Christ called us to a higher degree when He said: "If thou wilt be perfect, go sell what thou hast, and give to the poor, and thou shalt have treasures in heaven; and come follow me" (Mt. 19:21). This is the invitation that our Lord gave to the rich young man who was not satisfied with merely keeping God's commandments. It is an invitation to a life of close and intimate union with God. Such a life is called the life of higher perfection. It is based on the counsels which our Lord gave over and above the commandments.

For those who wish to love God with all their hearts, our Saviour especially recommends the observance of the Evangelical Counsels. This is the invitation that our Lord gave to the rich young man.

For those who wish to love God with all their hearts, *our Saviour especially recommends the observance of the Evangelical Counsels—voluntary poverty, perpetual chastity, and perfect obedience*. They are called "evangelical" because they appear in the Gospels; and they are called "counsels" because they are an invitation and not a command. All are invited to practice them, but no one is forced. As our divine Saviour says: "Not all can accept this teaching; but those to whom it has been given" (Mt. 19:11).

## Summary

To be saved we must not only believe what God has revealed, but must also keep God's laws. The two great commandments that contain the whole law of God are: (1) Thou shalt love the Lord thy God with thy whole heart, and with thy whole soul, and with thy whole mind, and with thy whole strength; (2) Thou shalt love thy neighbor as thyself.

We love God, our neighbor, and ourselves: (1) by keeping the commandments of God and of the Church; (2) by performing the spiritual and corporal works of mercy. There are ten command-

Everyone is obliged to perform the works of mercy, according to his own ability and the need of his neighbor.

ments of God, five precepts of the Church, seven chief corporal works of mercy, and seven chief spiritual works of mercy. We should not be satisfied with merely keeping the commandments of God, but should always be ready to do good deeds, even when they are not commanded. Everyone, however, is obliged to perform the works of mercy, according to his own ability and the need of his neighbor.

 **FOR ME TO REVIEW**

*Catechism Lesson*

**1127. Q. Which are the commandments that contain the whole law of God?**

A. The commandments which contain the whole law of God are these two: 1st, Thou shalt love the Lord thy God with thy whole heart, with thy whole soul, with thy whole strength, and with thy whole mind; 2nd, Thou shalt love thy neighbor as thyself.

**1128.** Q. Why do these two commandments of the love of God
and of our neighbor contain the whole law of God?

A. These two commandments of the love of God and of
our neighbor contain the whole law of God because all
the other commandments are given either to help us
to keep these two, or to direct us how to shun what is
opposed to them.

**819.** Q. Which are the chief corporal works of mercy?

A. The chief corporal works of mercy are seven: To feed
the hungry, to give drink to the thirsty, to clothe the
naked, to ransom the captive, to harbor the harborless,
to visit the sick, and to bury the dead.

**813.** Q. Which are the chief spiritual works of mercy?

A. The chief spiritual works of mercy are seven: To
admonish the sinner, to instruct the ignorant, to
counsel the doubtful, to comfort the sorrowful, to bear
wrongs patiently, to forgive all injuries, and to pray for
the living and the dead.

**812.** Q. How can we know spiritual from corporal works
of mercy?

A. We can know spiritual from corporal works of mercy,
for whatever we do for the soul is a spiritual work, and
whatever we do for the body is a corporal work.

**1130** Q. Which are the commandments of God?

A. The commandments of God are these ten:

1. I am the Lord thy God, who brought thee out of the
land of Egypt, out of the house of bondage. Thou shalt
not have strange gods before me. Thou shalt not make
to thyself a graven thing, nor the likeness of any thing
that is in heaven above, or in the earth beneath, nor
of those things that are in the waters under the earth.
Thou shalt not adore them, nor serve them.

2. Thou shalt not take the name of the Lord thy God in vain.

3. Remember thou keep holy the Sabbath day.

4. Honor thy father and thy mother.

5. Thou shalt not kill.

6. Thou shalt not commit adultery.

7. Thou shalt not steal.

8. Thou shalt not bear false witness against thy neighbor.

9. Thou shalt not covet thy neighbor's wife.

10. Thou shalt not covet thy neighbor's goods.

**310.** **Q. Is it enough to belong to God's Church in order to be saved?**

A. It is not enough to belong to the Church in order to be saved, but we must also keep the commandments of God and of the Church.

**109.** **Q. What is Charity?**

A. Charity is a theological virtue by which we love God above all things for His own sake, and our neighbor as ourselves for the love of God.

**111.** **Q. Is grace necessary to salvation?**

A. Grace is necessary to salvation, because without grace we can do nothing to merit heaven.

*Questions and Exercises*

## **Part 1**: Multiple Choice

1. Another name for the Ten Commandments is:
   A. counsels.
   B. gifts.
   C. the Beatitudes.
   D. the Decalogue.

2. The laws of God bind:
   A. all men.
   B. only Catholics.
   C. Protestants and Catholics.
   D. only those who believe He exists.

3. Poverty, chastity, and obedience are called:
   A. evangelical counsels.
   B. the Beatitudes.
   C. laws.
   D. gifts.

4. To bear wrongs patiently is one of the:
   A. corporal works of mercy.
   B. commandments of God.
   C. spiritual works of mercy.
   D. precepts of the Church.

5. The Ten Commandments of God were given by God Himself to:
   A. Abraham.
   B. Moses.
   C. Jacob.
   D. St. Peter.

6.  The commandments are divided into two divisions.
    The first division indicates our duties to:
    A. ourselves.
    B. our neighbor.
    C. God.
    D. nature.

7.  All ordinary deeds to help others in body and soul, if done
    in the name of Christ, are:
    A. gifts of the Holy Spirit.
    B. works of mercy.
    C. theological virtues.
    D. the Beatitudes.

8.  To "counsel" means:
    A. to command.
    B. to reprove.
    C. to desire.
    D. to give advice.

9.  God's law is expressed in the:
    A. commandments.
    B. counsels.
    C. the Beatitudes.
    D. gifts of the Holy Spirit.

**Part 2**: Problems for Discussion

1.  Marie has great influence over her friend, Rita. She knows that Rita is watching television shows that celebrate and portray sinful behavior, and hanging out with friends who encourage similar behavior. Is there a spiritual work of mercy which Marie might perform in Rita's regard? How might she go about it?

2.  Before the arrival of the early Catholic missionaries in the New World, could the Indians of our country have known anything about any of the Ten Commandments? Explain.

3.  What spiritual and corporal works of mercy can we, at our age and state in life, perform?

### FOR ME TO DO

1.  In a short paragraph of three or four sentences explain: "Why I should love God above all things."

2.  List ways in which the commandments are a means to happiness in the family, Church, and State.

3.  Use the word "commandment" to make an acrostic.

4.  Make a mural showing the works of mercy performed, e.g., in hospitals, in charitable institutions, by social workers, in parishes and schools.

5.  Report incidents showing how Catholic missionaries today practice the corporal works of mercy. Consult reports describing the work in the foreign missions.

6.  Write a list of occasions on which you are expected to be a Good Samaritan.

7.  Report on the Works of Mercy illustrated in the life of one of the following or similar saints: St. Vincent de Paul, St. Peter Claver, St. Elizabeth, St. John Bosco.

# CHAPTER 2

# Jesus Christ and the First Three Commandments

# The First, Second, and Third Commandments of God

## The First Commandment

*I am the Lord your God, who brought you out of the land of Egypt, out of the house of slavery; you shall have no other gods before me.*

This commandment is concerned chiefly with the worship and adoration God deserves. As the verse where we first find the first commandment makes clear, God is most deserving of our whole hearted worship, for he has brought us "out of the house of slavery"(Ex. 20:2). This commandment means that we must show our love for God in the highest possible way. In our everyday life we honor people who are outstanding because they have done great things. We look upon Washington and Lincoln as great men and we try to show them the respect and honor we feel they deserve. We love and honor Mother Mary and the saints too. But we never adore or worship them, for only God is worthy of this. He is the Supreme Being, Creator of heaven and earth and all things. He alone merits the worship of adoration and, in adoring Him, we acknowledge that He is the Sovereign Lord, the one to whom we owe all we are and have.

## We Worship God by Faith

You can likely think of countless instances where you have shown "faith" in other people. You believe your parents when they answer your questions. You believe your teachers and the books you read in school. You believe your friends when they tell you what they have been doing. If we believe men when they tell us things, then how much more should we believe all that God has revealed? He is God, and there is no question of being deceived, for He can neither deceive nor be deceived. Nevertheless, spiritual faith (a theological virtue that comes by grace) is not the same thing as merely believing something without understanding it or possessing concrete evidence. Faith, or a deeper faith, is something we ought to pray for which gives us a special kind of spiritual "vision"; we cannot increase our faith merely by telling ourselves we should believe something even if we feel no reason to believe it.

God alone merits the worship of adoration. Like the centurion in the Gospel, we offer this worship through faith.

Do you recall how the centurion came to Jesus and asked Him to cure his servant? The centurion's faith in Christ's power was so firm that our Lord healed his servant and praised his faith publicly: "Amen, I say to you, not even in Israel have I found such great faith" (Lk. 7:9).

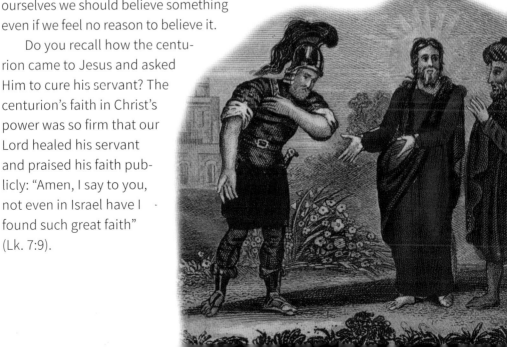

In every Mass the priest uses the words of the centurion in making his great act of faith. What are they?

Again, our faith in God is not something purely natural; in Baptism we received the supernatural virtue of faith, a gift from God. *Faith obliges us: to make efforts to find out what God has revealed; to believe firmly what God has revealed; and to profess our faith openly whenever necessary.*

*A Catholic can best safeguard his faith by making frequent acts of faith, by praying for a strong faith, by studying his religion very earnestly, by living a good life, by good reading, by refusing to associate with the enemies of the Church, and by not reading books and papers opposed to the Church and her teaching.*

Our faith can become weak through lack of exercise; it can be lost by neglecting it or by sinning against it. *A Catholic sins against faith by apostasy, heresy, and indifferentism.*

**We Worship God by Hope**
*Hope obliges us to trust firmly that God will give us eternal life and the means to obtain it.*

We sin against hope by presumption and despair. *A person sins by presumption when he trusts that he can be saved by his own efforts without God's help, or by God's help without his own efforts.* An attitude of presumption sounds like the following: "Well, God is good and merciful and even if I have not led a good life, I can go right on doing as I please and when I come to die, I am sure that God will give me a last-minute chance to repent." Or, "Oh, I am doing all right; I do not need God's help. I can manage pretty well by myself."

Another abuse of this gift of hope is to be found in the tragic story of Judas. In what way did he sin against hope? His case is one of despair. A *person sins by despair when he deliberately refuses to trust that God will give him the necessary help to save his soul.* There is never a valid reason to despair in this way, precisely because Christ has overcome sin for us and has the power to save even those who are most far from God. Paul testified to God's perfect ability to save us when he said, "I can do all things through him [Christ] who strengthens me" (Phil. 4:13).

How can one commit the sin of sacrilege? *A person sins by sacrilege when he mistreats sacred persons, places, or things.* For instance, an example of sacrilege would be to intentionally use an icon or crucifix as a doorstop.

### We Worship God by Charity

Completing the group of virtues relating to the first commandment is charity. *Charity, also known as Christian love, obliges us to love God above all things because He is infinitely good, and to love our neighbor as ourselves for the love of God.* There is no better way to understand what this love looks like, and indeed to begin to attain it, than to look upon and imitate the life of Christ; Christ's love for the Father, and for us, is perfect.

The saints also teach us the love of God. We can honor the saints *first, by imitating their holy lives; second, by praying to them; third, by showing respect to their relics and images.*

Let us pray that God may daily increase in our hearts the virtues of faith, hope, and charity. These virtues will enable us to live in a manner most pleasing to God, and will insure our happiness for all eternity.

*"So we have come to know and to believe the love that God has for us. God is love, and whoever abides in love abides in God, and God abides in him."*

—1 John 4:17

Among all the words of Revelation, there is one which is unique: the revealed name of God. God confides his name to those who believe in him; he reveals himself to them in his personal mystery. The gift of a name belongs to the order of trust and intimacy. "The Lord's name is holy." For this reason man must not abuse it. He must keep it in mind in silent, loving adoration. He will not introduce it into his own speech except to bless, praise, and glorify it.

—*Catechism of the Catholic Church, 2143*

## The Second Commandment

*Thou shall not take the name of the Lord your God in vain.*

The second commandment, like the first, has to do with man's relation toward his Creator. *By the second commandment we are commanded always to speak with reverence of God, of the saints, and of holy things, and to be truthful in taking oaths and faithful to them and to our vows.* For the Jews of the Old Testament, God's name was considered so holy that they refrained from using it even in prayer. They used a substitute for it. Did the coming of Christ make any difference in the way God's name was used? When Christ taught the Apostles the Our Father, how did He bring in the idea of reverence for God's name?

Consider this story.

A young man was lying in a hospital. The doctors and nurses were gathered around him. The chief surgeon spoke, "My young friend, I think that I should tell you frankly that your malady has been diagnosed as cancer of the tongue. In order to save your life it will be necessary to remove your tongue. We must operate at once. Is there anything you wish to say? Do so now as you will be speechless the rest of your life."

The young man grew pale and trembled with fright for a moment. Then he looked into the faces of those around him and said in a calm, earnest voice, "I

want my last words to be: Praised be the sacred name of Jesus."
Wouldn't you consider this an example of one who had tremendous love and reverence for the Holy Name? This commandment obliges us to show reverence whenever we use the Holy Name, or speak of the saints or holy things. It includes also the taking of only lawful oaths. *An oath is the calling on God to witness to the truth of what we say.* Do you know what things are necessary to make an oath lawful? *To make an oath lawful, three things are necessary: first, we must have a good reason for taking an oath; second, we must he convinced that what we say under oath is true; third, we must not swear, that is, take an oath, to do what is wrong.* What sin would a person be guilty of if he were to lie after taking an oath? This is the grievous sin of perjury.

Some years ago a man's business was completely ruined because of the dishonest handling of funds by his trusted partner. In his anger the injured man took an oath that some day he would get even with his partner. Was this oath pleasing to God? Explain.

The making of a vow is also included under this commandment. Do you remember that *a vow is a deliberate promise made to God by which a person binds himself under pain of sin to do something that is especially pleasing to God?* Ordinarily what group of people take vows?

Perhaps you have heard an individual use the words "hell" and "damn" in moments of anger. Would it be correct to say that the individual was guilty of cursing? What is cursing? How does it differ from using profane language?

Did you ever hear of the atheist, Robert Ingersoll? He traveled about the country giving lectures against God wherever he could get an audience. On one occasion, he took out his watch and challenged God to strike him dead at the end of three minutes. At the end of the allotted time, he showed his utter contempt for any belief in a Supreme Being. How was the second commandment violated? Sometimes, speaking vainly is more obvious: *blasphemy is insulting language which expresses contempt for God, either directly or through His saints and holy things.*

To conclude our consideration of the second commandment, it is important to point out that the name of a person in a very special way stands for the person himself. The second commandment, then, reminds us of this fact and tells us that by showing respect and reverence for the name of God, the saints, and holy things, we are honoring God Himself and His beloved friends.

## The Third Commandment

*Remember the Sabbath day, to keep it holy.*

The third commandment requires that a day be devoted to the external worship which we, as creatures, owe to God. The quotation that follows confirms this: " For in six days the LORD made heaven and earth, the sea, and all that is in them, and rested the seventh day; therefore the Lord blessed the sabbath day and hallowed it" (Exod. 20:11).

> *"If we really understood the Mass, we would die of joy."*
>
> —St. Jean Vianney

Every man is obliged to worship God, not only in his heart, but outwardly and publicly. Through all ages men have set aside certain times for public worship. In the Old Law the Jews observed the seventh day as the day set aside for the worship of God. How did Christ observe the law? Why do we worship God on Sunday?

### Keep Holy the Lord's Day

*By the third commandment we are commanded to worship God in a special manner on Sunday, the Lord's Day.* This does not merely mean that we must go to Mass on Sunday, nor does it mean that

What are some ways that we can keep the Lord's Day holy?

on other days God is to be ignored. God is to be worshiped on all days, but a certain day is set aside for special public worship. How then, do we worship God on Sunday? The Church tells us to participate actively in the Holy Sacrifice of the Mass. Sunday Mass is an obligation binding on all Catholics who have reached the age of reason. Is one ever excused from the obligation to attend Mass on Sunday? Yes; for instance, those may be excused who are ill or who must tend to the illness of another. Or, as another example, a bishop may dispense the members of his diocese of the Sunday obligation because of a problem endangering the community (e.g., a virus pandemic). Even if the Sunday obligation is lifted for someone, they remain obliged, if possible, to prayerfully take part in the Liturgy of the Word (the Scripture readings for Mass that day). Members are also encouraged to make a "spiritual act of communion" whenever it is not possible to receive the Eucharist physically. Can you suggest other acts one could perform in devoting this day to the worship of God? Why does the Church command us to keep Sunday as the Lord's Day? *The Church commands us to keep Sunday as the Lord's day, because*

*on Sunday Christ rose from the dead,
and on Sunday the Holy Spirit descended
upon the Apostles.*

### Rest From Work On the Sabbath

In addition to obeying the command
to worship God on Sunday by attending Mass, we must also refrain from
all unnecessary work or activities that
hinder the worship owed to God. By
resting on the seventh day, we imitate
the rhythm of life which God Himself
modeled for us in the book of Genesis:
"And on the seventh day God finished
the work that he had done, and he
rested on the seventh day from all
the work that he had done. So God
blessed the seventh day and hallowed
it, because on it God rested from all
the work that he had done in creation"
(Gen. 2:2–3). Not only should we rest on
Sunday in order to worship God at Mass,
but—in addition to this—we are also
encouraged to engage in leisurely activities that are spiritually joyful, to allow
ourselves to do good works of mercy
and charity, and to do things conducive
to the relaxation of mind and body. For
instance, many Christians in our busy
and noisy modern world find it appropriate to go on a nature walk since it is a
peaceful opportunity to admire and rest
in God's creation. Is work forbidden in
every case on Sunday? Meeting import-

## TERMS TO KNOW

- commandments
- spiritual
- presumption
- superstition
- counsels
- corporal
- apostasy
- heresy
- sacrilege
- scandal
- despair
- indifferentism
- faith
- charity
- images
- perjury
- cursing
- blasphemy
- oath
- vow
- deliberate
- swearing
- covet
- rejection
- idolatry
- apostate

ant needs for the individual or family can validly excuse persons from Sunday rest. That being said, everyone should take care not to make a habit of leaving tasks to be done on Sunday that could have been prudently done on another day. Sometimes, as Christ showed us, laboring on the Sabbath may be required in order to honor God and to love our neighbor: Recall the incident of our Lord's curing the man with the withered hand (Mk. 2:1–6). How did Christ answer those who claimed He broke the Sabbath?

One Sunday morning a farmer and his wife were on their way to attend Mass at their parish church. They saw an accident in which the driver was apparently seriously injured. By stopping to give assistance they would have to miss Mass. Would the farmer and his wife be justified in doing so? Why?

## Summary

The first commandment requires us to offer to God alone the supreme worship that is due to Him. We worship God by acts of faith, hope, and charity, and by adoring Him and praying to Him.

Faith obliges us: (1) to make efforts to find out what God has revealed; (2) to believe firmly what God has revealed; (3) to profess our faith openly whenever necessary. A Catholic sins against faith by apostasy, heresy, indifferentism, and by taking part in non-Catholic worship.

Hope obliges us to trust firmly that God will give us eternal life and the means to obtain it. The sins against hope are presumption and despair.

Charity obliges us to love God above all things because He is infinitely good, and to love our neighbor as ourselves for the love of God. The chief sins against charity are hatred of God and of our neighbor, sloth, envy, and scandal.

Besides the sins against faith, hope, and charity, the first commandment also forbids superstition and sacrilege.

The second commandment requires us always to speak with

reverence of God, of the saints, and of holy things. It also commands us to be truthful in our oaths, and faithful to them and to our vows.

The third commandment requires us to worship God in a special manner on Sunday, the Lord's Day. The Church commands us to worship God on Sunday by attending with attentiveness the Holy Sacrifice of the Mass. By the third commandment of God we are forbidden to do any unnecessary work on Sunday. Work is allowed on Sunday when the honor of God, our own need, or that of our neighbor requires it.

 **FOR ME TO REVIEW**

*Catechism Lesson*

**315. Q. What is the first commandment?**

A. The first commandment is: "I am the Lord thy God: thou shalt not have strange gods before Me."

**317. Q. How do we adore God?**

A. We adore God by faith, hope, and love, by prayer and sacrifice.

**318. Q. How may the first commandment be broken?**

A. The first commandment may be broken by giving to a creature the honor which belongs to God alone; by false worship; and by attributing to a creature a perfection which belongs to God alone.

**465. Q. What is faith?**

A. Faith is a theological virtue by which we firmly believe the truths which God has revealed.

**1164. Q. How does a person sin against faith?**

A. A person sins against faith: 1st, By not trying to know what God has taught; 2nd, by refusing to believe all that God has taught; 3rd, by neglecting to profess his belief in what God has taught.

**466. Q. What is hope?**

A. Hope is a theological virtue by which we firmly trust that God will give us eternal life and the means to obtain it.

**1182. Q. Which are the sins against hope?**

A. The sins against hope are presumption and despair.

**1183. Q. What is presumption?**

A. Presumption is a rash expectation of salvation without making proper use of the necessary means to obtain it.

**1184. Q. How may we be guilty of presumption?**

A. We may be guilty of presumption 1) By putting off confession when in a state of mortal sin; 2) by delaying the amendment of our lives and repentance for past sins; 3) by being indifferent about the number of times we yield to any temptation after we have once yielded and broken our resolution to resist it; 4) by thinking we can avoid sin without avoiding its near occasion; 5) by relying too much on ourselves and neglecting to follow the advice of our confessor in regard to the sins we confess.

**1185. Q. What is despair?**

A. Despair is the loss of hope in God's mercy.

**1186. Q. How may we be guilty of despair?**

A. We may be guilty of despair by believing that we cannot resist certain temptations, overcome certain sins or amend our lives so as to be pleasing to God.

**467. Q. What is Charity?**

A. Charity is a theological virtue by which we love God above all things for His own sake, and our neighbor as ourselves for the love of God.

1188. Q.  **How do we sin against the love of God?**

A.  We sin against the love of God by all sin, but particularly by mortal sin.

472.  Q.  **What mortal sins are opposed to faith?**

A.  Atheism, which is a denial of all revealed truths, and heresy, which is a denial of some revealed truths, and superstition, which is a misuse of religion, are opposed to faith.

556.  Q.  **Of what sin are persons guilty who put firm belief in religious or other practices that are either forbidden or useless?**

A.  Persons who put a firm belief in religious or other practices that are forbidden or useless are guilty of the sin of superstition.

1148. Q.  **How do we offer God false worship?**

A.  We offer God false worship by rejecting the religion He has instituted and following one pleasing to ourselves, with a form of worship He has never authorized, approved or sanctioned.

1151. Q.  **Do those who make use of spells and charms, or who believe in dreams, in mediums, spiritists, fortune-tellers, and the like, sin against the first commandment?**

A.  Those who make use of spells and charms, or who believe in dreams, in mediums, spiritists, fortune-tellers, and the like, sin against the first commandment, because they attribute to creatures perfections which belong to God alone.

600.  Q.  **In what other ways besides the unworthy reception of the sacraments may persons commit sacrilege?**

A.  Besides the unworthy reception of the sacraments, persons may commit sacrilege by the abuse of a sacred person, place or thing; for example, by willfully wounding a person consecrated to God; by robbing or destroying a church; by using the sacred vessels of the altar for unlawful purposes, etc.

**1189. Q. Does the first commandment forbid the honoring of the saints?**

A. The first commandment does not forbid the honoring of the saints, but rather approves of it; because by honoring the saints, who are the chosen friends of God, we honor God Himself.

**1195. Q. What do we mean by praying to the saints?**

A. By praying to the saints we mean the asking of their help and prayers.

**1203. Q. How can we best honor the saints, and where shall we learn their virtues?**

A. We can best honor the saints by imitating their virtues, and we shall learn their virtues from the written accounts of their lives. Among the saints we shall find models for every age, condition or state of life.

**1204. Q. Does the first commandment forbid us to honor relics?**

A. The first commandment does not forbid us to honor relics, because relics are the bodies of the saints or objects directly connected with them or with our Lord.

**1197. Q. How do we know that the saints hear us?**

A. We know that the saints hear us, because they are with God, who makes our prayers known to them.

**1198. Q. Why do we believe that the saints will help us?**

A. We believe that the saints will help us because both they and we are members of the same Church, and they love us as their brethren.

**1211. Q. Does the first commandment forbid the making of images?**

A. The first commandment does forbid the making of images if they are made to be adored as gods, but it does not forbid the making of them to put us in mind of Jesus Christ, His Blessed Mother, and the saints.

**1212. Q. How do we show that it is only the worship and not the making of images that is forbidden by the first commandment?**

A. We show that it is only the worship and not the making of images that is forbidden by the first commandment, 1) Because no one thinks it sinful to carve statues or make photographs or paintings of relatives or friends; 2) because God Himself commanded the making of images for the temple after He had given the first commandment, and God never contradicts Himself.

**1213. Q. Is it right to show respect to the pictures and images of Christ and His saints?**

A. It is right to show respect to the pictures and images of Christ and His saints, because they are the representations and memorials of them.

**1215. Q. Is it allowed to pray to the crucifix or to the images and relics of the saints?**

A. It is not allowed to pray to the crucifix or images and relics of the saints, for they have no life, nor power to help us, nor sense to hear us.

**1216. Q. Why do we pray before the crucifix and the images and relics of the saints?**

A. We pray before the crucifix and the images and relics of the saints because they enliven our devotion by exciting pious affections and desires, and by reminding us of Christ and of the saints, that we may imitate their virtues.

**1217. Q. What is the second commandment?**

A. The second commandment is: Thou shalt not take the name of the Lord thy God in vain.

**1218. Q. What do you mean by taking God's name in vain?**

A. By taking God's name in vain I mean taking it without reverence, as in cursing or using in a light and careless manner, as in exclamation.

**1219. Q. What are we commanded by the second commandment?**

A. We are commanded by the second commandment to speak with reverence of God and of the saints, and of all holy things, and to keep our lawful oaths and vows.

**1239. Q. What is forbidden by the second commandment?**

A. The second commandment forbids all false, rash, unjust, and unnecessary oaths, blasphemy, cursing, and profane words.

**1221. Q. What is an oath?**

A. An oath is the calling upon God to witness the truth of what we say.

**1231. Q. What is necessary to make an oath lawful?**

A. To make an oath lawful it is necessary that what we swear to be true, and that there be a sufficient cause for taking an oath.

**1222. Q. How is an oath usually taken?**

A. An oath is usually taken by laying the hand on the Bible or by lifting the hand towards Heaven as a sign that we call God to witness that what we are saying is under oath and to the best of our knowledge really true.

1223. Q. **What is perjury?**

A. Perjury is the sin one commits who knowingly takes a false oath; that is, swears to the truth of what he knows to be false. Perjury is a crime against the law of our country and a mortal sin before God.

1232. Q. **What is a vow?**

A. A vow is a deliberate promise made to God to do something that is pleasing to Him.

1241. Q. **What is blasphemy, and what are profane words?**

A. Blasphemy is any word or action intended as an insult to God. To say He is cruel or find fault with His works is blasphemy. It is a much greater sin than cursing or taking God's name in vain. Profane words mean here bad, irreverent or irreligious words.

1242. Q. **What is the third commandment?**

A. The third commandment is: Remember thou keep holy the Sabbath day.

1243. Q. **What are we commanded by the third commandment?**

A. By the third commandment we are commanded to keep holy the Lord's day and the holy days of obligation, on which we are to give our time to the service and worship of God.

1245. Q. **How are we to worship God on Sundays and holy days of obligation?**

A. We are to worship God on Sundays and holy days of obligation by hearing Mass, by prayer, and by other good works.

1250. Q. **Why does the Church command us to keep the Sunday holy instead of the Sabbath?**

A. The Church commands us to keep the Sunday holy instead of the Sabbath because on Sunday Christ rose from the dead, and on Sunday He sent the Holy Spirit upon the Apostles.

**1252. Q. What is forbidden by the third commandment?**
A. The third commandment forbids all unnecessary work and whatever else may hinder the due observance of the Lord's day.

*Questions and Exercises*

## Part 1: Yes or No

1. Is the belief that all religions are equally good known as indifferentism?

2. Is Catholic veneration of holy pictures and statues similar to the American devotion to historical pictures and statues?

3. Is a false oath called a "calumny"?

4. Are oaths used in courts of justice?

5. Has Sunday always been a day of worship dedicated to God?

6. Is it a sin of presumption to believe that we can be saved without the help of God?

7. Do we honor God by honoring the saints?

8. Is it a violation of the second commandment to call down evil on a person?

9. Are you ever allowed to do work on Sunday?

10. Is the rejection of one or more truths of the Catholic faith known as "apostasy"?

## **Part 2**: Matching

| COLUMN A | COLUMN B |
|---|---|
| 1. Chief external act of worship | A. Scandal |
| 2. Catholics worship God on Sunday | B. By attending the Sacrifice of the Mass |
| 3. Careless and irreverent use of the names of God or the saints | C. Perjury |
| 4. Unnecessary work | D. Helps to know God |
| 5. Anything leading another to commit sin | E. Profanity |
| 6. Attention to Catholic sermons, literature, and other Catholic media | F. Sloth, scandal, and envy |
| 7. Bodies of the saints or objects connected with the saints or with our Lord | G. Relics |
| 8. Catholics adore God | H. The Sacrifice of the Mass |
| 9. Sins against charity | I. But venerate the saints |
| 10. Deliberately calling on God to bear witness to a lie | J. Forbidden on Sundays |

## ✓ FOR ME TO DO

1. Group discussion: Explain why a Catholic might close his business on Sunday.

2. List ways in which members of the Church make open profession of their faith.

3. Write a letter to your friend and explain why Catholics have statues, pictures, and images in their homes and churches.

4. Write a paragraph on one of these topics: *Some Ways of Honoring Mary; Why It Is Right and Just to Thank God A Lesson From Mary's Life; How Jesus Worshiped His Father.*

5. Write a report on saints or outstanding characters who exemplify certain Christian virtues:

   A. Thomas More . . . served God and died for love of Him.

   B. St. Peter . . . performed a miracle through the power of the Holy Name.

   C. St. Monica . . . exemplified perseverance.

   D. Mary Magdalen . . . hoped in God's mercy.

# CHAPTER 3
## Jesus Christ and the Last Seven Commandments

*The last seven commandments teach us how to love God through love for our neighbor and ourself. We know that our fellow men have certain rights, among them: the right to honor, life, good reputation, and property. These rights are guaranteed by Divine Law. Now we shall see how our love of God is reflected in our respect for our neighbor's honor and welfare as well as our own.*

LESSON 3

# The Fourth Commandment of God

*Honor thy father and thy mother.*

## Obedience and Respect Are Due to Parents

You have learned that *by the fourth commandment we are commanded to respect and love our parents, to obey them in all that is not sinful, and to help them when they are in need.* These three duties of honor, love, and obedience are due to our parents because they are God's representatives and our greatest benefactors. We know that Christ was subject to Mary and Joseph until He was thirty years old. He showed great respect for His Mother at the marriage feast at Cana by complying with her request. He manifested His love for her by entrusting her to the care of St. John. He proved His obedience by fulfilling her wishes.

Jesus provides us with a perfect example of how we are to honor our own fathers and mothers.

The fourth commandment is addressed expressly to children in their relationship to their father and mother, because this relationship is the most universal. It likewise concerns the ties of kinship be- tween members of the extended family. It requires honor, affection, and gratitude toward elders and ancestors. Finally, it extends to the duties of pupils to teachers, employees to employers, subordinates to leaders, citizens to their country, and to those who administer or govern it.

—*Catechism of the Catholic Church, 2199*

We have many examples of saints, too, who showed obedience, love, and respect to their parents. For example, Pope Benedict XI always received his mother, a poor wash- erwoman, in the kindest manner. Can you mention others? Name some of the things you should do in order to live as an obedient child of God.

May our parents ever command us to do anything against the law of God? Take, for example, the case where parents without sufficient reason forbid their child to attend Mass on Sunday. Under such circumstances the child may dis- regard the command of the parent and let his conscience be his true guide. Parents and those in authority are never permitted to command anything sinful, because they cannot change God's law to suit themselves, and then force obedience. Is it wrong for a parent to command a child who is ill to stay home from Mass on Sunday? Why not?

If we are loving children, we will not hurt our parents' feel- ings, and will do nothing which will disgrace them. We will be willing as we grow older to help our parents when they are in need. Try as hard as we may we will never be able to repay them for all the love, labor, and energy they have spent on us.

## Respect and Obedience Are Due to All Lawful Superiors

*Besides our parents, the fourth commandment obliges us to respect and to obey all our lawful superiors.* Some of these superi- ors are the pope and the bishop of our diocese, the pastor of our parish, priests, teachers, and all lawful civil authorities. In all mat- ters *in which they have authority over us* we are obliged to obey them. We must be sure to have the correct attitude of respect, reverence, and loyalty toward our bishop and priests as ministers of Christ. Whose authority do they represent? What obligation do we have toward them?

The authority which parents and superiors have goes hand in hand with their responsibilities. Let us examine some of these duties. *Parents must provide for the spiritual and bodily welfare of their children; superiors, according to their varying degrees of responsibility, must care for those entrusted to them.* Children and all others subject to authority should be regarded by their superiors as a sacred trust. Therefore, parents, church rulers, and civil leaders have duties to perform.

## Lawful Superiors

A lawful superior is one who has God-given authority and who exercises this authority in a just manner. Saint Augustine of Hippo famously said, "An unjust law is no law at all." Thus, superiors can at times lose their moral right to obedience by the promulgation of unjust laws.

What are some of the obligations of fathers and mothers in regard to the children, the home, its upkeep, meals, the family income and budget, and so forth? Superiors who appreciate their obligations realize that good example helps the soul as well as the body. Would the obligation of parents to care for the spiritual welfare of their children include the duty of having them promptly baptized? Frequent the sacraments? Give them good example?

Superiors have sacred duties to fulfill toward those under their care. Children likewise have duties toward their parents and other lawful superiors. *The fourth commandment forbids disrespect, unkindness, and disobedience to our parents and lawful superiors.*

Jesus gives us a model for how to honor our mother and father. In the second chapter of Luke, we read about how he was obedient to Mary and Joseph: "And he went down with them, and came to Nazareth, and was subject to them" (Lk 2:51).

Can you mention ways in which one might fail in this regard? Disrespect and unkindness to parents are not allowed even when we are grown up; but obedience changes as we approach maturity and especially after we leave home. This is not true, however, of the obedience owed to other lawful superiors. Why?

## Good Catholics Are Good Citizens

Good members of the Church are also good citizens of their country. Those who exercise lawful authority in the state have a right to obedience and respect. They may expect a good citizen to perform certain duties. What are they? *A citizen must be sincerely interested in his country's welfare and respect and obey its lawful authority in those areas that they have actual authority.* In a famous letter to his son Jack, Commander Shea, a hero of World War II, wrote: "Be a good Catholic, and you can't help being a good American." Good Catholics do what the Church teaches. It teaches us to love our country and to do those things which good citizens should do. Jack's father was a good American. He gave his life for his fellow country men and taught his son how to be a good American, too.

*A citizen shows a sincere interest in his country's welfare by voting honestly and without selfish motives, by paying just taxes, and by defending his country's rights when necessary.* Can you think of other ways? How can each of these duties be for the good of the country?

Why must we obey civic rules and regulations? *We must respect and obey the lawful authority of our country because it comes from God, the Source of all authority.*

We must remember that *we are obliged to take an active part in works of good citizenship because right reason requires citizens to work together for the public welfare of the country.*

What would you say about this as an example of citizenship?

**TERMS TO KNOW**

- just laws
- welfare
- citizens
- motives
- disrespect
- civil authority
- unkindness
- reverence
- obedience
- stubbornness
- contempt
- just wage

The fourth commandment requires of us certain duties as citizens. A citizen must be sincerely interested in his country's welfare, and respect and obey its just laws.

Matthew voted for a senator who had shown that he (the senator) was not fit for the office because the senator gave him (Matthew) a job with the government although he did not qualify.

As citizens must respect and obey civil rulers, so public officials must realize their obligations toward the public they serve. *The chief duties of those who hold public office are to be just to all in exercising their authority and to promote the general welfare.* If a public official is willfully unjust in the exercise of his authority he is guilty of sin. For example: Jack Browne is an official in his city. He caused an unjust law to be enacted because his political party chief told him to do so. Is Jack sinning against the fourth commandment? Does the fact that many people will be harmed by the unjust law make his responsibility greater?

There are some political situations that arise which make living a Christian life very difficult, or even impossible. In this case, love for our country will look different. The early Church martyrs provide a vivid example of what it means to live as a Christian under the rule of one hostile to the truths of the faith. In the very last moments leading up to his beheading, St. Thomas

More famously said, "I die the king's good servant, but God's first." It is possible for the truths of our faith to contradict the demands of the state. When this happens, we too, like St. Thomas More, must choose God over the law. In this way we continue to love our country by setting an example of the truths which it ought to uphold.

God, in creating man, made obedience a fundamental law of his nature. Man must obey God and all who represent Him. Occasionally obedience may be difficult, but as we grow in this virtue our will and the will of God become one. To obey God becomes desirable to us, as the psalmist says, "I take joy in doing your will, my God, for your instructions are written on my heart" (Ps. 40:8).

*"I die the king's good servant, but God's first."*

—*St. Thomas More*

## Summary

By the fourth commandment we are commanded to respect and love our parents, to obey them in all that is not sinful, and to help them when they are in need. Besides our parents the fourth commandment obliges us to respect and to obey all our lawful superiors. By this same commandment parents and superiors are required to provide for the spiritual and bodily welfare of those under their care. The fourth commandment requires of us certain duties as citizens. A citizen must be sincerely interested in his country's welfare, and respect and obey its just laws.

**FOR ME TO REVIEW**

*Catechism Lesson*

**1257. Q.** **What is the fourth commandment?**

    **A.** The fourth commandment is: Honor thy father and thy mother.

**1259. Q.** **What are we commanded by the fourth commandment?**

    **A.** We are commanded by the fourth commandment to honor, love and obey our parents in all that is not sin.

**1261. Q.** **Are we bound to honor and obey others than our parents?**

    **A.** We are also bound to honor and obey our bishops, pastors, magistrates, teachers, and other lawful superiors.

**1263. Q.** **Who are meant by lawful superiors?**

    **A.** By lawful superiors are meant all persons to whom we are in any way subject, such as employers or others under whose authority we live or work.

**1265. Q.** **Have parents and superiors any duties toward those who are under their charge?**

    **A.** It is the duty of parents and superiors to take good care of all under their charge and give them proper direction and example.

**1268. Q.** **What is forbidden by the fourth commandment?**

    **A.** The fourth commandment forbids all disobedience, contempt, and stubbornness towards our parents or lawful superiors.

**1269. Q.** **What is meant by contempt and stubbornness?**

    **A.** By contempt is meant willful disrespect for lawful authority, and by stubbornness is meant willful determination not to yield to lawful authority.

*Questions and Exercises*

## Part 1: Completion

1. We are obliged to obey our parents in everything _____.
2. All lawful authority comes from _____. God
3. A good citizen shows his interest in his country's welfare especially by _____. ing its laws

## Part 2: Multiple Choice

1. In addition to obeying our parents we are obliged to obey lawful superiors because:

   A. they are older than we are.

   B. they have authority from God.

   C. we like them.

2. The most important thing the fourth commandment tells us to do is to:

   A. be kind to our parents.

   B. obey lawful authority.

   C. respect our parents.

## Part 3: Yes or No

1. There is no sin in evading the payment of just taxes. No
2. Children contribute to their country's welfare by obeying safety laws. Yes
3. It is right to disobey playground regulations provided no one gets harmed by our nonobservance. No

4. At no time has the State any right to insist that young men join the armed forces. *No*

5. It is all right to vote for an unworthy candidate if your motive in doing so is to keep your job. *?*

## Part 4: Questions for Discussion

*How many "fives" can you answer?*

1. What are five ways in which you show honor and respect for your superiors?

2. What five people besides your parents must you honor and obey?

3. What are five ways in which parents provide for the spiritual and bodily welfare of those entrusted to their care?

4. Tell five ways in which you can be a good citizen.

5. Name five duties of those who hold public office.

## Part 5: Scripture Hunt

*Find the following quotations on obedience. List the quotations. Discuss them.*

| | | |
|---|---|---|
| Eph. 6:2–3 | Sir. 3:5–7 | Col. 3:20 |
| Hebr. 13:17 | Lk. 20:25 | Acts 5:29 |
| Rom. 13:7 | Prov. 8:15–16 | |

LESSON ·4

# The Fifth Commandment of God

*Thou shalt not kill.*

Life is one of the most precious gifts that God has given us. It is given to us to serve Him, and to use according to His plans. A man who rents a house or a truck has certain rights and duties in regard to it. In like manner we have the right of using God's gift of life and also the duty of using it properly and preserving it from danger.

"What have you done? The voice of your brother's blood cries to me from the earth."

We may not put an end to our life or take that of our neighbor, for these are powers of ownership which belong to our divine Maker. Neither may we do things that would endanger or cripple our own or our neighbor's body, health, life, or spiritual well-being. From conception to natural death, life ought to be protected and reverenced. All this and more is included in the fifth commandment: *Thou shalt not kill.*

## Jesus Christ Teaches Us How to Observe This Commandment

In the New Testament Christ teaches us how to respect human life and to live in peace. He says: "Blessed are the meek . . ." "Blessed are the merciful . . ." "Blessed are they who suffer persecution . . ." (Mt. 5:3–10). "Whosoever shall murder shall be liable to judgment" (Mt. 5:21). We know that Christ carried out in His own life what He told others they should do. Can you recall some of the incidents which show Christ's perfect love of neighbor?

> "Human life is sacred because from its beginning it involves the creative action of God and it remains for ever in a special relationship with the Creator, who is its sole end. God alone is the Lord of life from its beginning until its end: no one can under any circumstance claim for himself the right directly to destroy an innocent human being."
>
> —*Catechism of the Catholic Church*, 2258 (*Donum Vitae*, Congregation for the Doctrine of the Faith)

During His public life Christ went about healing the sick, curing the blind, the deaf, the dumb, and raising the dead to life. He did not become impatient with His Apostles when they could not watch with Him during His agony in the Garden. Christ forbade His Apostles to use force and restored the ear of Malchus after it had been cut off by St. Peter. How do the following references bring out the charity of Christ: Jn. 5:1–14; 11:1–44; Mk. 4:24; 12:33?

Christ showed perfect love for all and tried to help men spiritually and physically. No matter how sinful their lives may have been, He was always ready to forgive them. "Father, forgive them"

(Lk. 23:34). "Love your enemies, do good to those who hate you" (Mt. 5:44). In the Sermon on the Mount Christ called those who would help preserve or bring about peace, "blessed."

The motive behind all Christ's actions was love, and love should be the mark distinguishing all His followers. Our Lord commands us to love all our neighbors, whether friends or enemies. He says: "Thou shalt love thy neighbor as thyself" (Mt. 22:39). "As you would that men should do to you, do you also to them in like manner" (Mt. 7:12).

## Care of Our Physical and Spiritual Welfare Is Required

*By the fifth commandment we are commanded to take proper care of our own spiritual and bodily well-being and that of our neighbor.*

### We have duties toward ourselves.
This commandment, as we already know, binds us to take ordinary care of our health and life. There is, however, no duty to use extraordinary means in the preservation of life and health.

Work—steady, hard, physical labor—is good for man, spiritually as well as physically. St. Joseph, the Workman, shows us the necessity and dignity of labor. Physical labor, as well as exercise and recreational sports, builds up our body. We must take care of our bodies to the best of our abilities. Our body is a temple of the Holy Spirit because it is the place where our soul resides––it deserves reverence and care. We must be temperate in eating and drinking, and in case of sickness provide medical attention, according to our means, for ourself and others committed to our care.

### We have duties toward our neighbor.
Do you remember the story of the Good Samaritan? What is the important thing that Christ wanted to impress upon our minds and hearts in this parable? We must be kind to our neighbors. We

must help our neighbors who are in distress or in need.

But who is our neighbor? In one way, it can be anyone in the world. But more importantly, our neighbor is the one "nearest" to us, as the roots of the word "neighbor" connote––from the Old English *nēah,* meaning "near," + *gebūr, meaning* "dweller." Before we consider those furthest from us, we should ask ourselves the question, "have I shown charity to those nearest to me? To those I live with? To those in my church community?" Being kind and charitable to those closest to us is often more difficult than showing charity to someone we've never met.

By the fifth commandment we are commanded to take proper care of our own spiritual and bodily well-being and that of our neighbor.

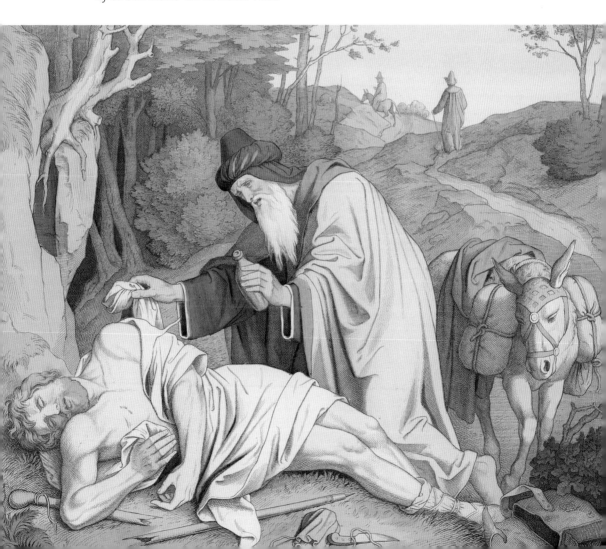

*"Whosoever hates his brother is a murderer. And you know that no murderer have eternal life abiding in himself."*

*—1 John 3:15*

We know that we must live in peace with our neighbor and respect him as the image of God. Our neighbor is a creature of God even as we are, gifted with a body and endowed with a soul like ourselves. God respects and loves him. Christ died on the cross for him, as He did for each and every one of us. He was created to be with God in heaven. Therefore, our general conduct toward all men must be respectful. Our actions must be in harmony with the laws of God and man; our speech, kind and charitable; our behavior, right and just. How do we fulfill our duties toward our neighbor?

From your study of the two great Commandments you learned that we show our love of neighbor by performing the corporal and the spiritual works of mercy in his behalf. How many works of mercy can you mention? Which corporal works of mercy did the Good Samaritan practice? Is it possible to presume that he practiced the spiritual works of mercy also? Did he speak words of comfort to the wounded man? Can you give examples of how children can practice the spiritual and corporal works of mercy?

Our Lord can never be outdone in generosity. Remember how Christ repaid St. Veronica's kind act by imprinting His image on her veil? His promise for the widow's small coin? If we love our neighbors and do good to them, Christ will imprint His image in our hearts. Christ says: "By this will all men know that you are my disciples, if you have love one for another" (Jn. 13:35).

Thus far we have considered the good acts commanded by the fifth commandment. We are to live in peace and union with our neighbor, to respect his rights, to seek his spiritual and bodily welfare, and to take proper care of our own life and health.

## Sins Forbidden by the Fifth Commandment

If we fulfill Christ's command to love our neighbor, we will find it easy to avoid sins forbidden by the Fifth Commandment. Do you know what these sins are? Our catechism tells us: *The fifth commandment forbids murder and suicide, hatred, revenge, drunkenness, bad example, and also unjustified fighting and anger.*

### Murder

Recall how Cain killed his brother Abel because he was jealous of his sacrifice. When God asked Cain, "Where is your brother Abel" he answered "I do not know, am I my brother's keeper?" (Gen. 4:9.) God told him that his brother's blood cried to Him from the earth. Why? Because it was shed in murder. For this sin of murder God punished Cain severely. He put on him the brand of a murderer and made him a wanderer on the face of the earth.

From Cain's example we see how far a man can fall if he gives in to his wicked inclinations or passions. Cain, as we know, was a slave to jealousy and anger. He planned the attack and then of his free will carried out the killing.

What is murder? Murder is the unjust, intentional, and deliberate killing of our neighbor. It is a grievous sin, because it violates God's right over life and death. God gave bodily life to man and He alone has supreme dominion over it. The murderer robs his victim of his most treasured earthly possession, life. He also robs him of the opportunity of gaining merits for heaven and preparing himself for a holy death.

Would a surgeon be guilty of murder if his patient died under an operation? Would a bricklayer who accidentally dropped a few bricks and killed one of the men working below? What about the driver of a car who kills a person? What about the driver who exceeds the speed limit, especially in a residential zone, even if he doesn't hit anyone?

> *"Whoever shall shed man's blood, his blood shall be shed."*
>
> —*Genesis 9:6*

Murder is the unjust killing of one human being by another. Is there such a thing as a just killing which is not forbidden by the fifth commandment? When is it lawful to take another's life? Would a man who shot a thief because he stole a small amount of money from him be justified in killing?

It is lawful to take another's life:

1. In a just war when the protection of one's country and the general good of society require it. Not all wars are just. But when a nation is unjustly attacked, its citizens are in conscience permitted to fight the attacking enemy. Is it possible for soldiers during war to be guilty of the sin of murder? Under what circumstances?

2. In self-defense when we are unjustly attacked and have no other means of saving our own life. For example: if you were to wake up at night and find a robber ready to strangle you, you would have a right to fight for your life, and kill, if necessary, to escape.

However, we may not do more than is needed for defense. If inflicting a wound would be sufficient to repel the attack, it would be wrong to kill. Let us suppose that a man was attacked by an unarmed man. Would he be allowed to beat him to death, if he were able to knock him out?

We are also permitted to defend ourselves against persons who attempt to rob us of something of great value which is necessary to maintain our own life or the lives of our family. But we would not be justified in killing another in order to protect property of small value.

Let us remember that every human life is important to God, to society, and to the individual who possesses it. Therefore, it must be carefully guarded as a jewel of great price.

## Abortion

The grave sin of abortion is the most prevalent form of murder in our day. Hundreds of innocent lives are taken through this sin. Abortion is a great evil, and has been foreshadowed by such atrocities as Pharaoh's command to lessen the Hebrew population, or Herod's massacre of the innocent. In our day, often a mother, when discovering that she is pregnant, feels helpless and unable to bear the weight of her new parental responsibility. In desperation, she may decide to kill the child within her, with the help of a doctor. No situation justifies the murder of an innocent child in the womb. How can we help mothers who are pregnant and are in desperation? How can we better the laws of our country to ensure that such an option is not available to women? How can we come together as a community to support women in need? A woman should never feel alone in such a situation.

*"Any country that accepts abortion is not teaching its people to love, but to use any violence to get what they want. This is why the greatest destroyer of love is abortion."*

—*St. Teresa of Calcutta*

In addition to protecting the life of the innocent child, the fifth commandment also
asks us to care for and support the mother
in need. See how you can become more
involved in pro-life ministries in your area.

### Sins Which Lead to Murder

We know that by the fifth commandment
God forbids not only the crime of actually
taking the life of another, but also everything which leads toward that crime. Which
sins lead to murder? You already know
that the *fifth commandment forbids hatred,
revenge, drunkenness, bad example, and
also unjustified fighting and anger.*

Let us consider an example of how an
act, probably not seriously sinful in itself,
may lead to other acts which are more
serious and sinful, and can involve
other people.

The brothers of Joseph, as you probably recall from the story
in the Bible, were jealous of him because of his dreams and his
father's preference for him. They planned to kill him. The oldest
brother, Ruben, realizing the seriousness of the act, persuaded
them to change their plans and urged them to throw Joseph
into a pit, hoping to rescue him later. But Joseph was sold by his
brothers to some merchants passing by. The brothers further
sinned when they deceived their father by telling him that the
boy had been devoured by wild beasts. Thus the jealousy of the
brothers, begun in anger, and prodded by pride, led to many
other sins.

**TERMS TO KNOW**

- murder
- suicide
- scandal
- anger
- temperance
- meekness
- patience
- just war
- welfare
- abortion
- mildness
- desperation
- motives
- bad example
- hatred
- self-defense

**Anger**

What are the sins of anger, hatred, and revenge?
Why are they sinful?

Anger, as we understand, is that strong feeling aroused by a real or imagined insult or injury. If not constantly held in check it can grow to enormous proportions. It can become a mortal sin. At times it leads to very serious consequences, even to murder. For example: King Saul, without a just cause, in a fit of rage, commanded that eighty-five priests to be tortured to death.

Anger is contrary to the spirit of Christ who was meek and humble of heart. But is anger always sinful? Anger is not always sinful, as St. Paul tells us, "Be angry and do not sin" (Eph. 4:26). Can you explain what he means by this statement? You may remember from Scripture that our Lord was angry with the money-changers in the temple and drove them out. A father may be angry with his son whom he has found guilty of some wrong-doing or serious neglect of duty. Can you think of other occasions when one's anger is justified? What is the meaning of the advice given by St. Paul in one of his letters to the Ephesians, "Do not let the sun go down upon your anger; do not give place to the devil"? (Eph. 4:26.)

If you have a tendency to lose your temper, perhaps this story about St. Francis de Sales will help you to conquer your habit. St. Francis was known to have a very violent temper. One day, some of his friends noticed how meek and quiet he remained all through an evening's entertainment without showing his temper even once. Finally one of the more courageous men—the others were afraid to ask—questioned

Francis on his victory over his passionate angry temper. "How did you do it?" Francis smilingly answered, "I just take my temper in both hands; then put my hands into my pockets."

Learn to control your temper as early as possible. With that comes control of the "tongue." Cultivate a sense of humor, for it will keep you from taking yourself too seriously, and will enable you to ignore things which you would otherwise consider an insult to your dignity. Jealousy and foolish pride cause much anger. If you control your temper, you will certainly do yourself and others a great favor: "Blessed are the meek," says our Lord. And St. Paul at Ephesus: "Do not let the sun go down on your anger" (Eph. 4:26).

### Fighting

Unjustified fighting is also forbidden by the fifth commandment. One reason for this is that fighting frequently causes bodily harm to ourselves or to others. But more important is the fact that fighting is a sin against the love we owe our neighbor.

What do you think of a boy who must use his fists to win? We know that in defense of the weak or of virtue, or to protect our possessions, fighting is often justified. However, street quarrels, fist fights, and other forms of physical violence are contrary to God's law. Frequently a person who uses his fists to win cannot win an argument with his mind. God, as we know, gave each of us an intellect or mind. Why not use this power to settle our arguments? Fighting, like anger, may lead to serious consequences.

### Hatred

You may have heard someone say: "I hate John. I can't stand him." Usually such a person does not mean what he says. For really to hate a person is a serious sin. In what does the sin of hatred consist?

Hatred is a sin directly against love of our neighbor. It not only leads us to forget every duty toward him, but positively creates a desire to injure him. In other words, hatred is a strong dislike of or ill-will toward anyone.

When it is directed against the person of our neighbor, hatred is always grievously sinful. If it is directed against the evil qualities of our neighbor, it may be without sin, for evil qualities are really hateful. In the example above, no doubt the person hated the bad qualities of John rather than John himself. Perhaps if he knew how and why John developed his bad habits he would pity John and try to help him. Hatred, when directed against the person himself, violates the law of God, "Thou shalt love thy neighbor as thyself" (Mt. 22:39).

**Revenge**

Have you noticed children in school making remarks similar to these? "Ruth insulted me." "Bob slapped me." "Jane squealed on me." "I'll get even."

Revenge is the desire to do evil to someone because we feel he has done evil to us. Before Christ came on earth many people did not think it sinful to seek revenge. They often improperly applied the Scripture phrase, "An eye for an eye; a tooth for a tooth" (Lev. 24:19–20; cf. Mt. 5:38). But Christ, as we know, has commanded us to love our enemies and to do good to them. "As you would that men should do to you, do you also to them in like manner." (Mt. 7:12). Christ told us to forgive. "But if you do not forgive men, neither will your Father forgive you your offenses" (Mt. 6:15). If someone should injure us or do some other wrong to us, we must forgive this person, and not injure him any in return or even wish the least harm to come to him. We may do all that is right in getting justice for ourselves. We may bring the case to court, but we may not commit a sin to avenge ourselves. "Vengeance is mine; I will repay, says the Lord" (Rom. 12:19).

In the story of Joseph we see a remarkable example of mercy. If Joseph had held any grudge against his brothers or sought revenge for their malicious deeds, he could have punished them

Joseph could have used his position to take revenge on his brothers. Instead, he treated them with mercy.

severely. Instead, like Christ our model, he really practiced mercy. He forgave them and helped them. Do we do good to those who have done evil to us?

If we keep in mind Christ's words of forgiveness as He hung on the cross, we will find it easier to forgive those who do us wrong. We have offended God more than anyone has offended us. But God has forgiven us repeatedly. We must also forgive, or we will not be forgiven. Read the story of the unmerciful servant and call to mind the last half of the Our Father.

Many persons today keep brooding over imaginary wrongs or even real but small wrongs that have been done to them. This is not good for one's bodily or mental health. Never hold a grudge. Learn to forgive and say a friendly word quickly. For example, "Let's forget it."

### Drunkenness and Drug Abuse

Drunkenness and drug abuse are sins. Through them we may endanger the life and property of others as well as ourselves. They often lead to other serious sins. Moderate use of intoxicating drink is not sinful but it can be dangerous to many people. Do you remember Noah?

We have just completed our study of various sins against the welfare of our neighbor. We have seen how they are contrary to the spirit of the fifth commandment which calls for humility, patience, charity, and good will. If we practice these virtues we will have a calm and unruffled mind; we will not provoke another to anger; we will command the respect of everybody, and we will be a source of peace and good cheer. Try to develop a pleasant and cheerful disposition.

God is patient with us and our many sins and shortcomings. We should show our gratitude by being patient and kind to our fellow men.

*"Woe to you that rise up early in the morning to follow drunkenness, and to drink till the evening, to be inflamed with wine."*

*—Isaiah 5:11*

### Suicide

Suicide is the taking of one's own life. It is a sin of grave matter because it destroys a life which belongs to God. We have life solely because God gave it to us. Only the Lord God may take it away. A person who commits such an act with full knowledge and consent dies in a state of mortal sin.

Since life is man's greatest physical gift, we must do everything to protect it and to avoid everything injurious to it. If we are discouraged and inclined to self-pity, brooding, and despon-

To put your life or health at risk without sufficient cause is a violation of the fifth commandment.

dency, we ought to think of Christ in the garden and on the cross. By contemplating His love for us we can overcome all things.

Perhaps you have asked yourself whether we are ever permitted to expose our life or our health to danger. On occasion, yes. We are permitted to expose or risk our life and health to danger when a greater or a higher good requires it. It is then the greatest act of love. For example, a man who bravely dashes into a burning building to rescue a trapped person commits no sin. Why? However, a boy who jumps from a second story building to show how daring he is, is sinning against the commandment. Why?

We have countless examples of martyrs who sacrificed their lives for their faith, and many saints who suffered rather than commit sin. By so doing they merited life eternal, for our Lord says: "He who loses his life for my sake, will find it" (Mt. 10:39). St. Aloysius died of the plague while nursing the sick in the hospitals. Missionaries in faraway lands are in constant danger of death and many of them ruin their health because of the hardships they undergo. The same may be said of priests, doctors, and nurses who attend those who have an infectious disease.

It is an act of charity to risk or lay down one's life to save another's life. Christ Himself knowingly gave His life to save souls. "Greater love than this no man has, that one lay down his life for his friends" (Jn. 15:13).

**Scandal**

It is possible to injure the spiritual life of our neighbor as well as his physical life. Accordingly, bad example of every kind is also forbidden by the fifth commandment because it injures or kills the life of grace in the soul.

Not only is bad example forbidden but every form of scandal such as immoral words or cursing, bad books or bad pictures, suggestive or indecent dress and drunkenness. In general all words, deeds, or omissions leading others to sin are forbidden by the fifth commandment.

> *"The sin of scandal consists not only in directly advising others to do evil, but also in inducing them indirectly by acts to the commission of sin."*
>
> —St. Alphonsus Liguori

Do you remember the scriptural quotation which Abraham Lincoln used in his second inaugural address as President of the United States: "Woe to the world because of scandals. For it must needs be that scandals come, but woe to the man through whom scandal does come" (Mt. 18:7). Can you explain what is meant by the quotation?

To damage or destroy our neighbor's property is sinful. To injure or take away life is more so. To ruin the supernatural life of our neighbor is most serious of all. It is far better to save our neighbor's soul than to rush into a burning building to save his body. To help send our neighbor to hell is an awful thing.

## Summary

By the fifth commandment of God, we are commanded not to kill, and also to avoid everything that may endanger our own or our neighbor's spiritual and bodily well-being. We are commanded by the fifth commandment to live in peace and union with our neighbor, to respect his rights, to seek his spiritual and bodily welfare, and to take care of our life and health.

Therefore, all willful murder, unjust fighting, unjust anger, hatred, revenge, and bad example, are forbidden by this commandment, and love and charity, forgiveness and mercy are commanded. We must not only keep our hands unstained, but our hearts pure and undefiled.

 **FOR ME TO REVIEW**

*Catechism Lesson*

**1270. Q. What is the fifth commandment?**

    A. The fifth commandment is: Thou shalt not kill.

**1271. Q. What killing does this commandment forbid?**

    A. This commandment forbids the killing only of human beings.

**1273. Q. What are we commanded by the fifth commandment?**

    A. We are commanded by the fifth commandment to live in peace and union with our neighbor, to respect his rights, to seek his spiritual and bodily welfare, and to take proper care of our own life and health.

*Questions and Exercises*

## Part 1: Matching

**COLUMN A**

1. The fifth commandment forbids *C*

2. He who has hatred in his heart for his brother *E*

3. We may expose or risk health and life *F*

4. A soldier who takes the life of an enemy in a just war *B*

5. We are commanded by the fifth commandment not only not to kill *A*

6. It is wrong to take revenge *D*

**COLUMN B**

A. but also to avoid everything that may put human life in danger.

B. is not guilty of a violation of the fifth commandment.

C. unjust fighting, unjust anger, hatred, revenge, drunkenness, and bad example.

D. against one who may have offended or hurt us in any way.

E. is guilty of sin.

F. to rescue our neighbor from physical or spiritual death.

## Part 2: Completion

1. The taking of one's own life is called _suicide_

2. The unjust taking of another's life is _murder_.

3. A strong feeling of displeasure, combined with a desire to punish the offender, is _Revenge_

4. The most precious natural gift given by God to us is _grace_.

5. A strong dislike of or ill-will toward anyone is _hatred_.

6. Any external act which occasions another to commit a venial or mortal sin is _a sin_.

7. A desire to injure others because they have injured us is _Hatred_

## Part 3: True or False

1. We must protect our life by caring for our health. *T*

2. The taking of life is a very serious offense against God and man. *T*

3. Revenge, or "getting even" with another for a good reason, is right. *F*

4. We must try to get along in peace with everyone regardless of race, color, or creed. *T*

5. We are obliged to give good example. *T*

6. The taking of one's own life is equally as serious as taking the life of another. *F*

7. Unjust fighting, quarreling, anger, and revenge are contrary to the fourth commandment. *F*

8. We must help others to save their souls. *T*

## ☑ FOR ME TO DO

1. Give an oral report on: "Who is my neighbor?"

2. If a dog is run over by a bus, a policeman usually shoots the dog to end its misery. If the same accident happened to you, could a doctor end your misery in the same way? Explain. Can a doctor end the life of a person suffering from incurable cancer? Why not? *because I have a soul*

3. In a paragraph of five or six sentences, tell what a man could do to an armed robber who breaks into the house.

4. Are we allowed to endanger the health or safety of others by practical jokes? *no*

*if needed in self defence the man could kill the robber. otherwise he could detain him until police show up*

67

LESSON 5

# The Sixth and Ninth Commandments of God

*Thou shalt not commit adultery.*

*Thou shalt not covet thy neighbor's wife.*

The sixth and ninth commandments are closely related. Both protect marriage, the home, husband and wife, children, and the source of new human life. Both have to do in a special way with the virtues of modesty, purity, and chastity. Both commandments refer to the violations of these virtues. The sixth commandment, "Thou shalt not commit adultery" forbids external actions; and the ninth, "Thou shalt not covet thy neighbor's wife," forbids willful thoughts and desires contrary to modesty and purity.

"Those whose hearts are pure are temples of the Holy Spirit."
—St. Lucy

Our Lord teaches us by word and example to observe these laws. In His sermon on the Mount, He holds out to us the reward for the pure of heart when He says, "Blessed are the clean of heart, for they shall see God" (Mt. 5:8). He chose a most pure virgin to be His mother. In His public life and Passion, He was falsely accused of many sins, but never once did His tormentors dare to accuse Him of a sin of impurity. He chose St. John, the virgin disciple, as His favorite companion.

St. John in his Apocalypse showed his respect for the virginal state when he mentioned the special reward of virgins in heaven, for these "follow the Lamb wherever He goes" (Rev. 14:3).

## Impurity and Immodesty Are Forbidden

The sixth commandment governs our external acts. By it *we are commanded to be pure and modest in our behavior. It forbids all impurity and immodesty in words, looks, and actions, whether alone or with others.*

In the *Lives of the Saints* we read of the great virtue of St. Aloysius Gonzaga. From early childhood Aloysius practiced modesty, fleeing from the slightest situation that might cause uneasiness about purity. He made a vow to preserve his innocence throughout his whole life, and through his constant vigilance, he sanctified himself. Two other Jesuit saints, St. Stanislaus Kostka and St. John Berchmans, were also shining examples of these virtues.

A great saint of our own time showed that she realized the great importance which God has attached to the virtue of purity. She is St. Maria Goretti, who chose to die rather than submit to an impure act.

Oh Saint Maria Goretti, who, strengthened by God's Grace, did not hesitate even at the age of twelve to shed your blood and sacrifice life itself to defend your virginal purity, look graciously on the unhappy human race which has strayed far from the path of eternal salvation.

Teach us all, and especially youth, with what courage and promptitude we should flee for the love of Jesus anything that could offend Him or stain our souls with sin.

Obtain for us from our Lord victory in temptation, comfort in the sorrows of life, and the grace which we earnestly beg of thee (*pause, insert special intention here*), and may we one day enjoy with thee the imperishable glory of heaven. Amen.

Our Father ... Hail Mary ... Glory be ...

St. Maria Goretti, pray for us!

## Purity must be practiced in words, looks, and actions.

It is forbidden to look at indecent images, whether these be found on the internet, in movies, or any other kind of video, whether in books, newspapers, magazines, or elsewhere. A Chinese proverb says that one picture is worth a thousand words. How true! What a deep impression one picture can make on the mind! If the picture is indecent, the impression will be a source of temptation for a long time. Reading bad books is also sinful and very dangerous. It leads us into many terrible temptations.

Impure actions with oneself or with another are generally grave sins. A modest person resists every temptation against purity. He knows that God knows and sees all things. In his relationship with others, the good Christian never performs or allows any action that might endanger holy purity.

## There are many dangers to chastity.

Chastity is a virtue that can be easily tarnished. *The chief dangers to the virtue of chastity are: idleness, sinful curiosity, bad companions, drinking, drug abuse, immodest dress, and indecent books, plays, films, and videos.*

Idleness is a vice from which other dangers spring. The idle person does not have anything good, beautiful, or useful with which to occupy himself; he daydreams, and is not watchful over his thoughts. In this state it is easy to indulge sinful curiosity, since vigilance over self is wanting. He may seek the company of evil companions, because they, like himself, have nothing to do. This frequently results in sin.

If a person wears immodest clothing or wears modest clothing in such a way as to be immodestly exposed, he must mention this in confession. Women and girls especially, who are

## TERMS TO KNOW

- curiosity
- purity
- passion
- covet
- immodesty
- decency
- adultery
- modesty

immodest in the clothes they wear, or in the way they wear them, are responsible for many sins of evil thought and desire. Men and young boys must keep careful guard over their eyes and not allow even the sins of others to lead them into sin. Immodest dress not only hurts our Lord, but it hurts the one who dresses immodestly. When we choose to dress immodestly, we disregard the sacredness of our bodies, we allow ourselves to become mere objects of desire, and we thwart the possibility of true friendship between ourselves and our neighbor.

## How Chastity Can Be Preserved

*The chief means of preserving the virtue of chastity are to avoid carefully all unnecessary spiritual dangers, to seek God's help through prayer, frequent confession, Holy Communion, and assistance at Holy Mass, and to have a special devotion to the Blessed Virgin.*

By the destruction of Sodom and Gomorrah, God has warned us that sins of impurity have dreadful consequences. Here are some sure helps and safeguards for purity.

> "Chastity includes an apprenticeship in self-mastery which is a training in human freedom. The alternative is clear: either man governs his passions and finds peace, or he lets himself be dominated by them and becomes unhappy."
>
> —*Catechism of the Catholic Church, 2339*

The most powerful aid to purity is Christ in the Holy Eucharist. Holy Communion puts out the fire of impurity in our hearts and gives us over and over again new heavenly strength for the battle. Frequent reception of the sacraments strengthens us against the temptations that may arise. Teenagers especially should go to Communion weekly, and even daily if possible, and to confession at least once a month, though preferable every two weeks.

Another safeguard is prayer. In temptation we must recommend ourselves to God and the Blessed Virgin. Temptations come to all. Sometimes, the Sign of the Cross or simply saying the name of Jesus will be enough to drive them away. The lives of the saints prove that prayer can keep us free from the chains of vice. Do you recall the stories of such saints?

A sincere devotion to our Blessed Mother is another powerful help in overcoming temptation. She is our mother and, being the purest of creatures and ever a virgin, will help us in a special way if we ask her. "Mother most pure, pray for us."

Important also is the selection of good companions. "Tell me your friends, and I'll tell you what you are" is a truism that speaks volumes. "Birds of a feather flock together." One bad companion can overcome the influence of a dozen good ones unless the good ones band together and firmly oppose the bad influences and evil suggestions.

## Willful Thoughts About Impure Things Are Sinful

*By the ninth commandment we are commanded to be pure in thought and desire.*

As you may know, even the greatest of saints were bothered by serious temptations. St. Catherine of Siena, who did such hard things for God, was often sorely tempted against purity. On one occasion, after a temptation stronger than usual, our Lord appeared to her. "Where were You, Lord, when these evil thoughts were in my mind?" she asked. Jesus smiled and replied, "I was in your heart taking pleasure in the victorious battle you were waging." We can see from this incident that bad thoughts in themselves are not sinful unless we consent to them.

*"Chastity is a difficult, long term matter; one must wait patiently for it to bear fruit, for the happiness of loving kindness which it must bring. But at the same time, chastity is the sure way to happiness."*

—*Pope St. John Paul II*

## Thoughts About Impure Things Are Not Always Sinful

Bad thoughts are caused by things we read, or hear, or see. They are, however, not sins just because they enter the mind. *Mere thoughts about impure things are not always sinful in themselves, but such thoughts are dangerous.* An unclean thought may enter the mind and throw an unclean picture on the screen of the imagination, but we should not let it remain there. Since we can think of only one thing at a time, we can remove the distasteful picture by putting another in its place. Just as a video can be switched from one program to another, so can a new thought be placed in the imagination, erasing the disturbing thought. A sincere effort to do this helps strengthen in us the virtue of purity. However, if we neglect to banish the temptation once we recognize it, we may fall into sin.

## Bad Thoughts Are Sinful if Deliberate

When we deliberately permit an impure thought to remain in our mind after a warning from our conscience, and fully welcome and enjoy the thought, we commit a sin. *Thoughts about impure things become sinful when a person thinks of an unchaste act and deliberately takes pleasure in so thinking, or when unchaste desire or passion is aroused and consent is given to it.*

Dancing, dating, and parties often cause temptations. The passions are powerful. We must cultivate the virtue of temperance when we feel that our passions have been aroused.

## Summary

By the sixth commandment we are commanded to be pure and modest in our outward behavior. This commandment forbids all impurity in words, looks, and actions, whether alone or with others.

The ninth commandment requires us to be pure in thought and in desire. Thoughts about impure things are sinful if deliberately entertained.

 **FOR ME TO REVIEW**

*Catechism Lesson*

**1281. Q. What is the sixth commandment?**

    A. The sixth commandment is: Thou shalt not commit adultery.

**1282. Q. What are we commanded by the sixth commandment?**

    A. We are commanded by the sixth commandment to be pure in thought and modest in all our looks, words, and actions.

**1284. Q. What is forbidden by the sixth commandment?**

A. The sixth commandment forbids all unchaste freedom with another's wife or husband; also all immodesty with ourselves or others in looks, dress, words, and actions.

**1315. Q. What is the ninth commandment?**

A. The ninth commandment is: Thou shalt not covet thy neighbor's wife.

**1316. Q. What are we commanded by the ninth commandment?**

A. We are commanded by the ninth commandment to keep ourselves pure in thought and desire.

**1317. Q. What is forbidden by the ninth commandment?**

A. The ninth commandment forbids unchaste thoughts, desires of another's wife or husband, and all other unlawful impure thoughts and desires.

**1318. Q. Are impure thoughts and desires always sins?**

A. Impure thoughts and desires are always sins, unless they displease us and we try to banish them. Impure thoughts are not always sinful, though if we do not resist them, they become sinful.

**300. Q. What is lust?**

A. Lust is an excessive desire for the sinful pleasures forbidden by the sixth commandment.

**301. Q. What effect has lust on our souls?**

A. Lust begets in our souls a distaste for holy things, a perverted conscience, a hatred for God, and it very frequently leads to a complete loss of faith.

*Questions and Exercises*

## Matching

**COLUMN A**

1. The sixth commandment forbids all impurity C

2. By the ninth commandment we are A

3. Mere thoughts about impure things B

4. Chastity can be preserved by E

5. We should be F

6. Impure thoughts are not sinful unless D

7. Sinful curiosity I

8. We should have great respect for our bodies J

9. Idleness and daydreaming may cause G

10. The sixth commandment forbids H

**COLUMN B**

A. commanded to be pure in thought and desire.

B. are not always sinful in themselves but such thoughts are dangerous.

C. whether alone or with others.

D. consent is given.

E. avoiding unnecessary dangers, by prayer, and by frequent reception of the sacraments.

F. pure and modest in our outward behavior.

G. impure thoughts and desires.

H. impure external acts.

I. is dangerous because it can lead us into mortal sin.

J. because they are temples of the Holy Spirit.

## ✓ FOR ME TO DO

1. Read about and report on saints who exemplify the virtue of purity, such as St. Aloysius and St. Maria Goretti.

2. Name five sins forbidden by the sixth and ninth commandments.

3. List near occasions that might lead to serious sins against the sixth and ninth commandments.

4. Before viewing, evaluate movies, TV programs, books, video games, websites, etc., to determine if they are morally harmful.

5. Pray that God may bless you with pure and holy friendships.

LESSON 6

# The Seventh and Tenth Commandments of God

*Thou shalt not steal.*

*Thou shalt not covet thy neighbor's goods.*

The fact that we are human beings gives us certain rights. The fact that we must live and work together with others who have similar rights places upon us certain obligations. We wish our

rights to be respected. The law of justice demands that we respect the rights of others and that they respect ours. Charity demands that we help in time of need. These two virtues of justice and charity form the basic foundation of our relationship with our fellow men. The duty of justice and charity was clearly brought out in the story of Dives and Lazarus (Lk. 16:19–31). Who can tell the story?

How did the rich man, traditionally known as Dives, fail in his duty of justice and charity toward Lazarus?

## Respect What Belongs to Others

In our study of the seventh commandment one of the first things we note is that *we are commanded to respect what belongs to others*. Why? To understand the idea a little better we might go back to the virtue of justice. It is one of the cardinal virtues that regulates the relationship between man and his neighbor. It keeps rights and duties in balance. You have the right to things which you have justly obtained and you also have the obligation to respect that same right which belongs to your neighbor.

Perhaps you have a job after school. It might be a paper route or baby sitting or running errands. You have worked hard at that job and are quite happy that you have earned money to pay your high school tuition. Would you resent someone taking all the money you had worked so hard to earn? Why would you? You were paid for your work and you have the God-given right to call that money your own. God made the world and all that is in it for all men. He meant that every man, by working, should be able to acquire for his use those created things which could enable him to lead a life that would make it possible for him to save his soul.

> "The seventh commandment forbids unjustly taking or keeping the goods of one's neighbor and wronging him in any way with respect to his goods. It commands justice and charity in the care of earthly goods and the fruits of men's labor. For the sake of the common good, it requires respect for the universal destination of goods and respect for the right to private property. Christian life strives to order this world's goods to God and to fraternal charity."
>
> —*Catechism of the Catholic Church*, 2401

## Keep Our Business Agreements

The seventh commandment also obliges us to keep our business agreements. Ordinarily these agreements center around a formal contract or informal agreement entered into by two or more persons or organizations. Keeping such agreements is a matter of justice. Deliberately failing to live up to such a contract might mean financial loss and consequently would certainly violate the commandment. If, for instance, a man agrees to buy your automobile and fails to keep his word, you may have to sell it at a lower price. Suppose violation of the contract didn't involve financial loss. Is it still a violation and, if it is, what about restitution?

We must be just in our individual dealings. Modern high pressure salesmanship and advertising lead many unthinking people into backbreaking debts and high interest charges which ruin their individual or family lives. Discuss the obligation of both buyer and seller in this matter.

## Pay Just Debts

The seventh commandment speaks of our obligation *to pay our just debts*. Many people live beyond their means. Some individuals involve themselves in heavy debts by buying costly homes, vehicles, or fashionable clothes, or furniture, and indulging in expensive forms of amusement which they could never possibly enjoy if they lived within their means. Do you think it a good policy to run up big bills even though you intend to pay them at some future date? Here it is well to remember that wise people live by the principle "pay-as-you-go." What does this mean?

Some people get out of paying debts by moving away. Even if they are able to "get away with it," have they not violated the seventh commandment? Do they still have an obligation to pay what they owe?

Not too long ago, a store was almost completely destroyed by a fire. The ledger containing charge accounts was destroyed. According to the seventh commandment every individual was obliged to pay what he owed even though he knew the owner of the store could not send a bill. If one were to use the destruction of the record of his account as an excuse for not paying what he owed, he most certainly would be guilty of violating the command "to pay our just debts."

## Dishonesty Is Forbidden

*Besides stealing, the seventh commandment forbids cheating, unjust keeping of what belongs to others, unjust damage to the property of others, and the accepting of bribes by public officials.*

### Stealing

Stealing is the unjust taking or keeping of what belongs to another. The act is serious or slight depending on what has been taken and from whom it has been taken.

*"He that stole, let him now steal no more; but rather let him labour, working with his hands the thing which is good, that he may have something to give to him that has need."*

—*Ephesians 4:28*

The story is told of robbers who forced their way into an orphanage at Christmas time and took the food that had been sent to the children by generous benefactors. Would the guilt be the same if they had broken into the home of a family in comfortable circumstances and taken things belonging to the children of the family?

Some children think there is no harm in taking small amounts of money when they go to the store and know there will be no account kept of the change. They seem to have the attitude, "Oh, mother will never miss it." Does that make it right? What is the real danger in such an attitude? Such an act, even though it involved an amount small in itself, remains dishonest. Additionally, it can lead to a habit of stealing difficult to break.

Some years ago, the chaplain in one of the state prisons conducted a survey among a group of men who were confined there because of big robberies. He wanted to find out how these men ever got started on such a career. The results of his survey were startling. He discovered the greatest number had started by taking amounts less than a dollar.

One can violate the seventh commandment without actually stealing. Assisting someone in the unjust taking or keeping of anything, for instance, by acting as "lookout," would make you guilty with the person who committed the theft. If one of your neighborhood friends came to you and shared with you something which you knew he had stolen, would you be guilty in any way of sinning against the seventh commandment? Would it make any difference if you did not know it was stolen?

**TERMS TO KNOW**

- restitution
- bribe
- robbery
- goods
- contract
- covet
- detachment
- debt
- covetousness
- theft

Now we come to a point relating to this commandment that is very often forgotten completely. It is restitution, which means giving back the stolen goods or their value as far as one is able. It also includes paying for damage we have unjustly caused.

Sometimes boys and girls feel they have satisfied their obligation simply by confessing the theft. This is not so. *We are obliged to restore to the owner stolen goods, or their value, whenever we are able.* The general rule is that restitution must be made to the person or company on whom the loss was unjustly inflicted.

But suppose that you had taken a large sum of money and wished to make restitution, only to discover that the person from whom you had taken the sum had left the city and you had absolutely no way of locating him. What are you to do then? If all sincere efforts to locate the person had failed then the money could be given for some charitable cause. If the owner had died, the money could be given to his heirs, or used for Masses for the repose of his soul.

**Cheating**

Cheating is another form of dishonesty forbidden by the seventh commandment. Many examples might be given. Perhaps a boy has neglected to do an assigned task. Before class he manages to get another's finished work and after copying it hands it in as his own. Or again, during the time of an examination a girl may not be able to answer the questions given and, watching her chance, may copy the answers of another and submit them as her own. In both instances these individuals are guilty of cheating.

In the field of industry an employer may violate the seventh commandment by failing to pay a just wage to his employee. Could the employee also be guilty of injustice as far as the employer is concerned? He, too, could fail in that respect by not putting in the required work or time or by deliberately producing inferior work.

Merchants and clerks, too, could be guilty of defrauding their customers regarding quantity or weight, or by deceiving them in regard to the quality of the article. All these instances are failures in observing the commandment that calls for the practice of the virtue of justice.

**Unjust Keeping of What Belongs to Others.**

Perhaps in your own neighborhood you have witnessed this particular form of injustice. A neighbor might approach your father and borrow a lawn mower and then fail to return it. Again, you may know of some person who found money or some article of value and did not make a sincere effort to find the owner.

**Unjust Damage to the Property of Others.**

Damaging the property of another can be a sin. Violations of this particular phase of the seventh commandment are countless. A very common one is the damage done to lawns, hedges, and flower beds of property owners. The next time you feel inclined to take a short cut through some neighbor's yard or to play ball there, stop for a moment and think. The man who planted that lawn has put in valuable time and money to improve his property. You may label him a "neighborhood crank" but he has every right to resent the destruction of his property and you have the obligation to respect his ownership of that property. An apology for damage done to property is not sufficient. *We are obliged to repair damage unjustly done to the property of others, or to pay the amount of the damage, as far as we are able.*

### Accepting of Bribes by Public Officials

The accepting of bribes by public officials is unjust. Public officials are obliged in conscience to be honest and just in carrying out the duties of their office. At no time are they allowed to use that office as a means of personal gain.

"The tenth commandment forbids greed and the desire to amass earthly goods without limit. It forbids avarice arising from a passion for riches and their attendant power. It also forbids the desire to commit injustice by harming our neighbor in his temporal goods."

—*Catechism of the Catholic Church, 2536*

## The Tenth Commandment

The tenth commandment might be looked upon as a safeguard for the seventh commandment. This commandment *forbids all desire to take or to keep unjustly what belongs to others, and also forbids envy at their success*. The seventh commandment forbids actual stealing. The tenth commandment also forbids the desire to steal and cheat. One would less likely be guilty of violating the seventh commandment if such unlawful desires were kept under control.

To overcome envy at another's success it might be well to form the habit of being happy when others gain some little recognition for their work. If one of your classmates wins a prize which you were striving to get, show your good will and offer him your hearty congratulations.

## Summary

The seventh commandment requires us to respect what belongs to others, to live up to our business agreements, and to pay our just debts. This commandment forbids all dishonesty such as: (1) stealing, (2) cheating, (3) unjust keeping what belongs to others, (4) unjust damage to the property of others, and (5) the accepting of bribes by public officials.

The tenth commandment forbids all desire to take or keep unjustly what belongs to others, and also forbids envy at their success.

 **FOR ME TO REVIEW**

*Catechism Lesson*

**1290. Q. What is the seventh commandment?**

A. The seventh commandment is: Thou shalt not steal.

**1295. Q. What are we commanded by the seventh commandment?**

A. By the seventh commandment we are commanded to give to all men what belongs to them and to respect their property.

**1298. Q. What is forbidden by the seventh commandment?**

A. The seventh commandment forbids all unjust taking or keeping what belongs to another.

**1301. Q. Are we bound to restore ill-gotten goods?**

A. We are bound to restore ill-gotten goods, or the value of them, as far as we are able; otherwise we cannot be forgiven.

**1304. Q. Are we obliged to repair the damage we have unjustly caused?**

A. We are bound to repair the damage we have unjustly caused.

**1319. Q. What is the tenth commandment?**

A. The tenth commandment is: Thou shalt not covet thy neighbor's goods.

**1323. Q. What is forbidden by the tenth commandment?**

A. The tenth commandment forbids all desires to take or keep wrongfully what belongs to another.

**309. Q. What is envy?**

A. Envy is a feeling of sorrow at another's good fortune and joy at the evil which befalls him; as if we ourselves were injured by the good and benefited by the evil that comes to him.

**310. Q. What effect has envy on the soul?**

A. Envy begets in the soul a lack of charity for our neighbor and produces a spirit of detraction, backbiting and slander.

*Questions and Exercises*

## Yes or No

1. Is adulteration of goods a permissible practice in business?

2. Is failure to give full pay for service, or vice versa, a form of stealing? yes

3. Do industriousness and regularity in work promote faithfulness to the seventh commandment?

4. May you keep a gift which you know has been stolen? no

5. Do you have to pay your bus fare even though you can slip past the conductor? yes

6. Is stealing always a mortal sin? no

7.  Are you violating the seventh commandment when you damage the seats in a bus? *no*

8.  Is envy of the success of another a violation of the tenth commandment? *yes*

9.  Does the seventh commandment require us to restore to the owner stolen goods or their value? *yes*

10. Does the seventh commandment forbid the accepting of bribes by persons in public office? *yes*

## ✓ FOR ME TO DO

1.  Group discussion: How the seventh commandment may be violated by a family, a workingman, and by corporations, a storekeeper, a voter, a man in public life, a nation.

2.  Cite examples from daily living showing how we can practice justice, obedience, filial devotion, honesty, truthfulness, gratitude, friendliness.

LESSON 7

# The Eighth Commandment of God

*Thou shalt not bear false witness against thy neighbor.*

A game of baseball was in progress. Terry hit the ball and ran. Just as he slid into third base, Tim caught the ball and swung to tag Terry. Terry's team called him "Safe" while Tim's team yelled "Out." Then came Tim's voice, "He's safe. I missed him." The game went on. A spectator was quite astonished. He spoke to one of the boys about it. "Well, sir," said the boy, "that's Timmy and he always tells the truth." Praise like that is worthwhile and yet Tim was only doing what he knew was right, keeping the eighth commandment.

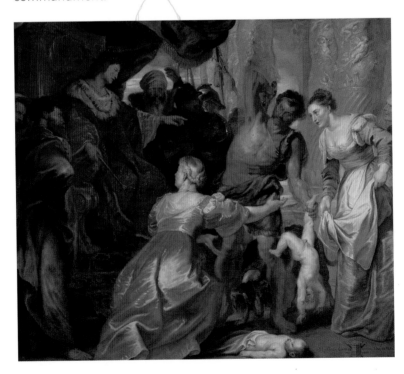

The Judgment of Solomon, 1 Kings 3:16—28

## Christ Teaches by Word and Example the Virtue of Truthfulness

Life in human society would be practically impossible unless we could presume that people generally tell the truth to one another. The eighth commandment confirms this societal need for honesty. *By the eighth commandment we are commanded to speak the truth in all things, but especially in what concerns the good name and honor of others.* To speak the truth often demands great heroism. We have a perfect example in Christ Himself. At the time when the high priests asked Him if He were the Son of God, He courageously answered that He was. Can you recall other such incidents in the life of our Lord?

As we continue our study of this commandment, we shall see how Christ detests all that is against truth and charity. St. James in his Epistle wrote, "If anyone does not offend in word, he is a perfect man" (James 3:2). What do you understand by this statement?

## We Are To Be Truthful in Speech

There are certain things, you know, which are forbidden by the eighth commandment. How many can you name? *The eighth commandment forbids lies, rash judgment, detraction, calumny, and the telling of secrets we are bound to keep.* Now let us take each one and see whether we understand it.

### Lies—"Lying lips are an abomination to the Lord" (Prov. 12:22).

As the Book of Proverbs shows, God hates lying. What is a lie? When does one lie? There are three things necessary to constitute a lie: (1) a spoken untruth; (2) the knowledge that it is untrue; and (3) the intention to deceive and lead others into error. There are different kinds of lies. Let us study them through examples.

John tells a "tall story" which everyone knows is just a joke. Did John sin? Such a story, told in jest, is not a lie for it is told to amuse, and without intention to deceive. It is not sinful if its purpose or character is obvious to the listeners.

*"He who speaks rightly should recognize that he receives the words from God. For the truth belongs not to him who speaks, but to God who is energizing him."*

—*St. Mark the Ascetic*

Paul tells his classmates that Dale copied in an examination. Paul, however, knows this is not true but his classmates believe him and will have nothing to do with Dale. Was Paul's action wrong? Why? Do you recall from your Old Testament study how the chaste Susanna would have been stoned to death if the wisdom of Daniel had not saved her? When Jesus was before the Sanhedrin, false witnesses accused Him of terrible crimes. Read the account in Mark 14:55–59. These witnesses dishonored Christ's good name and reputation and thereby brought death upon Him. On what other occasions were lies told about our Lord?

Christ stressed the hatefulness of lying when, in speaking to the Jews, He said, "Why do you not understand my speech? The father from whom you are is the devil. . . . When he tells a lie he speaks from his very nature, for he is a liar and the father of lies. . . . The reason why you do not hear is that you are not of God" (Jn. 8:44–47).

Speaking is not the only way of lying. A person may act a lie, for example the kiss of Judas. How can you "act a lie"? Jerry hands in his homework assignment which he copied from another boy. Sue, very cleverly, gets the test answers from the

Jesus Christ
before Pontius
Pilate

person sitting across from her. Did these two children do the right thing? To copy or cheat in an exam would be a sin of falsehood because, in so doing, one acts a lie by claiming knowledge which he does not possess.

However, it would not be sinful to give an evasive answer when asked a question we are not obliged to answer. An evasive answer is one which avoids a direct response, in a clever or skillful manner.

During the persecution in Mexico, Father Pro disguised himself a number of times. One day when his persecutors caught up with him, not knowing to whom they were speaking, they asked whether he had seen a priest pass by. He admitted he had and they continued their search. For the time being he was safe. Perhaps you recall from your Church history how cleverly St. Thomas of Canterbury escaped his persecutors. When the soldiers asked him if he were the archbishop, he pointed to the old horse he was riding and asked whether it looked like an archbishop's horse. The soldiers went on their way. How else may one give an evasive answer which would not be sinful?

### Rash Judgment—"Do not judge, that you may not be judged" (Mt. 7:1–5).

We have just seen that one sins against the eighth commandment by lying. One also sins against this commandment by rash judgment. *A person commits the sin of rash judgment when, without sufficient reason, he believes something harmful to another's character.* Who are we to judge our neighbor? Everyone has a duty to think well of his neighbor until his neighbor proves himself unworthy of his good name. You want everybody to think well of you, don't you?

Many of the Jews were rash in their judgment of our Lord and John the Baptist. Read Luke 7:33–34 if you do not remember the occasion. Were the Jews justified? Are there any other examples of rash judgment that you know?

There is an old saying, "Sweep before your own door before you sweep before the doors of others." How can this be applied to rash judgment. It would be well to remember to be severe with self and lenient toward others.

The gravity of a sin of rash judgment depends on the harm done to another and the lack of charity involved.

### Detraction—Calumny or Slander—"With what measure you measure, it shall be measured to you" (Mk. 4:24).

Other sins forbidden by the eighth commandment are detraction and slander, which is also called calumny. In Holy Scripture we read that the detractor is an abomination of man (Prov. 29:9). When is one guilty of the sin of detraction? *A person commits the sin of detraction when, without a good reason, he makes known the hidden faults of another.* St. James warns us against the detractor: "He who speaks against a brother, or judges his brother, speaks against the law and judges the law" (James 4:11). A person can be guilty of detraction by revealing the secret faults of others. A child may have stolen a nickel once and we know about it. Does that give us the right to say that he is a thief?

*A person commits the sin of calumny or slander when by lying he injures the good name of another*. Calumny or slander is much worse than detraction because it injures or destroys a person's reputation by lies. Many of the Jews falsely accused Jesus of having a devil (Jn. 8:48–49). They even went so far as to invent lies to have Paul condemned to death (Acts 24:1–13).

If you have committed a sin of detraction or calumny, you must make reparation. Is it always easy? An ink spot is easily made on a sheet of paper, but no efforts will completely remove the blot. So, too, it is quite impossible to restore a good name once it has been ruined by detraction or calumny. Nevertheless, *a person who has sinned by detraction or calumny, or who has told a secret he is bound to keep, must repair the harm he has done to his neighbor, as far as he is able.*

Who are we to judge our neighbor? Everyone has a duty to think well of his neighbor until his neighbor proves himself unworthy of his good name.

### Keeping Secrets Is an Obligation

*We are obliged to keep a secret when we have promised to do so, when our office requires it, or when the good of another demands it.* Let us see what this means through examples.

Ronald and Ed are good friends and often confide secrets to each other. In the course of a conversation Ronald tells Ed about a temptation to which he yielded. Realizing what he has done, he makes Ed promise not to say anything about the matter. Is Ed under obligation to keep it a secret?

Are doctors or lawyers obliged to keep professional secrets? If a person seeks professional advice from a doctor or lawyer, or seeks counsel in a matter of conscience, he expects this information to be kept secret. To disclose important secret information, generally speaking, would be a serious sin against justice, and often against charity.

What about sins told in confession? May a priest reveal a sin if it may mean the saving of his own or of another's life? Under no

condition can a priest break the seal of confession. St. John Nepomucene, whose feast we celebrate on May 16, lost his life because he refused to tell what the queen told him in the confessional. As a reward for his fidelity to the seal of confession, his tongue is miraculously preserved to the present day.

**TERMS TO KNOW**

- rash judgment
- detraction
- calumny

If you overhear someone's confession, would you be allowed to make known what you heard? Is it a violation of the seal of confession deliberately to try to overhear what is being said?

Are we ever justified in telling the faults of others? In general we should not bear tales, but there are times when it is necessary to talk about or reveal the faults of others. If you know that in your school there is a student whose presence is morally very harmful to the other pupils, you are obliged to make that known. The person to whom we tell the faults should be one who has a right to know, such as parents, teachers, and other lawful superiors.

We may also reveal secret faults when it is for the good of the guilty person. If John knows his brother is going with very bad companions, unknown to his parents, he is obliged to inform them. Another instance would be when it is necessary to protect ourselves or others.

Examples can be found in the Bible when the faults of others had to be made known. You remember that Joseph told his father of his brothers' wicked acts. Paul warned Timothy to shun a wicked man named Alexander. Heli was informed by the Israelites of the evil his sons had done. In each case were the individuals justified in making known the faults of others?

## Charity Covers a Multitude of Sins

There is an old saying well worth remembering:

*"There's so much good in the worst of us,*

*And so much bad in the best of us*

*That it behooves none of us*

*To speak about the rest of us."*

In his first Epistle to the Corinthians, St. Paul gives a beautiful lesson on charity. "Charity is patient, is kind; charity does not envy . . ." Read the rest in 1 Cor. 13:4–7. Why is charity the greatest virtue? It makes us most like God.

Whenever anyone spoke about the faults of another, St. Thérèse always managed to change the conversation. What do you do? What opportunities do you have to practice charity, in word and in deed? We have a beautiful example of this virtue in our Blessed Mother. Recall instances from the New Testament showing how Mary practiced charity. Are you charitable in thought, word, and deed?

## Summary

The eighth commandment requires us to speak the truth in all things, but especially in what concerns the good name and honor of others. The eighth commandment forbids: (1) lies, (2) rash judgment, (3) detraction, (4) calumny, and (5) the telling of secrets we are bound to keep. A person who has sinned by detraction or calumny, or has told a secret he is bound to keep, must repair the harm he has done to his neighbor, as far as he is able.

**FOR ME TO REVIEW**

*Catechism Lesson*

**1305. Q. What is the eighth commandment?**

A. The eighth commandment is: Thou shalt not bear false witness against thy neighbor.

**1306. Q. What are we commanded by the eighth commandment?**

A. We are commanded by the eighth commandment to speak the truth in all things, and to be careful of the honor and reputation of everyone.

**1310. Q. What is forbidden by the eighth commandment?**

A. The eighth commandment forbids all rash judgments, backbiting, slanders, and lies.

**1311. Q. What are rash judgment, backbiting, slander and detraction?**

A. Rash judgment is believing a person guilty of sin without a sufficient cause. Backbiting is saying evil things of another in his absence. Slander is telling lies about another with the intention of injuring him. Detraction is revealing the sins of another without necessity.

**1314. Q. What must they do who have lied about their neighbor and seriously injured his character?**

A. They who have lied about their neighbor and seriously injured his character must repair the injury done as far as they are able, otherwise they will not be forgiven.

*Questions and Exercises*

## Matching

| COLUMN A | COLUMN B |
|---|---|
| 1. Calumny C | A. To make known the hidden faults of another |
| 2. Lie D | B. Believing something harmful to another's character without sufficient reason |
| 3. Rash judgment B | C. Injuring the good name of another |
| 4. Detraction A | D. Telling an untruth |

## ☑ FOR ME TO DO

1. Write a paragraph on the proverb: "A good name is better than great riches."

2. Make a collection of pictures illustrating the virtues of kindness and love of neighbor.

3. Cite examples from daily living for the practice of truthfulness.

4. Read and describe the trial of Jesus in Mt. 26:59–64.

5. Are there times when the truth must be told about a person even though it will injure his good name? Discuss.

6. Report on the trial of Joan of Arc. Tell the story of Father Pro.

7. With your parents, watch the film *I Confess*, directed by Alfred Hitchcock

## Prayer of Resolution

*O my God: Henceforth I resolve to strive earnestly to be patient and gentle, and not allow the waters of contradiction to extinguish the fire of that charity which I owe to my neighbor.*

*Amen.*

# CHAPTER 4
# The Laws of Christ's Church

*The Ten Commandments, as you know, were given by God to Moses as the laws of love to direct us on the road to salvation. Since they regulate our duties toward God, our neighbor, and ourselves, they are extremely important, for we can attain union with God only by fulfilling His will.*

*Since these laws come from God, they are binding on all men. But, as you remember, in establishing the Church, God gave it the power to make laws. These laws will be considered in this section to enable you to understand better your duties and responsibilities. They will also help you appreciate the interest of the Church in your salvation.*

*Laws of the Church which repeat or explain God's laws may not change what God intended. But other laws of the Church may be abridged, changed, or added to, as the need arises.*

God gave us the Ten Commandments through Moses, but He also gave authority to the Church to make her own laws.

# The Precepts of the Church

Do you recall how Christ organized His Church, and the instructions He gave to His Apostles? When Christ said, "He who hears you, hears me," He delegated His authority to the Church.

We are fortunate to be members of the Catholic Church. We belong to the great Christian family of which the pope is the father. When the father commands, the children are bound to obey. So must we, the obedient children of a loving father, be guided by the wisdom and the authority of the Church, and keep her commandments.

Suppose someone asks: Where does the Church get her authority to make laws? The answer is: *The Catholic Church has the right to make laws from Jesus Christ, who said to the Apostles, the first bishops of His Church: "Whatever you bind on earth shall be bound also in heaven."*

Another question might be: Who exercises this authority? In reply we would say, *This right to make laws is exercised by the bishops, the successors of the Apostles, and especially by the Pope, who as the successor of the chief of the Apostles, St. Peter, has the right to make laws for the universal Church.*

The Church has given us many laws. Some of these apply to certain members of the Church; others to all Catholics without exception. Chief among the laws of the Church are the five precepts:

1. You shall attend Mass on Sundays and holy days of obligation.

2. You shall confess your sins at least once a year.

3. You shall receive the sacrament of the Eucharist at least during the Easter season.

4. You shall observe the days of fasting and abstinence established by the Church.

5. You shall help to provide for the needs of the Church.

*"Know, O Christian, that the Mass is the holiest act of religion. You cannot do anything to glorify God more, nor profit your soul more, than by devoutly assisting at it, and assisting as often as possible."*

—*St. Peter Julian Eymard*

## The First Precept of the Church

The first precept of the Church is to attend Mass on Sundays and holy days of obligation.

God is the Supreme Being, and worship and honor are due to Him. In order that man may gain eternal life by giving God the reverence due to Him, the Church has set aside a certain day of the week for the worship of God. On this day man is obliged under pain of mortal sin to perform his duty of worship to his Creator.

Mass at
St. Peter's
Square

We learn in the catechism that *a Catholic who through his own fault misses Mass on a Sunday or holy day of obligation commits a mortal sin.*

It is possible for us to be present physically at Mass and still fail in our duty to actively participate. To fulfill this obligation we must give the Mass our attention, uniting our hearts and minds with the priest and all those present. The Mass is the public prayer of Christ's Church, and because it is a prayer it is necessary for us to use our minds and wills in offering it to God. If, for example, a person sleeps through the entire Mass he does not fulfill the obligation.

In addition, we can fulfill the letter of the law requiring us to assist at Mass and still not offer the Mass in the spirit in which we should. If we look around during Mass or deliberately allow our thoughts to wander from one subject to another, we are being disrespectful to God. Merely by giving sufficient attention to realize what is being done at the altar we can, it is true, fulfill the obligation to assist at Mass. But we are not giving God the worship He deserves if we voluntarily allow ourselves to be distracted. The best way for us to assist at Mass is to use a missal, as it helps us to follow the actions of the priest and unite our prayers with his.

In addition to Sundays the Church asks us to attend Mass on the holy days of obligation. There are ten holy days observed by the Church. Those celebrated in the United States are these six:

**Holy Days of Obligation**

*Christmas Day (December 25)*

*Mary, Mother of God (January 1)*

*The Ascension (The Sixth Week of Easter)*

*The Assumption (August 15)*

*All Saints' Day (November 1)*

*The Immaculate Conception (December 8)*

You may be sure that the Church, knowing the forgetfulness of her children, had good reason for designating certain days to be days of special devotion. *Holy days were instituted by the Church to remind us of the mysteries of our faith and of the important events in the lives of Christ and of His Blessed Mother, and to recall to us the virtues and the rewards of the saints.*

Many events in the life of our Lord and His mother are celebrated as great feasts, but not all are holy days. The Church prescribes that all these feasts be celebrated with fitting solemnity.

Many saints, too, have their proper feast days. The number of martyrs, confessors, and virgins who have entered heavenly glory is countless. They do not all have a special feast day, so the Church honors them all on one day near the end of the ecclesiastical year, on November first—All Saints' Day.

We have been considering attendance at Mass on Sundays and holy days of obligation, but the Lord demands also keeping His days holy in other ways. God Himself gave us one example when He rested after six days of work. Following His example, *the Church obliges us to abstain from work on holy days of obligation, just as on Sundays, as far as we are able.* You have learned that on Sundays and holy days some kinds of work are permissible while others are forbidden. How do some people sin by working on Sunday, while others work and commit no sin?

In the preceding paragraphs we find another proof of God's love for us. He gave the Church the power to make certain laws which make clear our obligations, and make it easier to obey the commandments of God. Governments pass laws contributing to the general welfare of their citizens. So, too, the Church, with the power vested in her since the time of St. Peter, legislates for the spiritual welfare of her children.

## The Second and Third Precepts of the Church

The second precept of the Church is to confess our sins at least once a year. The third precept of the Church is to receive the Holy Eucharist during the Easter Time.

The second and third precepts of the Church are closely related, and will be considered together in this section. Christ gave the command, "Except you eat the flesh of the Son of Man, and drink his blood, you shall not have life in you" (Jn. 6:54). From this we learn that Christ desires this intimate union with His beloved children so greatly that He commands us to come to Him. One of the reasons why Christ instituted the sacrament of Penance and Reconciliation was to enable us to receive Holy Communion worthily.

> *"In failing to confess, Lord,*
> *I would only hide You from*
> *myself, not myself from You."*
>
> —*St. Augustine*

### We Are Strictly Obliged to Make a Good Confession at Least Once a Year

*You know that by the commandment to confess our sins at least once a year is meant that we are strictly obliged to make a good confession within the year, especially if we have a mortal sin to confess.* Whoever fails in observing this commandment sins grievously. But the sacrament of Penance and Reconciliation does more than take away sin.

*We should go to confession frequently because frequent confession greatly helps us to overcome temptation, to keep in the state of grace, and to grow in virtue.* We can see from this why the Church encourages frequent confession.

A garment must be washed over and over again. The soul, too, must be cleansed repeatedly from mortal and venial sin in order to keep it spotless. A good housekeeper does not wait for spring housecleaning to put her house in order, but makes it a regular task to give it a cleaning each week to get rid of the dust and dirt.

Many people never commit a mortal sin, yet they go to confession once a week. Why? They realize that grace received from a good confession is a safeguard for the supernatural life of the soul. If a person is in danger of death, he is obliged to go to confession if he has a mortal sin of his soul.

Let us reflect on the goodness of God and resolve to use every opportunity to gain grace through penance.

## To Neglect to Receive Holy Communion During the Easter Time Is a Grave Sin

Christ's parting gift to His Apostles was the Holy Eucharist. He wanted to be with men for all ages, and in His love He instituted this tremendous sacrament. In it Christ is really present—body and blood, soul and divinity—on our altars. It is our greatest privilege to receive our Lord in Holy Communion; and the Church, in order to emphasize our need for Christ's help, has commanded the faithful to receive Holy Communion at least once a year. The law is: *A Catholic who neglects to receive Holy Communion worthily during the Easter time commits a grave sin.*

*The Easter time in the United States begins on the first Sunday of Lent and ends on Trinity Sunday.* Not only must we perform our own Easter duty, but we must see to it that others under our care receive Communion. All Catholics should know that sickness does not excuse them from the obligation of making their Easter duty. It is well for all to make their Easter duty in their own parish church. Why?

The Eucharist is a great gift which we would do well to receive often.

While it is a precept of the Church that we receive Holy Communion during the Easter time, a practicing Catholic will not be satisfied with a mere observance of this commandment. He will satisfy his longing for union with Christ by receiving Him at every opportunity.

St. Pius X, who is called the "Pope of the Blessed Sacrament," allowed children to receive Holy Communion at an early age, and recommended frequent, even daily, Communion for all.

In the Old Testament we read that God commanded every Jew under pain of death to partake of the Paschal Lamb. The Paschal Lamb was a prototype of the "Lamb of God," Jesus Christ.

## The Fourth Precept of the Church

The fourth precept of the Church is to observe the prescribed days of fasting and abstinence.

You know the words of our Lord requiring penance and self-denial from His followers (Lk. 9:23; 13:5).

The early Christians were very religious people. On vigils of feasts they frequently fasted until five o'clock in the evening. Later these severe customs were modified somewhat, and a full meal at noon, with a lighter evening meal, was permitted. Today it is much easier. But penance is still necessary, for many reasons.

*The Church commands us to fast and to abstain in order that we may control the desires of the flesh, raise our minds more freely to God, and make satisfaction for sin.*

Abstinence from flesh meat is commanded on Fridays during Lent. In the United States, it is a binding discipline to practice some form of penance on all Fridays of the year (excepting solemnities). *The Church makes Friday a day of penance to remind us of our Lord's death on Good Friday.* The example of Christ's suffering makes us reflect on His goodness in suffering so much for us. It should make us want to offer sacrifice for His sake.

There is no excuse for anyone's not knowing the laws concerning fast and abstinence. *We can know the days appointed for*

*"The scripture is full of places that prove fasting to be not the invention of man but the institution of God, and to have many more profits than one. And that the fasting of one man may do good unto another, our Saviour showeth himself where he saith that some kind of devils cannot be cast out of one man by another "without prayer and fasting." And therefore I marvel that they take this way against fasting and other bodily penance."*

*—St. Thomas More*

*fast or abstinence from the instructions of our bishops and priests*. These are made public through the diocesan newspapers, bulletins, websites, and announcements at Sunday Mass, especially at the beginning of Lent.

**Certain Days Are Set Aside as Fast Days**

Certain days are fast days. Others are days of abstinence. Others still, are both.

*A fast day is a day on which only one full meal is allowed; but in the morning and evening some food may be taken, the quantity and quality of which are determined by approved local custom.* Ash Wednesday and Good Friday are days of fasting. *All baptized persons between the ages of twenty-one and fifty-nine are obliged to observe the fast days of the Church, unless they are excused or dispensed.*

Pastors and confessors have the power of dispensing from the obligation of fasting. Those requesting it must have a good reason. If a person wishes a dispensation for Lent it should be obtained before Ash Wednesday and need not be asked for in the confessional. In case of a dispensation, the priest usually asks the penitent to perform some other act of penance in place of fasting.

**All Fridays of the Year Are Days of Penance**

The fourth precept of the Church also commands us to abstain from flesh meat on certain days. *A day of abstinence is a day on which we are not allowed the use of meat.* By meat is meant the flesh of warm-blooded, breathing, land animals, including birds and fowl. All Fridays of the year are abstinence days. In the United States, Catholics may substitute some other form penance for abstinence on Fridays. *All baptized persons seven years of age or over who have attained the use of reason are obliged to observe the abstinence days of the Church, unless they are excused or dispensed.* The Church allows the ill, the convalescent, the very old, and the poverty-stricken sometimes to be given a dispensation from the obligation of abstinence.

Although the law of fast and abstinence is universal, the observance is not the same in all parts of the world. With the permission of the Holy See, the bishops have the power to interpret and sometimes to modify the regulations concerning fast and abstinence. Some bishops have allowed all within their jurisdiction to substitute abstaining from meat with some other penance.

On one occasion when the Fourth of July fell on Friday, the bishop dispensed his diocese from the law of abstinence. A Protestant was heard to remark: "You Catholics think it is a sin to eat meat on Friday, and then your priests tell you to go ahead and eat meat. If a thing is a sin, it is always a sin." Can you explain? Can the Church change her own laws? Can she change God's laws? Can she change natural law? What is the difference between a legislator changing the speed limit and declaring that murder is now permissible?

## The Fifth Precept of the Church

The fifth precept of the Church is to help provide for the needs of the Church.

*By this precept is meant that each of us is obliged to bear his fair share of the financial burden of the Church.* This obligation is contained in both the Old and the New Testaments.

In the Old Testament the Holy Land was divided among eleven of the twelve tribes of Israel. One of the tribes, the Levites, was made up entirely of priests and persons who served in the temple. They received none of the land, but were to be supported by the other eleven tribes. The people were obliged by law to bring first fruits and tithes, that is, one tenth of income in goods or money, each year to the temple.

In the New Law we are not required to contribute a definite amount. However, every Christian is obliged to give to God's Church according to his ability and the Church's needs. It has

The widow's mite,
Luke 21:1-4

been recommended that every person who is working, or has an income, give one day's wage or income each month to the various needs of God's Church. Do you think that this is too much? Is it more than the average family spends for recreation each month? If this were done, the ordinary expenses of the Church could easily be met.

Read the story of the Widow's Mite (Lk. 21:1–4). What lesson can be derived from it?

### The Faithful Must Share in the Support of the Diocese

The diocese is a definite territory under the pastoral jurisdiction of a bishop. In carrying out his work he depends on the financial support of all the members of the diocese.

The maintenance of the cathedral, the support of the bishop, the salaries of various diocesan officials, and expenses of the various offices of the chancery, are borne by the diocese. In addition to these, schools, hospitals, seminaries, depend upon the contributions of the faithful. There are other numerous requests that must be met by the generosity of the Catholic people.

### The Faithful Must Share in the Support of the Parish

The ordinary expenses of the parish are those which any business firm would incur. The expenses of heat, light, water, the cleaning and maintenance of the church and school, the salaries of the priests, teachers, and employees, are a financial obligation on the parish which the pastor must pay from the contributions of the faithful.

In addition to his salary, which is a nominal one, the priest accepts Mass offerings, and voluntary contributions for baptisms and weddings. These are not payments for the spiritual advantages received but rather a contribution to the living expenses of the priest.

A member of the Church is entitled to all its services and privileges, and should be willing to contribute to its support according to his means. "If you have much, give abundantly; if you have little, take care even to bestow a little" (Tob. 4:9). What kind of sin would it be to neglect to support the Church?

## Other Laws of the Church

Besides the five precepts of the Church, there are many other laws that are important and binding on all Catholics. These you will study in more detail when you are in high school.

## Summary

The Catholic Church has received the right to make laws from her founder, Jesus Christ. Our Lord said to the Apostles, the first bishops of the Church: "Whatever you bind upon earth shall be bound in heaven." The right to make laws is exercised by the bishops, the successors of the Apostles. There are five precepts of the Church.

1   You shall attend Mass on Sundays and holy days of obligation.

2   You shall confess your sins at least once a year.

3   You shall receive the sacrament of the Eucharist at least during the Easter season.

4   You shall observe the days of fasting and abstinence established by the Church.

5   You shall help to provide for the needs of the Church.

The precepts of the Church are binding on all Catholics, and must be obeyed with the same strictness and care as the commandments of God. Unlike the commandments of God they may be changed or discontinued by the Church as she judges best.

 **FOR ME TO REVIEW**

*Catechism Lesson*

**545.   Q. Did our Lord Himself make all the laws of the Church?**
   A. Our Lord Himself did not make all the laws of the Church. He gave the Church also power to make laws to suit the needs of the times, places or persons as it judged necessary.

**546.** **Q.** **Can the Church change its laws?**

    **A.** The Church can, when necessary, change the laws it has itself made, but it cannot change the laws that Christ has made. Neither can the Church change natural law, or any doctrine of faith or morals.

**1244.** **Q.** **What are holy days of obligation?**

    **A.** Holy days of obligation are special feasts of the Church on which we are bound, under pain of grave sin, to attend Mass and to keep from labors when it can be done without great loss or inconvenience. Whoever, on account of their circumstances, cannot give up work on holy days of obligation should make every effort to attend Mass and should also explain in confession the necessity of working on holy days.

**1332.** **Q.** **Why were holy days instituted by the Church?**

    **A.** Holy days were instituted by the Church to recall to our minds the great mysteries of our faith and the virtues and rewards of the saints.

**1337.** **Q.** **What do you mean by fast days?**

    **A.** By fast days I mean days on which we are allowed but one full meal.

**1338.** **Q.** **Is it permitted on fast days to take any food besides the one full meal?**

    **A.** It is permitted on fast days, besides the one full meal, to take two other meatless meals, to maintain strength, according to each one's needs. But together these two meatless meals should not equal another full meal.

**1339.** **Q.** **Who are obliged to fast?**

    **A.** All persons over 18 and under 59 years of age, and whose health and occupation will permit them to fast.

1344. Q. **What do you mean by days of abstinence?**
    A. By days of abstinence I mean days on which no meat at all may be taken. This is explained in the regulations for Lent. All the Fridays of the year are days of abstinence or penance except when a solemnity falls on a Friday.

1346. Q. **Why does the Church command us to fast and abstain?**
    A. The Church commands us to fast and abstain, in order that we may mortify our passions and satisfy for our sins.

1347. Q. **What is meant by our passions and what by mortifying them?**
    A. By our passions are meant our sinful desires and inclinations. Mortifying them means restraining them and overcoming them so that they have less power to lead us into sin.

1348. Q. **Why does the Church command us to abstain from flesh-meat or do some other penance on Fridays?**
    A. The Church commands us to abstain from flesh-meat on Fridays or perform some other penance in honor of the day on which our Saviour died.

1349. Q. **What is meant by the precept of confessing at least once a year?**
    A. By the precept of confessing at least once a year is meant that we are obliged, under pain of grave sin, to go to confession within the year.

1350. Q. **Should we confess only once a year?**
    A. We should confess frequently, if we wish to lead a good life.

1353. Q.  What sin does he commit who neglects to receive Communion during the Easter time?

A.  He who neglects to receive Communion during the Easter time commits a grave sin.

1356. Q.  Are we obliged to contribute to the support of our pastors?

A.  We are obliged to contribute to the support of our pastors, and to bear our share in the expense of the Church and school.

1357. Q.  Where did the duty of contributing to the support of the Church and clergy originate?

A.  The duty of contributing to the support of the Church and clergy originated in the Old Law, when God commanded all the people to contribute to the support of the temple and of its priests.

*Questions and Exercises*

## Part 1: Completion

1.  A Catholic who misses Mass on a Sunday or holy day of obligation commits a _____ sin.

2.  The holy days of obligation in the United States are ____(a)____, ____(b)____, ____(c)____, ____(d)____, ____(e)____, ____(f)____.

3.  The pastor and confessor have the power to dispense from laws of ____(a)____(b)____.

4.  Easter time in the United States begins on the ____(a)____ Sunday of____(b)____ and ends on ____(c)____.

## Part 2: Matching

**COLUMN A**

1. Abstinence day

2. November 1 *D*

3. Persons between twenty-one
   and fifty-nine *C*

4. August 15 *E*

5. Fast day *B*

**COLUMN B**

A. Day on which one full meal
   is allowed

B. Day on which meat is
   not allowed

C. Are obliged to fast

D. The feast of All Saints

E. The feast of the Assumption
   of the Blessed Virgin

### ☑ FOR ME TO DO

1. Look up the following Scripture texts and discuss what our Lord did on the Sabbath: Mk. 2:23–28; 3:1–6; Lk. 13:10–17; Jn. 9:1–41.

3. Compare the laws of the Church protecting our spiritual health with health and safety rules caring for bodily health.

4. Discuss why the following fasted: our Lord, St. John the Baptist.

5. Scripture Hunt: Show how the following texts are applied to the precepts of the Church: Lk. 15:1–7; 15:8–10; 15:11–32; 18:9–14; 19:1–10; 12:13–21; Mt. 6:16–18; 17:23–26; Mk. 12:41–44; 2:18–22; Jn. 10:1–21; Acts 4:34–35.

## Acceptance of God's Will

*In all things may the most holy, the most just, and most lovable will of God be done, praised, and exalted above all forever. Your will be done, O Lord, your will be done. The Lord has given and the Lord has taken away; blessed be the name of the Lord now and always.*

*Amen.*

# Achievement Test

*Write your answers on a separate sheet of paper*

 **I.** Multiple Choice

1.  We owe God our homage and adoration because He is:
    A. Triune.
    B. good to us.
    C. merciful.
    D. infinitely perfect.

2.  We are observing the first commandment of God when we:
    A. pray or offer sacrifice.
    B. take an oath in court.
    C. vow to make a pilgrimage.
    D. give good example to others.

3.  The calling down of some evil on a person, place, or thing is:
    A. blasphemy.
    B. lying.
    C. cursing.
    D. perjury.

4.  We violate the second commandment if we:
    A. participate in false worship.
    B. give bad example to others.
    C. wish evil upon someone.
    D. believe in fortunetelling.

5.  When a person trusts that he can be saved by his own efforts without God's help, or by God's help without his own efforts, he commits sin by:
    A. sloth.
    B. distrust.
    C. despair.
    D. presumption.

6.  The calling on God to witness to the truth of what we say is:
    A. cursing.
    B. blasphemy.
    C. an oath.
    D. a vow.

7.  Our test of love for God is:
    A. keeping the commandments.
    B. thinking of Him.
    C. praying to Him.
    D. knowing our religion well.

8.  We must love:
    A. only those whom we know personally.
    B. only those in the state of grace.
    C. communism.
    D. all men.

9.  Another name for the Ten Commandments is:
    A. the creed.
    B. the Decalogue.
    C. the precepts of the Church.
    D. counsels.

10. The sin of perjury is committed by one who:
    A. deliberately calls on God to bear witness to a lie.
    B. calls on God to send evil to someone.
    C. expresses contempt for God.
    D. uses God's name without reverence.

11. The virtue or power by which we love God and our neighbor in a supernatural way is called:
    A. faith.
    B. hope.
    C. charity.
    D. fortitude.

12. The false doctrine which teaches that all religions are equally good is called:
    A. apostasy.
    B. indifferentism.
    C. infidelity.
    D. spiritism.

13. The highest form of worship in the Catholic Church is the:
    A. Benediction of the Blessed Sacrament.
    B. Sacrifice of the Mass.
    C. adoration of the cross.
    D. recitation of the rosary.

14. Children must obey their parents in:
    A. all commands which are not sinful.
    B. all commands without exception.
    C. only those matters which they consider reasonable.
    D. the choice of a state of life.

15. Render to Caesar the things that are Caesar's means to:
    A. respect our parents.
    B. pray for those who offend us.
    C. care for the sick.
    D. obey the civil law.

16. A deliberate promise made to God by which a person binds himself under pain of sin to do something that is especially pleasing to Him is:
    A. an oath.
    B. a vow.
    C. a precept.
    D. a beatitude.

17. The best way to assist at Mass is to:
    A. unite our prayers with those of the priest by using the missal.
    B. watch the actions of the priest.
    C. read various prayers from a prayer book.
    D. recite the rosary.

18. Careless and irreverent use of the name of God is called:
    A. profanity.
    B. cursing.
    C. blasphemy.
    D. swearing.

19. A Catholic who willfully and with full knowledge neglects his Easter duty commits:
    A. a sacrilege.
    B. a venial sin.
    C. no sin.
    D. a mortal sin.

20.  A person who, without a good reason, makes known the hidden faults of another commits the sin of:
     A. detraction.
     B. rash judgment.
     C. calumny.
     D. perjury.

21.  By the sixth commandment we are commanded to:
     A. be modest in our outward behavior.
     B. practice charity.
     C. speak the truth at all times.
     D. take proper care of our physical welfare.

22.  Theft and robbery are opposed to the virtue of:
     A. prudence.
     B. temperance.
     C. justice.
     D. fortitude.

23.  The eighth commandment tells us to:
     A. respect the property of others.
     B. speak the truth in all things.
     C. make known the faults of others.
     D. lie if we can save someone.

24.  We are bound under penalty of grave sin to assist at Mass on the feast of the:
     A. Nativity of the Blessed Virgin Mary.
     B. Epiphany.
     C. Assumption.
     D. Presentation of the Blessed Virgin.

25. A permission, officially given, which excuses one from keeping the law is called:
    A. restitution.
    B. a contract.
    C. abstinence.
    D. dispensation.

 **II. True / False**

1. The secret of happiness is summed up in the great commandment—love of God and love of neighbor. T

2. The commandments are just as binding today as they were when God first made them known. T

3. Parents are obliged to correct and punish their children for wrongdoing. T

4. God has promised a special blessing on those who are obedient to their parents. T

5. Immodest dress is a cause of scandal. F

6. A false oath is called calumny. T

7. The three evangelical counsels are faith, hope, and charity. T

8. We are obliged to use reasonable means to safeguard our lives. T

9. Influencing others to sin by word or example is scandal. T

10. We may tell a deliberate lie for our neighbor's good. F

11. Failure to give full pay for service, or vice versa, is a form of stealing. T

12. To shelter the homeless is one of the spiritual works of mercy. F

13. Unnecessarily exposing oneself to harm or danger is a sin. T

14. We adore Christ; we venerate the saints. T

15. Industriousness and regularity in work promote faithfulness to the seventh commandment. F

16. The development of habits of pure and modest living safeguards us against disorders in adult life. T

17. A child's stubbornness against his parents is a sin against the second commandment. F

18. The sixth commandment forbids all impurity in words, looks, and actions, whether alone or with others. T

19. The welfare of the whole country depends upon the individual's observing the Ten Commandments. T

## III. Matching

| COLUMN A | COLUMN B |
|---|---|
| 1. Injuring others because they have injured us J | A. Vow |
| 2. Every man, woman, and child in the world E | B. Cursing |
| 3. Rejection of one or more truths of the Catholic Faith F | C. Scandal |
| 4. Insulting language which expresses contempt for God, either directly or through His saints and holy things G | D. Profanity |
| 5. A deliberate promise made to God by which a person binds himself under pain of sin to do something that is especially pleasing to God A | E. Neighbor |
| 6. The calling down of some evil on a person, place, or thing B | F. Heresy |
| 7. Careless and irreverent use of the names of God or the saints D | G. Blasphemy |
| 8. Anything leading another to commit sin C | H. Rest from work |
| 9. Judging ill of our neighbor without sufficient proof or reason I | I. Rash judgment |
| 10. Required on Sundays and holy days H | J. Revenge |

Additional Statements for the Multiple Choice Test

1. Days of abstinence are those on which we are forbidden to eat:
   A. fish.
   B. food between meals.
   C. three full meals.
   D. meat.

2. We should avoid profanity, blasphemy, and all unnecessary oaths chiefly because:
   A. it shows a lack of self-respect.
   B. it shows respect for God's Holy Name.
   C. it advertises our ignorance.
   D. it develops better control of our tongues.

3. To give back what one has taken from another unjustly is:
   A. robbery.
   B. restitution.
   C. stealing.
   D. usury.

4. In trying to overcome a temptation to steal an article from a store, the best motive John might have would be: I won't do this because:
   A. I really love God.
   B. it is a sin.
   C. I may get caught.
   D. I will have to return it.

5. The ability to accept the teachings of the Church on God's authority comes from:
   A. hope.
   B. faith.
   C. justice.
   D. charity.

6. If you wish to keep pure:
   A. receive Holy Communion frequently.
   B. have plenty of time on your hands.
   C. read all kinds of books.
   D. be indifferent about your companions.

7. The prayer which we say especially to make reparation for profanity is called the:
   A. Our Father.
   B. Angel of God.
   C. Act of Faith.
   D. Divine Praises.

8. The last seven commandments point out the duties we owe:
   A. the saints.
   B. ourselves and our neighbor.
   C. the souls in purgatory.
   D. God.

## Exercises for Further Study

1. Why has the Church the right to make laws binding on her members?

2. Without the virtue of faith can we know that God exists? (See Rom. 1:29.)

3. In heaven, will there be any need for the virtues of faith and hope? Explain.

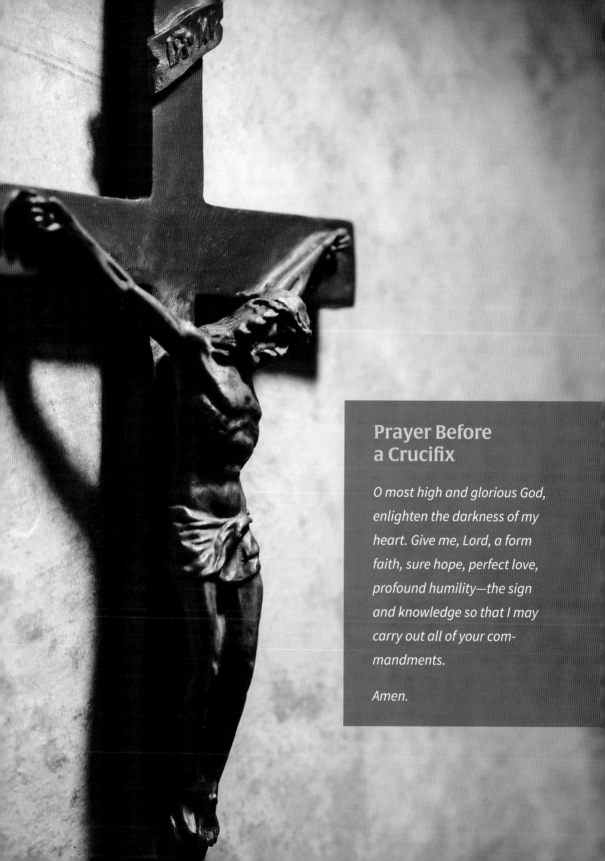

## Prayer Before a Crucifix

*O most high and glorious God, enlighten the darkness of my heart. Give me, Lord, a form faith, sure hope, perfect love, profound humility—the sign and knowledge so that I may carry out all of your commandments.*

*Amen.*

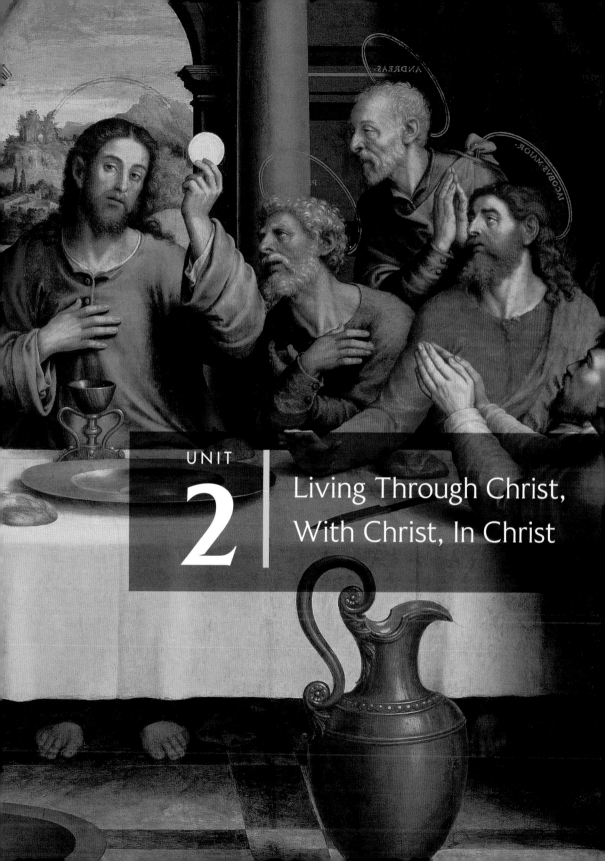

# UNIT 2

## Living Through Christ, With Christ, In Christ

# CHAPTER 5
## Christ's Sacraments in General

In unit 1, we studied the commandments, which tell us how a person who believes those doctrines should live.

Keeping the commandments and practicing the virtues and the works of mercy is no easy task. Indeed it cannot be done without supernatural assistance. God gives us this needed help through the means of grace. Chief among these are the sacraments. There are also the sacramentals, indulgences, and most importantly prayer.

We already know much about the sacraments. We studied them from the smaller catechism in an earlier grade. Now it is time to get a more grown-up knowledge of these very important channels of the graces of the Redemption.

# The Sacraments

The life of Christ comes to us through the seven sacraments. They are the channels through which the grace of Christ flows into the soul. It is the life-giving grace of the sacraments that we need to enable us to live through Christ, with Christ, and in Christ.

*What Do We Already Know About the Sacraments?*

- What is grace?

- What is sanctifying grace?

- How can the sacraments give grace?

- How was each of the sacraments instituted?

- What are the sacraments of the living? of the dead?

- What are the requirements for each of the sacraments?

- What is the sacramental character?

- Which sacraments imprint this sacramental character?

- Can you give scriptural quotations for each of the sacraments?

- What is the formula for the administration of Baptism?

- Who is the ordinary minister of each of the sacraments?

## A Sacrament Is an Outward Sign

A sacrament is an outward or visible sign instituted by Christ to give grace. Since it is a visible sign, it can be perceived by our senses. Thus, for example, water is part of the visible sign of Baptism; bread and wine are the visible signs of Holy Eucharist; chrism (consecrated oil) is part of the visible sign of Confirmation, and so forth.

And it is fitting for God to communicate His grace to men through visible signs. For God provides for man according to man's nature, which is such that he is led to grasp the spiritual through the senses. In addition, God redeemed man by taking on human flesh, and therefore it is only fitting that He should continue the work of redemption by making use of visible nature.

But it is necessary to show the difference between the sacraments as signs in contrast with other kinds of natural signs that we come across in the world. For example, smoke signifies fire, but the smoke is not the fire itself; a portrait portrays a certain person, but the portrait is not the same things as the person. Such signs merely signify objects, but they do not produce the object or cause it to exist.

"The sacraments are efficacious signs of grace, instituted by Christ and entrusted to the Church, by which divine life is dispensed to us."

—*Catechism of the Catholic Church, 1131*

The sacraments, on the other hand, both signify or manifest grace *and* actually produce it in us. Or, to quote a traditional phrase, the sacraments "effect what they signify." In Baptism the water that is poured over our heads not only signifies what is being done (i.e., the washing away the filth of sin) but actually produces the effect (the remission of sin). The power of the sacrament is in the sign. When the priest pours baptismal water over the head of a child, the water is not only a sign of cleansing, but actually produces the spiritual cleansing of the soul from original sin. Therefore these signs have in themselves the power to produce the grace which they signify. They produce and increase supernatural life in the soul. No material sign could do so unless God willed it. God chooses to confer these graces through a sign, in order to make the sacrament visible. He wanted us to have some definite proof and assurance that we had received grace. He is always thinking of us.

## Christ Instituted Seven Sacraments

We know that there can be no more than seven sacraments because Christ instituted only seven. This is proved from Scripture, testified to by the Tradition handed down to us from the Fathers, and authoritatively restated at the Council of Trent. The seven sacraments are: *Baptism, Confirmation, Holy Eucharist, Penance and Reconciliation, Anointing of the Sick, Holy Orders, and Matrimony.*

Adoration of the Blessed Sacrament is one way we can encounter our Lord in the sacrament of Holy Eucharist.

Because the sacraments produce grace which is a gift of God, Christ alone could institute the sacraments and give the outward sign the power to sanctify the soul. In instituting the seven sacraments Christ had in mind the principal needs of our supernatural life.

Through these seven sacraments we receive divine grace when we are most in need of it. As there are roadside inns where the traveler can pause to rest and regain his strength, so on the weary journey of life the sacraments are intended to nourish and strengthen our supernatural life.

## Source of the Power of the Sacraments

*The sacraments receive their power to give grace from God, through the merits of Jesus Christ.*

Think of our divine Saviour dying on the cross, suffering to gain grace for our souls. While Christ was hanging upon the cross after having paid the price of our redemption, Longinus opened His side with a spear. Immediately there came out blood and water (Jn. 19:34). The blood reminds us what it cost our Lord to do what He did—give up His life for us. The water reminds us of the effect He produced—the cleansing of our souls from sin.

Let us remember that the sufferings which our Lord endured have merited grace to cleanse and perfect every soul, from the beginning of the world until the end of time. Our Divine Redeemer has merited for us all the graces that we receive through the sacraments. All graces come to us through Christ, our Saviour and Redeemer.

### TERMS TO KNOW

- sacrament
- grace
- visible
- matter
- instituted
- sacramental
- spiritual
- sanctifying grace
- disposition
- imprint
- effect
- sacrilege
- supernatural
- redemption
- outward
- merits

## The Sacraments Give Sanctifying Grace

You know that Christ instituted the sacraments to give and to increase grace, which is the supernatural life of our soul. Sanctifying grace, as we know, makes our soul holy and pleasing to God. It also permits us to share in the life of God Himself. Thousands of martyrs have sacrificed their natural lives to preserve this divine life of sanctifying grace.

*"If the angels could be jealous of men, they would be for one reason: Holy Communion."*

—St. Maximillian Kolbe

It is very necessary to keep and strengthen this life by the practice of virtue because otherwise we cannot reach our eternal destiny. Our natural powers can never enable us to reach God. Only grace will do it. our Lord has told us: "No one can come to me unless drawn by the Father who sent me; and I will raise that person up on the last day" (Jn. 6:44).

## Sacraments Impart Sacramental Grace

As we have previously said, each sacrament gives us divine life (sanctifying grace) or an increase of it. But in addition, we know that *each of the sacraments also gives a special grace, called sacramental grace, which helps one to carry out the particular purpose of that sacrament.*

If each sacrament did not give some special, actual, or sacramental grace, there would be no need of more than one sacrament. The sacrament of Baptism gives us the grace to renounce the devil and guard against sin. Penance and Reconciliation gives us the grace to guard against falling again into sin. Confirmation gives us the grace to be brave in serving God, and if necessary, to die for the faith, besides giving us the seven gifts of the Holy Spirit. Holy Orders gives the grace to perform the duties of the priesthood of God. The Holy Eucharist nourishes and sustains supernatural life in us. Matrimony gives to husband and wife the grace to live a blessed married life, and to rear their children in the love of God. Anointing of the Sick gives us the grace not to fear death, strengthens us against temptations, and makes us resigned to God's will.

Since each sacrament confers a special grace to assist man at particular stages of his life, you can understand why Christ instituted the seven sacraments.

## Do the Sacraments Always Give Grace?

*The sacraments always give grace if we receive them with the right disposition.*

It is the teaching of the Catholic Church that the sacraments always give grace to those who receive them with the right dispositions and who fulfill the necessary conditions required by the Church for each sacrament. Christ Himself said this when He instituted the sacraments to give grace to men. "He who believes and is baptized shall be saved" (Mk. 16:16).

If we fail to comply with the necessary conditions, we place an obstacle in the way of receiving grace. A sinner, for instance, who does not intend to give up sin, might receive the sacrament of Confirmation or Matrimony, but he would not receive the grace of these sacraments. Also if we go to confession and have no contrition for our sins, we do not receive the grace of the sacrament. To be in a state of contrition has two essential components: firstly, to be sorry for, and sad about, the sin(s) committed; secondly, genuine contrition necessarily involves a resolution to not sin in the future. Even if our contrition is "imperfect" (i.e., if only some genuine sorrow is felt, and if only some resolution not to sin again is made—however weak that resolution may be), we can receive the grace of the sacrament. Again, it is important to remember that we can receive the sacrament, but not the grace it was instituted to impart, if we do not receive it under the right disposition and intention.

The sacraments may be compared to the sunshine. The sun cannot penetrate into a room if the shutters are closed. But as soon as the shutters are opened, the sunshine streams in, warming it and illuminating it. In like manner, a sacrament cannot produce the life of grace in the soul of the person receiving it if there is an obstacle. It is important, therefore, that nothing stop the flow of grace into our soul when receiving a sacrament.

## Sacraments Are Classified as the Sacraments of the Dead and of the Living

Some sacraments are called "sacraments of the living", others are called "sacraments of the dead."

*Baptism and Penance and Reconciliation are called sacraments of the dead because their chief purpose is to give the supernatural life of sanctifying grace to souls spiritually dead through sin.*

Confirmation, Holy Eucharist, Anointing of the Sick, Holy

Orders, and Matrimony are called sacraments of the living became their chief purpose is to give more grace to souls already spiritually alive through sanctifying grace.

The sacraments of the dead are chiefly intended for those without supernatural life, whereas the sacraments of the living are intended for those who are in the state of sanctifying grace. Again, while the sacraments of the dead give or restore supernatural life to the soul, the sacraments of the living ordinarily increase it.

For example, if we are spiritually dead through original or mortal sin, we must receive supernatural life if we are to obtain the grace of the sacraments. On the other hand, if we are already

Baptism and Penance and Reconciliation are called sacraments of the dead because their chief purpose is to give the supernatural life of sanctifying grace to souls spiritually dead through sin.

in the state of sanctifying grace, the sacraments of the living serve to increase it in us.

Make frequent use of the sacraments. May the Christlike life which is thus increased in us appear in all that we say and do. A human being enjoys fullness of life when he uses the means of health—air, food, rest. We glow with the life of God, with grace, when we receive the sacraments worthily.

Does a person commit a serious sin when he receives a sacrament of the living in the state of mortal sin? We know the sacraments were instituted by Christ Himself and that they are, therefore, holy and sacred. If a person knowingly receives a sacrament of the living in the state of mortal sin, he violates the sacredness of the sacrament. In accordance with what we learned earlier, we know that *he who knowingly receives a sacrament of the living in mortal sin commits a mortal sin of sacrilege, because he treats a sacred thing with grave irreverence.*

What should one do if through weakness he has received any sacrament of the living in the state of mortal sin? He should repent of his sin, confess it and regain the state of grace through the sacrament of Penance and Reconciliation.

## Sacraments Received Once; Sacraments Received More Than Once

Which sacraments may be received only once? We read in the catechism that *the sacraments that can be received only once are Baptism, Confirmation, and Holy Orders. Why? Because they imprint on the soul a spiritual mark, called a character, which lasts forever.* The "character," you will remember, implies a sign of official rank or distinction.

By the sacramental character we are dedicated to perform certain services in Christ's Church: Baptism marks us as members of His Mystical Body and gives us the right to take a part in the sacrificial worship it offers to God; Confirmation brings us to

## Sacraments That May Be Received Only Once

- Baptism
- Confirmation
- Holy Orders
  *(Imprint a character on the soul)*

## Sacraments That May Be Received More Than Once

- Holy Eucharist
- Reconciliation
- Anointing of the Sick
- Matrimony

adult life in the Church, making us soldiers of Christ; and Holy Orders seals those who receive it with authority to forgive sins and bring Christ down upon the altar. These sacramental characters distinguish Christians from non-Christians, and likewise from one another. Since these marks are spiritual they can never be destroyed, not even by serious sin. For those who are saved, these marks will be a special honor because the persons having them belong to God in a particular way. They will remain for all eternity. For those who are damned, they will be a double disgrace. The damned will be lost through their own fault, in spite of the extra help given them by their heavenly Father.

Let us consider briefly the sacraments that may be received more than once. Can you see why Holy Eucharist, Reconciliation, Anointing of the Sick, may need to be received more than once? They increase grace in our soul. In this way our souls become holier and more pleasing to God, and we become more fervent and zealous in our worship of Him. Matrimony may also be celebrated more than once, but only after the death of a spouse.

From this review of the sacraments in general we can realize the importance of grace for the attainment of eternal happiness. Grace gives us supernatural life. Grace brings us the power to act in a supernatural way. Grace gives us the needed help. Grace, merited for us by Christ's Passion and death and placed at our disposal, is inexhaustible because it is infinite. Let us turn to Him and ask His graces, and thus fulfill His will. Only then will we be able to share His company forever.

## Summary

A sacrament is an outward sign instituted by Christ to give grace. There are seven sacraments. The sacraments receive their power to give grace from God, through the merits of Jesus Christ. All the sacraments give sanctifying grace. Each of the sacraments also gives a special grace called sacramental grace. Sacramental grace helps one to carry out the particular purpose of the sacrament. The sacraments always give grace if we receive them with the right disposition.

 **FOR ME TO REVIEW**

*Catechism Lesson*

136.  **Q. What is a sacrament?**

   A. A sacrament is an outward sign instituted by Christ to give grace.

137.  **Q. How many sacraments are there?**

   A. There are seven sacraments: Baptism, Confirmation, Holy Eucharist, Penance and Reconciliation, Anointing of the Sick, Holy Orders, and Matrimony.

138.  **Q. Whence have the sacraments the power of giving grace?**

   A. The sacraments have the power of giving grace from the merits of Jesus Christ.

147.  **Q. Do the sacraments always give grace?**

   A. The sacraments always give grace, if we receive them with the right dispositions.

593.  **Q. Which are the sacraments that give sanctifying grace?**

   A. The sacraments that give sanctifying grace are Baptism and Penance and Reconciliation; and they are called sacraments of the dead.

**594. Q. Why are Baptism and Reconciliation called sacraments of the dead?**

A. Baptism and Reconciliation are called sacraments of the dead because they take away sin, which is the death of the soul, and give grace, which is its life.

**596. Q. Which are the sacraments that increase sanctifying grace in our soul?**

A. The sacraments that increase sanctifying grace in our souls are: Confirmation, Holy Eucharist, Anointing of the Sick, Holy Orders, and Matrimony; and they are called sacraments of the living.

**597. Q. What do we mean by sacraments of the dead and sacraments of the living?**

A. By the sacraments of the dead we mean those sacraments that may be lawfully received while the soul is in a state of mortal sin. By the sacraments of the living we mean those sacraments that can be lawfully received only while the soul is in a state of grace—i.e., free from mortal sin. Living and dead do not refer here to the persons, but to the condition of the souls; for none of the sacraments can be given to a dead person.

**598. Q. Why are Confirmation, Holy Eucharist, Anointing of the Sick, Holy Orders, and Matrimony called sacraments of the living?**

A. Confirmation, Holy Eucharist, Anointing of the Sick, Holy Orders, and Matrimony are called sacraments of the living because those who receive them worthily are already living the life of grace.

**148. Q. Can we receive the sacraments more than once?**

A. We can receive the sacraments more than once, except Baptism, Confirmation, and Holy Orders.

**599.** **Q.** What sin does he commit who receives the sacraments of the living in mortal sin?

**A.** He who receives the sacraments of the living in mortal sin commits a sacrilege, which is a great sin, because it is an abuse of a sacred thing.

**601.** **Q.** Besides sanctifying grace do the sacraments give any other grace?

**A.** Besides sanctifying grace the sacraments give another grace, called sacramental grace.

**602.** **Q.** What is sacramental grace?

**A.** Sacramental grace is a special help which God gives, to attain the end for which He instituted each sacrament.

**603.** **Q.** Is the sacramental grace independent of the sanctifying grace given in the sacraments?

**A.** The sacramental grace is not independent of the sanctifying grace given in the sacraments; for it is the sanctifying grace that gives us a certain right to special helps—called sacramental grace—in each sacrament, as often as we have to fulfill the end of the sacrament or are tempted against it.

*Questions and Exercises*

## **Part 1**: Multiple Choice

1. The sacrament that gives us the right to call God our Father is:
   A. Holy Orders.
   B. Baptism.
   C. Matrimony.
   D. Confirmation.

2. The greatest gift that Adam and Eve lost in the Garden of Eden was:
   A. strength of will.
   B. an enlightened understanding.
   C. immortality.
   D. sanctifying grace.

3. Grace is obtained especially through:
   A. prayer and sacraments.
   B. good works.
   C. the use of sacramentals.

4. The reception of the grace of the sacraments depends chiefly on:
   A. God's mercy.
   B. the prayer of the Church.
   C. the priest who administers them.
   D. our own disposition and co-operation.

5. An outward sign instituted by Christ to give grace is a:
   A. beatitude.
   B. commandment.
   C. sacrament.
   D. work of mercy.

6. One who knowingly receives a sacrament of the living in mortal sin commits:
   A. a sacrilege.
   B. a venial sin.
   C. no sin.

7. The special grace given by each sacrament to help one carry out the particular purpose of the sacrament is:
   A. sanctifying grace.
   B. sacramental grace.
   C. actual grace.

8. The sacraments that can be received only once are:
   A. Baptism and Reconciliation.
   B. Holy Orders, Confirmation, Baptism.
   C. Matrimony, Baptism, Confirmation.
   D. Anointing of the Sick, Holy Orders.

9. Actual grace:
   A. forces the will.
   B. was given to us in baptism.
   C. helps us to do good.
   D. comes from our first parents.

10. "I am the vine, you are the branches. He who abides in me and I in him, he bears much fruit, for without me you can do nothing," refers particularly to:
    A. sacramental grace.
    B. the necessity of good works.
    C. actual grace.
    D. sanctifying grace.

11. The seven sacraments were instituted by:
    A. the early Church.
    B. the apostles.
    C. the pope.
    D. Jesus Christ.

12. The best means of preserving and strengthening the supernatural life is to:
    A. avoid bad companions
    B. go to confession frequently and receive Holy Communion as often as possible.
    C. listen to the advice of priests, parents, and teachers.
    D. say morning and night prayers faithfully.

13. Baptism and Reconciliation are called sacraments of the dead because they:
    A. help one carry out the purpose of the sacrament.
    B. give more grace to persons already spiritually alive through sanctifying grace.
    C. imprint on a person a lasting character.
    D. give the supernatural life of sanctifying grace to persons spiritually dead through sin.

14. The sacrament that is called the "Gate of the Church" is:
    A. Anointing of the Sick.
    B. Confirmation.
    C. Penance and Reconciliation.
    D. Baptism.

15. The sacrament of "Catholic Action" is:
    A. Confirmation.
    B. Baptism.
    C. Holy Eucharist.
    D. Matrimony.

**Part 2**: Scripture Hunt

*Which sacraments are indicated by the following quotations?*

| | |
|---|---|
| Jn. 3:5 | Mt. 26:22–28 |
| 1 Cor. 11:23–25 | Jn. 20:23 |
| James 5:14–15 | Lk. 22:19 |
| Eph. 5:31 | |

### ✓ FOR ME TO DO

1. Make a mural of the seven sacraments showing the cross of Christ as the source of these channels of grace.

2. Choose any one of the seven sacraments and give a two-minute talk telling how it can assist you to become a good citizen as well as a good Christian.

3. Read Lk. 7:1–15 and retell the story in your own words.

4. Compare the restoration of life to a dead body and the restoration of the life of grace to a dead soul.

5. Write down a few of the thoughts which this verse from Scripture suggests to you: "I have fought the good fight, I have finished the course, I have kept my faith" (2 Timothy 4:7-8).

# CHAPTER 6

# Christ Incorporates Us Into the Life of His Mystical Body

LESSON 10

# Baptism

When God created Adam and Eve, He not only gave them natural life as beings composed of body and soul, but supernatural life as well. By this life they became sharers of His divine life and nature. Unfortunately, our first parents sinned and forfeited this supernatural life not only for themselves, but also for all their descendants. Because of their sin we are all conceived with original sin. This means that we are deprived of the divine life of grace which God intended us to have. Without it we cannot enter heaven.

> "Holy Baptism is the basis of the whole Christian life, the gateway to life in the Spirit, and the door which gives access to the other sacraments."
>
> —*Catechism of the Catholic Church, 1213*

Christ, by His death on the cross, made possible our eternal salvation. By His goodness He has provided for the restoration of supernatural life through the sacrament of Baptism. It is important that we know about Baptism and its effects.

## Baptism Is a Sacrament of "New Life"

*Baptism is the sacrament that gives our souls the new life of sanctifying grace by which we become children of God and heirs of heaven.* Baptism is the most necessary sacrament. Without it we cannot receive any other sacrament.

Baptism has the three essentials of a sacrament. (1) It was instituted by Christ. (2) It is an outward visible sign. (3) It confers grace. Let us now consider briefly each essential.

## Baptism Was Instituted by Christ

Although Holy Scripture does not tell us when Christ instituted Baptism, we are certain that, before His ascension, Christ gave His Apostles the commission to baptize. "All power in heaven and on earth has been given to me. Go, therefore, and make disciples of all nations, baptizing them in the name of the Father, and of the Son, and of the Holy Spirit" (Mt. 28:18). As you recall from your study of the growth of the Church, the Apostles did as they were commanded and baptized in the name of the Trinity. Do

The Baptism of
Jesus Christ

you remember the result of Peter's sermon on the first Pentecost? How many persons were baptized on that occasion?

### Baptism Is an Outward Sign
The outward sign of Baptism consists in the pouring of the water on the forehead while pronouncing the words: "I baptize you in the name of the Father, and of the Son, and of the Holy Spirit."

### Baptism Confers Grace
We know that Christ instituted Baptism to confer the new supernatural life of grace on the soul. "Unless a man be born again of water and the Spirit, he cannot enter into the kingdom of God" (Jn. 3:5).

## Baptism Produces Marvelous Effects in the Soul
Baptism, you will remember, remits sin. What sin does Baptism take away? The catechism gives the answer. *Baptism takes away original sin; and also actual sins and all the punishment due to them, if the person baptized be guilty of any actual sins and truly sorry for them.*

### Baptism Takes Away Original and Actual Sins
We know that water in the natural order cleanses the body, puts out fire, invigorates human life, gives fertility to the soil, and produces other effects. The water in Baptism does something similar in a supernatural way. As the water is poured on the head of a person to be baptized, the Holy Spirit comes down upon him and cleanses him from all sins, both original and actual, and also remits the eternal and temporal punishment due to them.

If a man who was perfectly disposed died immediately after Baptism, he would enter the kingdom of God without spending a single moment in purgatory. The reason for this is that Baptism is not merely a remedy. It is a new life which completely destroys sin and all punishment due to it.

Baptism takes away original sin and restores the sanctifying grace lost by our first parents.

### Baptism Confers Sanctifying Grace

The supernatural life conferred by Baptism is the beginning of our eternal life. Through this new life of grace we become God's adopted children. As such, we are heirs of heaven. An adopted child on earth inherits the earthly possessions when the parent dies. God's adopted children have a right to heaven and eternal happiness with God. That is why we are called "heirs of heaven." We belong to God's family. We are His adopted sons and daughters, and as such have a right to enter into God's kingdom, heaven. St. Paul says: "If sons, heirs also; heirs indeed of God and joint heirs with Christ" (Rom. 8:17).

*"Every baptized person should consider that it is in the womb of the Church where he is transformed from a child of Adam to a child of God."*

—*St. Vincent Ferrer*

With the reception of sanctifying grace, we begin our supernatural life as a member of Christ's Mystical Body. We are intimately united with Christ so that His life becomes ours. Just as your arms, legs, and hands are joined to your body, and live the same life as your heart and head live, so through sanctifying grace, we actually live supernaturally by participating in the life of Christ. We are sharers in the very life of God. As St. Paul tells us: "Do you not know that you are the temple of God, and that the spirit of God dwells in you" (1 Cor. 3:16). Do you know what he means by this statement?

St. Louis of France used to say: "I think more of the private chapel where I was baptized than of the Cathedral of Rheims where I was crowned. The dignity of a child of God, which was bestowed on me at Baptism, is greater than that of the ruler of a kingdom. The latter I shall lose at death; the former will be my passport to everlasting glory." It takes a saint to see this so clearly and to say it so plainly.

The final effect of the sacrament of Baptism is the imprinting of a spiritual mark or character on the soul. This character produces certain effects. Do you know what these effects are?

**Effects of the Baptismal Character**

We read in the catechism that *the effects of the character imprinted on the soul by Baptism are that we become members of the Church, subject to its laws, and capable of receiving the other sacraments.*

While the grace of Baptism makes us share in the divine life, the character of Baptism, a spiritual mark, shows us living members of Christ's Mystical Body, the Church. As members of any society must obey the regulations of that society, so we, as members of Christ's Church, must accept her teaching and obey her laws. This character also entitles us to receive the other sacraments, and to share in all the means of salvation which the Church administers.

## Baptism Is Administered In and Through the Church

### The Ordinary Ministers

From your previous study about Baptism you learned that *the bishop, priest, or deacon are the usual ministers of Baptism, but if there is danger that someone will die without Baptism, anyone else may and should baptize.* Ordinarily the bishop, priest, or deacon are the ministers in a solemn Baptism, that is, Baptism with all its rites and ceremonies. Traditionally, some of these ceremonies are: (1) the placing of salt on the tongue to signify wisdom; (2) the anointing of the breast, head, and back to signify strength given by Baptism; (3) the clothing with a white garment to signify the purity of the baptized soul; (4) the giving of the candle to signify the light of faith and the fire of love.

### Anyone May Baptize

The usual way to administer the sacrament of Baptism is to pour water on the head of the infant or person to be baptized in such a way that it flows on the skin. While doing this the person must say: *"I baptize thee in the name of the Father, and of the Son, and of the Holy Spirit."* All these words and actions are necessary. As said above, the ordinary minister of the sacrament is a priest but in cases of necessity anyone may administer the sacrament of Baptism, even a non-Catholic, provided he has the use of reason, and in baptizing does what the Church wants, and what Christ has ordered.

## Baptism Is Necessary For Salvation

*Baptism is necessary for the salvation of all men because Christ has said: "Unless a man be born again of water and the Spirit, he cannot enter into the kingdom of God" (Jn. 3:5).*

Here Christ speaks of our eternal salvation. It is through Baptism that we first receive supernatural life which enables us to save our souls. Baptism, therefore, is necessary for salvation because by it we are "born again" to the supernatural life which our first parents had and lost.

What happens to people who are not baptized? What about those who do not know the necessity of Baptism or are never

given the chance to have someone baptize them? Will they never enjoy eternal happiness? If the stray sheep cannot find the shepherd, the shepherd goes to the sheep. God "will have all men be saved." In His mercy, He will not refuse salvation to those who love Him and desire to do His holy will, even though they have not received Baptism of water through ignorance of it or because of impossibility.

When the man of good will does not know about the necessity of Baptism for salvation, or cannot receive it, God offers him a substitute for this most necessary sacrament. The Catholic Church teaches us: *Those who through no fault of their own have not received the sacrament of Baptism can be saved through what is called baptism of blood or baptism of desire.* When does an unbaptized person receive the baptism of desire? Baptism of blood?

## Baptism of Desire

*An unbaptized person receives the baptism of desire when he loves God above all things and desires to do all that is necessary for his salvation.* Can you explain this? Because such a person loves God, he would fulfill the command of baptism if he could. According to Christ's own promise, the Blessed Trinity will come to abide in the soul of such a one: "Love, therefore, is the fulfilling of the law" (Rom. 13:10).

The emperor Valentinian is a good example of one receiving this baptism. We are told that Valentinian ardently desired to be a Christian. He traveled to Milan to receive his instructions from St. Ambrose, Bishop of Milan. During his journey, he was assassinated. The holy bishop Ambrose in his funeral oration assured his loved ones that Valentinian had received a baptism of desire which was sufficient for his salvation. Can a non-Christian who leads a good life, but who has never heard of Baptism, receive baptism of desire? Explain.

Did the good thief who hung on the cross at Christ's right side receive baptism of desire? Explain.

## Baptism of Blood

*An unbaptized person receives the baptism of blood when he suffers martyrdom for the faith of Christ.* When a person who has never been baptized gives up his life for the sake of Christ, he gives the supreme proof of his love of God. He is saved through baptism of blood. Such has been the case of those martyrs who, being converted and confessing their faith in Christianity, have been put to death before there was any opportunity for Baptism. "He who loses his life," said Christ, "for my sake, will find it" (Mt. 10:39).

Baptism of blood and baptism of desire are not sacraments. Neither imprints the special character of the sacrament on the soul. In both cases, however, through the merits of Christ and the operation of the Holy Spirit, the individual is cleansed of original sin and born supernaturally as a child of God and brother of Christ, co-heir with Him to the kingdom of heaven.

## Babies Should Be Baptized At Once

Since Baptism is so necessary, *children should be baptized as soon as possible after birth.* Ordinarily, the child should be baptized within two weeks. It would be wrong for parents to postpone baptism for a long time without a good reason. Such parents expose their children to the danger of losing heaven and the vision of God for all eternity. The Church has great cause to hope that there is a way of salvation for all unbaptized children, but this hope never justifies failing to baptize infants in ordinary circumstances.

**TERMS TO KNOW**

- Baptism
- minister
- sponsor
- character
- danger
- renounce
- effects
- ordinary
- anoint
- obligation
- chrism
- regeneration
- private
- heirs
- martyrdom
- baptize

## The Role of a Sponsor and Godparents in Baptism

In your study of the history of persecutions in the early Church, you may recall that whenever a person wished to become a Christian he had to have a sponsor. The sponsor guaranteed that the candidate was sincere and would remain faithful to his religion in times of persecution.

Besides the priest who administers Baptism, it is ordinary practice that godparents are selected (usually by the child's parents or primary caretakers) to participate in the sacred ceremony. The kind of role godparents are expected to have in the godchild's life is derived historically from the role of a "sponsor." A sponsor is someone—normally in the case of adult baptism and confirmation—who attests before the Church to the sincerity and integrity of the convert, and also who functions as a mentor and assistant for them in the right practice of the faith. Similarly, godparents make themselves available to instruct and form their godchildren in the Catholic faith. Godparents are especially important if a child's parents or primary caretakers become incapable of bringing the child up in the faith themselves. Along with the parents, the godparents are present at the ceremony to "present" the Child to the Church for baptism. In doing so, both parents and godparents vow to take on certain responsibilities. Namely, godparents are asked by the Church to help the parents of the child in their "Christian duty as parents."

The persecutions of the Church by the Romans ceased many centuries ago, but the custom of having a sponsor at Baptism has continued. Today, godparents are chosen by the parents or guardians to act as official witnesses to the entry of their children into the Church. The children make certain promises through the godparents. What are these promises?

### Baptismal Promises

*We promise through our godparents in Baptism to reject Satan and to live according to the teachings of Christ and of His Church.* By the words "reject Satan" we understand that we shall try to avoid sin and the near occasions of sin. To live according to the teachings of Christ and of His Church means to obey God's commandments and those of the Church. This promise is called our baptismal promise, or baptismal vows. By the assistance of his grace God helps us keep it and merit an exceedingly great reward. In being fully conformed to the Church through the sacrament of Confirmation, a baptized Christian will make a "renewal" of these same baptismal vows.

### The Chief Duty of Godparents

*The duty of a godparent after Baptism is to see that the child is brought up a good Catholic, if this is not done by the parents.* Since godparents must see to the religious education of the child if the parents fail to do so, it is evident that they must be suffi-ciently qualified for this task. It is important that the right choice of godparents be made.

Who should be chosen as godparents for Baptism? *Only Catholics who know their faith and live up to the duties of their religion should be chosen as godparents for Baptism.* Catholics who do not practice their religion cannot be expected to fulfill the obligation nor can they be expected to be approved by the priest to act as sponsors.

## The Name of a Saint Is Given at Baptism

Through baptism we become members of the Communion of Saints. We are brothers or sisters of the saints in heaven. Since they are to be our protectors and intercessors with God through-out life, the Church tells us that *the name of a saint is given in Baptism in order that the person baptized may imitate his virtues and have him for a protector.* This saint, having become one's "patron saint", is to be a model as well as our protector for the baptized person.

Alexander, the famous Greek conqueror, used to say to soldiers who had the same name as himself, "Either take another name or see that you do credit to my name." Our patron saints may say the same to us: "Are you called Peter, John, or Ann? Then be like St. Peter, St. John, or St. Ann in your daily life; otherwise you are not worthy to bear our name." Let us pray to our patron saints each day to obtain their help to keep the promise made at Baptism. Can you tell the life of your patron saint? What virtues are exemplified in his life?

Saint Vincent and Saint Catherine of Siena are two examples of wonderful saintly names given at Baptism.

## Summary

The sacrament of Baptism gives our souls the new life of sanctifying grace. Through this sacrament we become children of God and heirs of heaven. Baptism takes away original sin. In those with the use of reason, it also takes away actual sins and all the punishment due to them, if the person baptized be guilty of any actual sins and is sorry for them. Baptism makes us certain members of the Church, and through it we become capable of receiving the other sacraments. Baptism is necessary for the salvation of all men, for Christ said: "Unless a man be born again of water and the Spirit, he cannot enter the kingdom of God" (John 3:5). However, those who through no fault of their own have not received the sacrament of Baptism can be saved through what is called baptism of blood or baptism of desire.

 **FOR ME TO REVIEW**

*Catechism Lesson*

**152.** **Q. What is Baptism?**

A. Baptism is a sacrament which cleanses us from original sin, makes us Christians, children of God, and heirs of heaven.

**637.** **Q. Can a person ever receive any of the other sacraments without first receiving Baptism?**

A. A person can never receive any of the other sacraments without first receiving Baptism, because Baptism makes us members of Christ's Church, and unless we are members of His Church we cannot receive His sacraments.

**153.** **Q. Are actual sins ever remitted by Baptism?**

A. Actual sins and all the punishment due to them are remitted by Baptism, if the person baptized be guilty of any, and is rightly disposed.

**155. Q. Who can administer Baptism?**

A. The bishop, priest, or deacon are the ordinary ministers of Baptism; but in case of necessity anyone who has the use of reason may baptize.

**156. Q. How is Baptism given?**

A. Whoever baptizes should pour water on the head of the person to be baptized, and say, while pouring the water: I baptize thee in the name of the Father, and of the Son, and of the Holy Spirit.

**154. Q. Is Baptism necessary to salvation?**

A. Baptism is necessary to salvation, because without it we cannot enter into the kingdom of heaven.

**650. Q. What is Baptism of desire?**

A. Baptism of desire is an ardent wish to receive Baptism, and to do all that God has ordained for our salvation.

**651. Q. What is Baptism of blood?**

A. Baptism of blood is the shedding of one's blood for the faith of Christ.

**652. Q. What is the Baptism of blood most commonly called?**

A. The Baptism of blood is most commonly called martyrdom, and those who receive it are called martyrs. It is the death one patiently suffers from the enemies of our religion, rather than give up Catholic faith or virtue. We must not seek martyrdom, though we must endure it when it comes.

**653. Q. Is Baptism of desire or of blood sufficient to produce the effects of Baptism of water?**

A. Baptism of desire or of blood is sufficient to produce the effects of the Baptism of water, if it is impossible to receive the Baptism of water.

654. **Q. How do we know that the Baptism of desire or of blood will save us when it is impossible to receive the Baptism of water?**

A. We know that Baptism of desire or of blood will save us when it is impossible to receive the Baptism of water, from Holy Scripture, which teaches that love of God and perfect contrition can secure the remission of sins; and also that our Lord promises salvation to those who lay down their life for His sake or for His teaching.

642. **Q. Is it wrong to defer the Baptism of an infant?**

A. It is wrong to defer the Baptism of an infant, because we thereby expose the child to the danger of dying without the sacrament.

657. **Q. Why is the name of a saint given in Baptism?**

A. The name of a saint is given in Baptism in order that the person baptized may imitate his virtues and have him for a protector.

658. **Q. What is the saint whose name we bear called?**

A. The saint whose name we bear is called our patron saint—to whom we should have great devotion.

660. **Q. Why are godfathers and godmothers given in Baptism?**

A. Godfathers and godmothers are given in Baptism in order that they may promise, in the name of the child, what the child itself would promise if it had the use of reason.

661. **Q. By what other name are godfathers and godmothers called?**

A. Godfathers and godmothers are usually called sponsors. Sponsors are not necessary at private Baptism.

665. Q. **What is the obligation of a godfather and a godmother?**

   A. The obligation of a godfather and a godmother is to instruct the child in its religious duties, if the parents neglect to do so or die.

666. Q. **Can persons who are not Catholics be sponsors for Catholic children?**

   A. Persons who are not Catholics cannot be sponsors for Catholic children, because they cannot perform the duties of sponsors; for if they do not know and profess the Catholic religion themselves, how can they teach it to their godchildren? Moreover, they must answer the questions asked at Baptism and declare that they believe in the Holy Catholic Church and in all it teaches; which would be a falsehood on their part.

667. Q. **What should parents chiefly consider in the selection of sponsors for their children?**

   A. In the selection of sponsors for their children parents should chiefly consider the good character and virtue of the sponsors, selecting model Catholics to whom they would be willing at the hour of death to entrust the care and training of their children.

*Questions and Exercises*

## **Part 1**: A "Because" Test

*Give the correct reasons. Prove, if possible.*

1. Everyone should know how to baptize because:

2. A name of a saint should be given in Baptism because:

3. It is impossible to enter heaven without Baptism because:

4. Baptized persons are heirs of heaven because:

5. Non-Catholics cannot be sponsors for a Catholic child because:

6. Children should be baptized as soon as possible because:

7. A person who dies immediately after Baptism can go straight to heaven without passing a single moment in purgatory because:

8. Christ's baptism by John was not a sacrament because:

9. Good practical Catholics should be sponsors in Baptism because:

10. Baptism of blood and baptism of desire are not sacraments because:

## Part 2: Completion

1. The final reward for those who are in the state of sanctifying grace at the time of death is _____ .

2. The ordinary ministers of the sacrament of Baptism are _____ .

3. The chief qualifications of a sponsor are _____ .

4. The baptism which an unbaptized person suffering martyrdom for Christ's sake receives is called _____ .

## ☑ FOR ME TO DO

1. Read the life of your patron saint and report to the class how imitating his virtues will make you a good Christian.

2. Read and report on stories of hardships undergone by missionaries at home and abroad to baptize a single soul.

3. Panel discussion: The difference between a baptized person and an unbaptized person.

4. Write a brief summary of the wonderful blessings received at Baptism.

5. Write a short letter to a missionary priest. Tell him two things you are going to do to help him.

6. Make a collage of pictures which illustrate the Church fulfilling the divine command: "Go teach all nations, baptizing them . . ."

7. Discuss the topic: "What Does Baptism Mean to Me?"

# Christ Strengthens Us to Advance From Supernatural Childhood to Supernatural Maturity

LESSON 11

# Confirmation

"Baptism, the Eucharist, and the sacrament of Confirmation together constitute the 'sacraments of Christian initiation,' whose unity must be safeguarded. It must be explained to the faithful that the reception of the sacrament of Confirmation is necessary for the completion of baptismal grace. For 'by the sacrament of Confirmation, [the baptized] are more perfectly bound to the Church and are enriched with a special strength of the Holy Spirit. Hence they are, as true witnesses of Christ, more strictly obliged to spread and defend the faith by word and deed.'"

—*Catechism of the Catholic Church, 1285*

Baptism, as we have seen, is the sacrament which first gives us the life of grace. The other sacraments are intended to impart their own particular graces and to help us in our spiritual life. By Baptism we are made members of Christ's Mystical Body, the Church. In Confirmation the Holy Spirit comes to us in a special way to strengthen us and make us soldiers in Christ's army. The Holy Spirit abides in each of us and brings us to spiritual maturity. He gives us the power for combat with the enemies of our soul.

## The Full Spiritual Growth to Perfection Is the Purpose and Effect of Confirmation

As our catechism tells us, *Confirmation is the sacrament through which the Holy Spirit comes to us in a special way and enables us to profess our faith as strong and perfect Christians and soldiers of Jesus Christ.*

### Confirmation Was Instituted by Christ

Even though we do not find the express words of the institution of Confirmation in the Bible, we do find the rite of the sacrament

described. At the Last Supper when our Lord was about to leave His Apostles, He promised that He would send the Paraclete (the Holy Spirit) to aid them (Jn. 14:16–18). Fifty days after Christ's Resurrection, the Apostles became changed men. Read Acts 8:14, 17. You will see it was through the coming of the Holy Spirit in this sacrament that the Apostles were filled with courage and made ready to teach and preach in the name of Christ.

As time went on, the Apostles confirmed others. The power of confirming was given by Christ to His Apostles. They, in turn, gave this power to their successors, the bishops.

Confirmation is the sacrament through which the Holy Spirit comes to us in a special way and enables us to profess our faith as strong and perfect Christians and soldiers of Jesus Christ.

As a rule, *the bishop is the ordinary minister of Confirmation.* If need arises, the bishop may grant the faculty of administering Confirmation to priests. Any priest can confirm in danger of death.

You recall Paul's experience as related in Acts 19:1–7. Read the story of Philip, the deacon, in the Acts of the Apostles 8:5–7. He baptized, but let the Apostles confirm.

### Confirmation Has an Outward Sign

There is something very chivalrous about a knight. You remember that before a young man became a knight, he had to be trained at the royal court for many years. He was dubbed knight at a beautiful ceremony at which he was given a sword, the outward sign of his knighthood. We, too, become knights or soldiers of Christ our King in the sacrament of Confirmation.

Let us consider the ceremony of Confirmation. *The bishop extends his hands over those who are to be confirmed, prays that they may receive the Holy Spirit, and, while laying his hand on the head of each person, anoints the forehead with holy chrism in the form of a cross.* You recall how Paul did this in the Acts 19:5–6. Note the significance of each action. *In anointing the person he confirms, the bishop says: "Be sealed with the gift of the Holy Spirit"*

In former times athletes' bodies were rubbed with olive oil. When a person is confirmed, he is anointed with holy chrism as a symbol of spiritual preparation.

What is chrism? *Holy chrism is a mixture of olive oil and balm, blessed by the bishop on Holy Thursday.* It has certain natural qualities. It flows, spreads, penetrates, softens, nourishes, and strengthens. These properties signify the inward effects of the Holy Spirit on the soul. The fragrance of balm signifies the sweet odor of virtue which should be diffused by those who have been confirmed. The strength and suppleness from the balm denotes the grace which helps one preserve oneself from the corruption of the world.

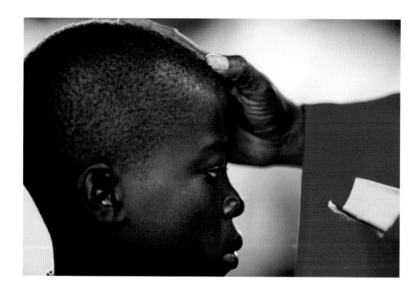

The anointing is done on the forehead. *The anointing of the forehead with chrism in the form of a cross signifies that the Catholic who is confirmed must always be ready to profess his faith openly and to practice it fearlessly.* Since the Church began we have countless examples of people who have done this. Can you name a few?

We have the story of Sebastian, a soldier of the Roman Emperor at the time of the persecutions. Through Confirmation he had also become a soldier of Christ. Discovered performing acts of charity in the name of Christ, Sebastian was brought before the Emperor and accused of being a Christian. The Emperor tried to induce him to sacrifice to the idols, but he refused. Sebastian was then delivered to the Roman archers. They tortured him by shooting him with arrows and finally killed him.

Perhaps you have asked yourself whether you could ever suffer the way the martyrs did. If the time came for you to suffer for your faith, would you have the strength of the Holy Spirit dwelling within you?

**The Effects of Confirmation Are Threefold**

What happened to you at Baptism? What did you receive? Who recalls what happens to a person when he is confirmed? *Confirmation increases sanctifying grace, gives its special sacramental grace, and imprints a lasting character on the soul. The sacramental grace of Confirmation helps us to live our faith loyally and to profess it courageously.* Besides this, we are strengthened and sanctified by the gifts and fruits of the Holy Spirit.

When the bishop confirms, he prays that we may receive the Spirit of Wisdom, so that we may have a relish for the things of God; the Spirit of Understanding, so that we may acquire a deeper knowledge of the mysteries of faith; the Spirit of Counsel, so that we may be enlightened concerning the dangers to our salvation; the Gift of Fortitude, so that we may be strengthened to do God's will; the Gift of Piety, so that we may be filled with love and obedience to God; the Spirit of Knowledge, so that we may be aided to know God's will; and the Spirit of Fear of the Lord, so that there may be enkindled in us a dread of offending Christ. The bishop also prays that our souls may be filled with the precious fruits described by St. Paul: "But the fruit of the Spirit is charity, joy, peace, patience, kindness, goodness, faith" (Gal. 5:22–23). How can the Gifts and Fruits be applied to our daily life?

As the bishop is anointing us, a mark is imprinted on our souls. *The character of Confirmation is a spiritual and indelible sign which marks the Christian as a soldier in the army of Christ.* Knights in the army of a king were recognized by their leader through their swords. We, who are enrolled in the army of Christ through Confirmation, are recognized by this spiritual mark imparted to us in Confirmation.

**TERMS TO KNOW**

- profess
- chrism
- anoints
- Holy Spirit
- indelible
- Christians
- imprint
- sacramental grace

## The Church Teaches Us How to Receive Confirmation Properly

In the early days of the Church, Confirmation was given immediately after Baptism. In our day it is administered to those who have the use of reason a sufficient understanding of their religion. *To receive Confirmation properly it is necessary to be in the state of grace, and to know well the chief truths and duties of our religion.*

It is a sin for a baptized person to neglect to receive Confirmation when the opportunity is offered. The more serious the neglect the more serious the sin.

If a baptized person should receive Confirmation in the state of mortal sin, he would be guilty of a sacrilege. Does such a person receive the sacrament validly? Yes. He will receive the graces of Confirmation after sin has been removed from his soul.

You remember that at Baptism, godparents were required. For Confirmation, a sponsor is also necessary. May anyone be a sponsor? There are certain qualifications necessary: (1) a sponsor must be someone other than the parent of the one to be confirmed; (2) a sponsor must have received all of the sacraments of initiation (Baptism, Confirmation, and the Eucharist); (3) a sponsor must be at least 16 years of age and may be male or female regardless of the sex of the candidate; (4) a sponsor, as a practicing Catholic, must not be living willingly and knowingly in a state of mortal sin.

The Catechism tells us that the sacrament of Confirmation "increases the gifts of the Holy Spirit in us" (1303). These gifts are:

- Wisdom
- Understanding
- Counsel
- Fortitude
- Knowledge
- Piety
- Fear of the Lord

## Additional Responsibilities

Because a person is confirmed this does not mean that there is no further need to study religion. The need, perhaps, is even greater. Why? There are many who after Confirmation are not more fervent in the practice of their faith than they were before they received Confirmation. The fault does not lie with the sacrament but with the individual who fails to co-operate with the graces of the sacrament. How do you stand in this regard? A man cannot paint the top of the house without using a ladder. So too, we cannot expect to reach heaven unless we make use of the graces given us.

*After we have been confirmed, we should continue to study our religion even more earnestly than before, so that we may be able to explain and defend our faith, and thus co-operate with the grace of Confirmation.* By fulfilling our duties, such as going to Mass, receiving the sacraments, practicing virtue, and praying for others, we can attract others to our religion.

*All Catholics should be confirmed in order to be strengthened against the dangers to salvation and to be prepared better to defend their Catholic faith.* Do you see a special need for it in these days? Are Catholics being persecuted anywhere?

## Summary

Confirmation is the sacrament through which the Holy Spirit, comes to us in a special way. This sacrament enables us to profess our faith as strong and perfect Christians and soldiers of Jesus Christ. The bishop is the ordinary minister of Confirmation.

Confirmation increases sanctifying grace, gives its special sacramental grace, and imprints a lasting character on the soul. The sacramental grace of Confirmation helps us to live our faith loyally and to profess it courageously. The character of Confirmation is a spiritual and indelible sign which marks the Christian as a soldier in the army of Christ.

To receive Confirmation properly it is necessary to be in the state of grace, and to know well—as far as can be reasonably expected in each case—the chief truths and duties of our religion.

All Catholics should be confirmed. With Confirmation we are strengthened against the dangers to salvation and are better prepared to defend our Catholic faith.

## ✓ FOR ME TO REVIEW

*Catechism Lesson*

**166.** **Q.** **What is Confirmation?**

**A.** Confirmation is a sacrament through which we receive the Holy Spirit to make us strong and perfect Christians and soldiers of Jesus Christ.

**167.** **Q.** **Who administers Confirmation?**

**A.** The bishop is the ordinary minister of Confirmation.

**168.** **Q.** **How does the bishop give Confirmation?**

**A.** The bishop extends his hands over those who are to be confirmed, prays that they may receive the Holy Spirit, and anoints the forehead of each with holy chrism in the form of a cross.

**170.** **Q.** **What does the bishop say in anointing the person he confirms?**

**A.** In anointing the person he confirms the bishop says: I sign thee with the Sign of the Cross, and I confirm thee with the chrism of salvation, in the name of the Father, and the Son, and of the Holy Spirit.

**169.** **Q.** **What is holy chrism?**

**A.** Holy chrism is a mixture of olive-oil and balm, conse-crated by the bishop.

171. Q. **What is meant by anointing the forehead with chrism in the form of a cross?**
     A. By anointing the forehead with chrism in the form of a cross is meant, that the Christian who is confirmed must openly profess and practice his faith, never be ashamed of it, and rather die than deny it.

176. Q. **Which are the effects of Confirmation?**
     A. The effects of Confirmation are an increase of sanctifying grace, the strengthening of our faith, and the gifts of the Holy Spirit.

177. Q. **Which are the gifts of the Holy Spirit?**
     A. The gifts of the Holy Spirit are Wisdom, Understanding, Counsel, Fortitude, Knowledge, Piety, and Fear of the Lord.

173. Q. **To receive Confirmation worthily is it necessary to be in the state of grace?**
     A. To receive Confirmation worthily it is necessary to be in the state of grace.

174. Q. **What special preparation should be made to receive Confirmation?**
     A. Persons of an age to learn should know the chief mysteries of faith and the duties of a Christian, and be instructed in the nature and effects of this sacrament.

175. Q. **Is it a sin to neglect Confirmation?**
     A. It is a sin to neglect Confirmation, especially in these evil days when faith and morals are exposed to so many and such violent temptations.

*Questions and Exercises*

## Completion

1.  The ordinary minister of Confirmation is the_____.

2.  The_____comes to us in a special way in the sacrament of Confirmation.

3.  The mixture of olive oil and balm used by the bishop in giving Confirmation is called_____.

4.  Confirmation marks the Christian as a_____.

5.  Confirmation is a sacrament of the_____.

## ☑ FOR ME TO DO

1.  Make two columns on paper. Above Column One write "Soldier of a Country"; above Column Two write "Soldier of Christ." List side by side as many likenesses as you can between the two.

2.  After reading the Acts of the Apostles 2:1–14, discuss how the sacrament of Confirmation changed the Apostles.

3.  Discuss why all Catholics should be confirmed.

4.  Discuss how the grace of Confirmation works in countries where Catholics are being persecuted.

5.  List the practices by which a Catholic professes his faith daily.

6.  Read and report on the lives of saints whose bravery was outstanding and find instances in their lives of bravery, for example, St. Thomas a Becket, and St. Perpetua.

7.  Draw symbols of the Holy Spirit.

# Achievement Test

*Write your answers on a separate sheet of paper*

## I. Completion

*Use the following words to complete the sentences below*

1. grace
2. Baptism
3. chrism
4. bishop
5. matter
6. anointing
7. baptism of desire
8. baptism of blood
9. sacraments of the dead
10. sacraments of the living

11. sacramental grace
12. sanctifying grace
13. merits
14. character
15. minister
16. Holy Thursday
17. Catholic action
18. sacrilege
19. right dispositions
20. practice

21. Confirmation
22. Catholics
23. godparents
24. faith
25. sacrament
26. effects
27. Christ
28. form
29. religion

____1____ is the supernatural gift bestowed on us through the merits of Jesus Christ for our salvation.

By the ____2____ we mean the proper motive in receiving the sacraments, and the good acts or habits by which we prepare for them, such as faith and contrition.

Baptism and Reconciliation are called ____3____ because their chief purpose is to give the supernatural life of sanctifying grace to persons spiritually dead through sin.

A __2 4__ is an outward sign instituted by Christ to give grace.

__2 5__ is the sacrament that gives us the new life of sanctifying grace by which we become children of God and heirs of heaven.

The ordinary minister of Confirmation is the __4 6__ .

__2 7__ is a mixture of olive oil and balm, blessed by the bishop on __22 8__ .

Each of the sacraments gives a special grace, called __1 9__ , which helps one to carry out the particular purpose of that sacrament.

The __6 10__ of Confirmation is a spiritual and indelible sign which marks the Christian as a soldier in the army of __2 11__ .

An unbaptized person receives __8 12__ when he suffers martyr-dom for the faith of Christ.

The sacrament of __2 13__ helps us to live our faith loyally and to profess it courageously.

The outward sign is composed of material things or actions and this element is called the __3 14__ of the sacrament, and of the words spoken by the person giving the sacrament and this element is called its __5 15__ .

As __16__ for Baptism only __2 17__ should be chosen who know their faith and live up to the duties of their __2 18__ .

An unbaptized person receives __7 19__ when he loves God above all things and desires to do all that is necessary for his salvation.

By __20__ the forehead with chrism in the form of a cross is meant that the Catholic who is confirmed must always be ready to profess his __21__ openly and to __2 22__ it fearlessly.

__23__ are the rewards Christ earned by His sufferings and death.

Confirmation especially prepares us for the work of __7 24__ .

__25__ is the supernatural life of the soul.

✠ **II. Yes or No**

1. Does God give us all the graces we need to gain heaven? *Yes*

2. Is it possible for you either to accept or to reject the graces God gives you? *Yes*

3. Will God's grace obtain for us eternal life without our co-operation? *No*

4. Can anyone gain heaven without actual grace? *No*

5. Would it be correct to say that after God Himself, sanctifying grace holds the most important place in your life? *?*

6. Can you gain heaven by your efforts alone? *No*

7. Were all the seven sacraments in use at the time of the Apostles? *No*

8. Is it correct to say: Sanctity is acquired by making use of the ordinary daily graces God gives us? *?*

9. Do all who receive the sacraments receive the same amount of grace? *No*

10. Is Baptism necessary for salvation? *Yes*

11. Can anything take the place by Baptism of water?

12. Did our Lord receive the sacrament of Baptism? *No*

13. May children who have the use of reason be baptized without their consent? *Yes*

14. Did the Apostles administer Confirmation? *?*

15. Is baptism of desire a sacrament? *Yes*

16. Is baptismal water necessary for Baptism in a case of necessity? *No*

17. May an infant ever be baptized without the consent of the parents?

18. Do sponsors assist at Baptism for the same reason that witnesses assist at a wedding? *no*

19. Is there spiritual relationship between you and your Confirmation sponsor? *yes*

20. Should all Catholics be confirmed? *yes*

21. Does Confirmation imprint an indelible mark on the soul? *yes*

22. Does mortal sin erase the sacramental character conferred by Baptism, Confirmation, Holy Orders? *no*

23. Is a sponsor required in Confirmation? *yes*

24. Is the Holy Eucharist the most necessary sacrament? *yes*

25. Do we receive the Holy Spirit for the first time in Confirmation? *no*

## Problems For Discussion

1. Mr. Anderson, whose mother is a devout Catholic but whose father is a Protestant, earnestly desires his parents to be godparents for his infant son in Baptism. May Mr. Anderson's parents be godparents? Explain.

2. John's family lives in an out-of-the-way district where a priest visits only once or twice a year. They want to wait six months for the priest to baptize their baby brother. Are they justified in delaying Baptism? What should they do? How should they do it?

3. Jack, a non-Catholic friend of yours, wishes to be a Catholic. He asks you to baptize him since there is no priest around. Eager for the opportunity, you obtain some fresh water and baptize him according to the rite of the Church. Did your friend receive the sacrament of Baptism?

4. In a bishop's sermon on Confirmation day, he said to all those confirmed, "Now you are soldiers of Christ's army." What did he mean?

LESSON 12

# The Holy Eucharist

The Holy Eucharist is the greatest of all the sacraments because it contains the Author of all the sacraments, Jesus Christ Himself. This sacrament is the center of Christian life.

## The Holy Eucharist Is a Sacrament and a Sacrifice

Christ instituted the Holy Eucharist at the Last Supper, the night before He died.

There is no sacrament which we should seek out more frequently than the Holy Eucharist. It is profitable therefore to use every means to learn more about it so that we will acquire a better understanding of it.

The Holy Eucharist is a sacrament and a sacrifice. As a sacrament, it is an outward sign instituted by Christ to give grace. In your previous study of the Mass, you learned the meaning of "sacrifice." Here is a fuller, precise definition. *A sacrifice is the offering of a victim by a priest to God alone, and the destruction of it in some way to acknowledge that He is the Creator of all things.*

> "The Eucharist is the 'source and summit of the Christian life.'"
>
> —*Catechism of the Catholic Church, 1324*

In a previous grade you learned: *The Holy Eucharist is a sacrament and a sacrifice. In the Holy Eucharist, under the appearance of bread and wine, the Lord Christ is contained, offered, and received.*

You know that in Jesus Christ there are two natures: the nature of God, His divine nature, and the nature of man, His human nature. The body, blood, and soul belong to His human nature; the divinity, to His divine nature. The Holy Eucharist contains Christ's body and blood, soul and divinity, whole and entire.

## The Institution of the Holy Eucharist Took Place at the Last Supper

From your study of the New Testament you know when Christ promised to institute the Holy Eucharist. Do you remember the occasion when Christ fed five thousand people with five barley loaves and two fishes? A clear account of it is related by St. John in Chapter 6. Perhaps you would like to look it up and refresh your memory.

On the day following the miracle of the loaves and fishes at Capernaum, Christ promised the Holy Eucharist. Many of the people who had seen the miracle came to Him again, hoping He would perform another miracle and again multiply the bread. Jesus knew their thoughts and reproved them for being so anxious for food for their bodies. He told them He would give them bread from heaven that would make them live forever. He said that the bread He would give would be His own body and blood.

Christ kept His promise when He instituted the Holy Eucharist. When did this happen? You know the answer. *Christ instituted the Holy Eucharist at the Last Supper, the night before He died*. His promise was made about a year before He died. He fulfilled the promise the very night before He died. Someone has said: "The Eucharist was Christ's secret; He kept it as long as He could, until His very last meeting with His friends."

Who were these friends whose great privilege it was to be present when Christ instituted this august sacrament? *When our Lord instituted the Holy Eucharist the Apostles were present*. We read in Holy Scripture (Mt. 26:20): "Now when evening arrived, he reclined at table with the twelve disciples." It was the evening before our Lord's Passion and death. Jesus and His twelve Apostles were gathered together to celebrate the Paschal Supper, a part of the Passover. The solemn moment was at hand. The actual institution of the Holy Eucharist was about to take place. How did Christ institute the Holy Eucharist? What did He say? What did He do?

*Christ instituted the Holy Eucharist in this way: He took bread, blessed and broke it, and giving it to His Apostles, said: "Take and eat; this is My body"; then He took a cup of wine, blessed it, and giving it to them, said: "All of you drink of this; for this is My blood of the new covenant which is being shed for many unto the forgiveness of sins": finally, He gave His Apostles the commission: "Do this in remembrance of Me."*

In the early days of His public life, Christ frequently spoke in parables. The parables often hid the meaning of His words. On occasion He would explain what they meant to those who would ask Him to explain. But that Holy Thursday was the last evening of His life. He did not speak in parables but quite plainly.

He spoke plainly because He was instituting a new covenant, a new testament, a new law. You will recall the Old Testament had been ratified, that is, sealed, by the blood of the paschal lamb, and that Moses had sprinkled the people with the blood. The New Testament (covenant) was ratified by the blood of Christ. The paschal lamb was a figure or type of Christ.

The Apostles believed the words of Christ when He said "This is My body; this is My blood." They believed them then, and so do we and millions of other Catholics now. It was the true body of Christ which the Apostles ate; it was the true blood of Christ which the Apostles drank, the blood which would be shed for the remission of sins.

## Transubstantiation

*When our Lord said, "This is My body," the entire substance of the bread was changed into His body and when He said, "This is My blood," the entire substance of the wine was changed into His blood.* A marvelous change took place. The substance of

the bread was changed into the substance of Christ's body. The substance of the wine was changed into the substance of Christ's blood. Both were changed into the substance of Christ.

*After the substance of the bread and wine had been changed into our Lord's body and blood, there remained only the appearances of bread and wine.* The substance of the bread and the substance of the wine had changed. Only the appearance of bread and wine remained. Christ's body and blood looked like bread and wine. Christ wanted the appearances to remain. They are the outward signs of this holy sacrament. They signify food, nourishment for our souls.

Do you understand what is meant by the appearances of bread and wine? *By the appearances of bread and wine we mean their color, taste, weight, shape, and whatever else appears to the senses.* For example, the eye sees shape and color; the ear can hear the breaking of the Host; the hand feels the weight; the taste and smell can also be known by the senses.

*The change of the entire substance of the bread and wine into the body and blood of Christ is called Transubstantiation.* Transubstantiation means a change of one substance into another substance without a change of appearance. Substance is that which makes a thing to be what it is. Appearances are accidents of a thing—its color, shape, taste, weight, and other properties that can be known by the senses. The substance is more essential than the appearances. It is the substance of the bread which makes it bread; it is the substance of the wine which makes it wine. The properties, or appearances, do not make the thing, but, because they are what our senses directly perceive, they help us know what the thing really is. The substance of a thing cannot be directly detected. We are directly aware only of the appearances.

Transubstantiation occurs only in the Eucharist. In everyday life when ordinary substances are changed, the appearances are changed also. For example, when food is eaten by us it becomes blood, bone, tissue, flesh, and muscle. There is not only a change of substance, but there is also a change in the appearances of the food. In Transubstantiation, the substance only is changed; the appearances remain what they were. The substance of the bread is changed into Christ's body. What appears to be bread, judging from the appearances, is not bread but Christ's body. What appears to be wine, judging from the appearances, is not wine but Christ's blood. Transubstantiation

> *"With all the strength of my soul I urge you young people to approach the Communion table as often as you can. Feed on this bread of angels whence you will draw all the energy you need to fight inner battles. Because true happiness, dear friends, does not consist in the pleasures of the world or in earthly things, but in peace of conscience, which we have only if we are pure in heart and mind."*
>
> —*Blessed Pier Giorgio Frassati*

is, therefore, a change of substance without a change of appearances.

Transubstantiation is a supernatural mystery, "a truth we cannot fully understand, but which we firmly believe because we have God's word for it."

How is Jesus Christ present under the appearances of bread and wine? *Jesus Christ is whole and entire both under the appearances of bread and under the appearances of wine*. The whole Christ—His body, blood, soul, and divinity—is present under the appearances of the wine as well as of the bread. Christ is present in the Eucharist with the same glorified body that He has in heaven. Christ in the Eucharist is alive and because He is alive, His body and soul are united. To be alive He must possess both body and blood. He is present whole and entire in the bread and whole and entire in the wine. The consecrated Host contains not only the body but also the blood. The consecrated wine contains the body and blood, too.

When the host and chalice are raised at the elevation in the Mass, we adore our Lord, body and blood, soul and divinity. We believe that Christ is whole and entire under both appearances because Jesus Christ, who is Truth itself, has made known to us this glorious truth. What wonderful things our Faith helps us to know! How grateful we should be!

How was it possible for our Lord to change bread and wine into His body and blood? *Our Lord was able to change bread and wine into His body and blood by His almighty power*. In one of the first lessons of the catechism you learn that God is "omnipotent" which means He can do all things. Our Lord is God. He who fed five thousand people with five loaves and two fishes; who

**TERMS TO KNOW**

- adorn
- harmony
- sacrifice
- commemorating
- covenant
- ministry
- supreme
- tremendous
- commission
- remission
- renewing
- testament
- divinity
- repetition
- supernatural

*"Every morning during meditation, I prepare myself for the whole day's struggle. Holy Communion assures me that I will win the victory; and so it is. I fear the day when I do not receive Holy Communion. This bread of the Strong gives me all the strength I need to carry on my mission and the courage to do whatever the Lord asks of me. The courage and strength that are in me are not of me, but of Him who lives in me—it is the Eucharist."*

—*St. Faustina*

changed water into wine, and brought back the dead to life, can change bread and wine into His body and blood.

The Holy Eucharist is a great mystery and therefore beyond human understanding. To the power of God this great gift of the Holy Eucharist is not impossible. With God all things are possible.

## Christ Gave to Priests the Power to Change Bread and Wine into His Body and Blood

*This change of bread and wine into the body and blood of Christ continues to be made in the Church by Jesus Christ, through the ministry of His priests.* What Jesus Himself once did at the Last Supper, He continues to do through His priests. Through them as His ministers, He changes bread and wine into His own body and blood. He speaks and acts through His priests. They receive this power in the sacrament of Holy Orders. Only ordained priests have the power to change bread and wine into the body and blood of Christ. At the Consecration in the Mass when this change takes place, priests act in the person of Christ *(in persona Christi)*. The priest does not say: "This is Christ's body: this is Christ's blood." He says: "This is My body"; "this is My blood." The Victim is Christ. He is also the priest.

Christ gave His priests the power to change bread and wine into His body and blood when He made the Apostles priests at the Last Supper by saying to them: "Do this in remembrance of Me." One of the greatest powers a priest has is the power of consecration. By making the Apostles priests Christ gave them

This change of bread and wine into the body and blood of Christ continues to be made in the Church by Jesus Christ, through the ministry of His priests.

the power to do what He had done. He had changed bread and wine into His body and blood. The Apostles did what Jesus commanded them.

Since they knew that the power of consecration was meant to last for all ages, the Apostles ordained other worthy men to be priests. Christ's Church was to last until the end of time. "Do this in remembrance of Me," was intended not only for the Apostles but also for the thousands of priests and bishops who were to guide the Church in the centuries to come.

*Priests exercise their power to change bread and wine into the body and blood of Christ by repeating at the Consecration of the Mass the words of Christ: "This is My body . . . this is My blood."*

What tremendous power a priest has! What great reverence and respect we should have for him. How great a privilege is ours to be present at the Consecration of the Mass. How do we show our appreciation of this great privilege?

## Christ Gives Us His Own Body and Blood in the Holy Eucharist for Many Reasons

*Christ gives us His own body and blood in the Holy Eucharist: first, to be offered as a sacrifice commemorating and renewing for all time the sacrifice of the cross; second, to be received by the faithful in Holy Communion; third, to remain ever on our altars as the proof of His love for us, and to be worshiped by us.*

As a sacrifice, the Holy Eucharist is the "unbloody" renewal of the sacrifice made by Christ on the cross. This sacrifice is offered to God only in the Mass. As a sacrifice, the Eucharist is therefore the same thing as the sacrifice of the Mass.

As a sacrament, the Holy Eucharist is called the Blessed Sacrament. The Sacrament of the Holy Eucharist is received in Holy Communion. By studying its effects, you will increase your knowledge of why we should receive the Eucharist in Holy Communion.

Believing that the Son of God is really present in the Holy

Eucharist, the Church builds churches
and chapels and adorns them with
beauty. She arranges ceremonies, too,
with which to honor our Lord in the
Blessed Sacrament.

As members of the Church, we
should express our devotion toward the
Holy Eucharist in a becoming manner.
We should adore our Lord and love Him
in return for the great love He showed
for us in instituting this wondrous sacrament. Our love for the Holy Eucharist
can be shown by attending at the Holy
Sacrifice of the Mass, by having Mass offered, by receiving Holy
Communion, and by making visits to adore our Lord in the Blessed
Sacrament.

## Summary

The Holy Eucharist is a sacrament and a sacrifice. It is the sacrament in which our Saviour, Jesus Christ, body and blood, soul
and divinity, whole and entire, under the appearances of bread
and wine, is contained, offered, and received.

Christ instituted the Holy Eucharist at the Last Supper, the
night before He died. First, He took bread, blessed and broke it,
and giving it to His Apostles said: "Take and eat; this is My body."
Then He took a cup of wine, blessed it, and giving it to them said:
"All of you drink of this; for this is My blood of the new covenant
which is being shed for many unto the forgiveness of sins." Finally,
Jesus said to His Apostles: "Do this in remembrance of Me."

When our Lord said, "This is My body," the entire substance
of the bread was changed into His body. When He said, "This is
My blood," the entire substance of the wine was changed into His
blood. Jesus Christ is whole and entire both under the appearances of bread and under the appearances of wine.

The change of bread and wine into the body and blood of Christ continues to be made in the Church by Jesus Christ, through the ministry of His priests. Christ gave His priests the power to change bread and wine into His body and blood at the Last Supper. At that time He ordained the Apostles priests by saying to them: "Do this in remembrance of Me." Priests use their power to change bread and wine into the body and blood of Christ at the Consecration of the Mass.

Christ gave us His own body and blood in the Holy Eucharist: (1) to unite us to Himself and to nourish our soul with His divine life; (2) to increase sanctifying grace and all virtues in our soul; (3) to lessen our evil inclination; (4) to be a pledge of everlasting life; (5) to fit our bodies for a glorious resurrection; (6) to continue the sacrifice of the cross in His Church.

## ✓ FOR ME TO REVIEW

*Catechism Lesson*

238.  Q.  **What is the Holy Eucharist?**

A.  The Holy Eucharist is the sacrament which contains the body and blood, soul and divinity, of our Lord Jesus Christ under the appearances of bread and wine.

239.  Q.  **When did Christ institute the Holy Eucharist?**

A.  Christ instituted the Holy Eucharist at the Last Supper, the night before He died.

240.  Q.  **Who were present when our Lord instituted the Holy Eucharist?**

A.  When our Lord instituted the Holy Eucharist the twelve Apostles were present.

241. Q. **How did our Lord institute the Holy Eucharist?**

A. Our Lord instituted the Holy Eucharist by taking bread, blessing, breaking, and giving to His Apostles, saying: "Take ye and eat, This is My body"; and then by taking the cup of wine, blessing and giving it, saying to them: "Drink ye all of this. This is My blood which shall be shed for the remission of sins. Do this for a commemoration of Me."

242. Q. **What happened when our Lord said, "This is My body; this is My blood?"**

A. When our Lord said, "This is My body," the substance of the bread was changed into the substance of His body; when He said, "This is My blood," the substance of the wine was changed into the substance of His blood.

243. Q. **Is Jesus Christ whole and entire both under the form of bread and under the form of wine?**

A. Jesus Christ is whole and entire both under the form of bread and under the form of wine.

244. Q. **Did anything remain of the bread and wine after their substance had been changed into the substance of the body and blood of our Lord?**

A. After the substance of the bread and wine had been changed into the substance of the body and blood of our Lord there remained only the appearances of bread and wine.

245. Q. **What do you mean by the appearances of bread and wine?**

A. By the appearances of bread and wine I mean the figure, the color, the taste, and whatever appears to the senses.

246. Q. What is this change of the bread and wine into the body and blood of our Lord called?

A. This change of the bread and wine into the body and blood of our Lord is called Transubstantiation.

247. Q. How was the substance of the bread and wine changed into the substance of the body and blood of Christ?

A. The substance of the bread and wine was changed into the substance of the body and blood of Christ by His almighty power.

248. Q. Does this change of bread and wine into the body and blood of Christ continue to be made in the Church?

A. This change of bread and wine into the body and blood of Christ continues to be made in the Church by Jesus Christ through the ministry of His priests.

249. Q. When did Christ give His priests the power to change bread and wine into His body and blood?

A. Christ gave His priests the power to change bread and wine into His body and blood when He said to the Apostles, "Do this in commemoration of Me."

250. Q. How do the priests exercise this power of changing bread and wine into the body and blood of Christ?

A. The priests exercise this power of changing bread and wine into the body and blood of Christ through the words of Consecration in the Mass, which are the words of Christ:

"This is My body; this is My blood."

**251. Q. Why did Christ institute the Holy Eucharist?**

    A.  Christ instituted the Holy Eucharist:

      1.  To unite us to Himself and to nourish our soul with His divine life.

      2.  To increase sanctifying grace and all virtues in our soul.

      3.  To lessen our evil inclinations.

      4. To be a pledge of everlasting life.

      5. To fit our bodies for a glorious resurrection.

      6. To continue the sacrifice of the cross in His Church.

*Questions and Exercises*

## Part 1: Matching

| COLUMN A | COLUMN B |
|---|---|
| 1. Appearances of bread and wine | A. The nature of God |
| 2. Transubstantiation | B. By means of them |
| 3. Through the ministry of His priests | C. Color, taste, weight, shape, and whatever else appears to the senses |
| 4. Divinity | D. New Testament |
| 5. New covenant | E. The change of the entire substance of the bread and wine into the body and blood of Christ |

## Part 2: Short Answer Exercise

1.  When did Christ institute the Holy Eucharist? *last supper*

2.  What is the name of the sacrament which contains the body and blood, soul and divinity, of our Saviour, Jesus Christ?

3.  For what purpose did Christ say His blood would be shed? *he was abt to be killed*

4. Who were present when Christ instituted the Holy Eucharist? *The Apostles*

5. At the Last Supper, to whom did Christ give His body to eat and His blood to drink? *Apostles*

6. At the Last Supper, what did Christ change into His body? *Bread*

7. At the Last Supper, what did Christ change into His blood? *Wine*

8. Today, who changes bread and wine into the body and blood of Christ? *Priest*

9. At what part of the Mass does a priest exercise his power to change bread and wine into the body and blood of Christ? *Transubstantiation*

10. What are the words the priest uses in exercising his power to change bread and wine into the body and blood of Christ? *This is my body which will be given up for you*

**Part 3**: Completion

1. Our Lord instituted the Holy Eucharist in this way: He took _Bread(a)___, blessed and broke it, and giving it to His Apostles, said: "Take and__eat(b)___; this is My__body(c)___." Then He took a cup of__wine(d)___, blessed it, and giving it to them, said: "All of you__drink(e)___ of this: for this is My __blood(f)___ of the new covenant which is being shed for many unto the forgiveness of__sin(g)___"; finally, He gave His___(h)___ the commission: "___(i)___ this in remembrance of Me."

2. The Holy Eucharist is a___(a)___ and a___(b)___; in it our Saviour, Jesus Christ,___(c)___ and___(d)___(e)___ and_ (f)___, is contained, offered, and received.

3. Christ gives us His own body and blood in the Holy Eucharist (1) to be offered as a sacrifice__to sin(a)___ and___(b)___ for all time the sacrifice of the cross; (2) to be received by the faithful in___(c)___; (3) to remain ever on our___(d)___ as a proof of His love for us, and to be worshiped by us.

## ☑ FOR ME TO DO

1. Write a report on Christ's reasons for giving us the Holy Eucharist.

2. Prepare a report on some saint who was a great lover of the Holy Eucharist.

3. Read and report to the class on one of the following: The history and meaning of the Feast of Corpus Christi, Forty Hours' Devotion, or Holy Hour.

4. Write an account of the Lord's promise to institute the Holy Eucharist (Jn. 6:48–59).

5. Get an understanding of the sacred vessels used in the service of the Blessed Sacrament. Make a list of them and write an explanation on the use of each.

6. Memorize the English translation of *O Salutaris Hostia*; of *Tantum Ergo*.

7. Prepare a presentation on the Last Supper.

## O Saving Victim

O saving Victim, opening wide
The gate of heaven to man below;
Our foes press hard on every side;
Thine aid supply; thy strength bestow.
To thy great name be endless praise,
Immortal Godhead, One in Three.
Oh, grant us endless length of days,
In our true native land with thee.

Amen.

LESSON 13

# The Holy Sacrifice of the Mass

"Attend to the service of Holy Church devoutly, with heart and mouth, especially at Mass, when the Consecration takes place . . . and lastly, take care, my son, that you have Masses sung for my soul." These were the last words spoken by St. Louis, King of France, as he lay dying in Africa.

> *"'The Mass is long,' you say, and I add: 'Because your love is short.'"*
>
> —St. Josemaria Escriva

In our study of the Holy Eucharist, we speak of the Holy Eucharist as a sacrifice as well as a sacrament; now, we will study it as a sacrifice, the Holy Sacrifice of the Mass. *Our Divine Saviour said the first Mass, at the Last Supper, the night before He died.*

## The Mass Is a Perfect Sacrifice

From the beginning of creation people offered sacrifice to God for all He had given unto them. Cain and Abel offered sacrifice to God. God specifically demanded sacrifices in the time of Moses, and even outlined the manner in which they were to be offered.

The first commandment of God begins with a statement of His divinity and His supreme lordship—*I am the Lord thy God.* This commandment obliges us to offer to God alone the supreme worship due Him. There are two considerations involved: God Himself and our dependence on God.

God is infinite in Himself; therefore, man is obliged to render worship to God.

From the beginning of creation people offered sacrifice to God for all He had given unto them. Cain and Abel offered sacrifice to God.

The next consideration is our dependence upon Him. We are in His debt for everything we possess, or shall possess. We owe Him our continuance in life as well as the means necessary to sustain it. God has redeemed us. We must atone for our sins if we wish to share in the graces of the Redemption. We see how great is our dependence upon God and how complete His lordship over us. What a priceless gift life is and how great a return we should make to God for it.

Man must give God adoration because of God's infinite excellence. We must also give Him worship because He is our supreme Lord.

Man owes himself and everything he has to God. God could demand a complete return from man of himself and all that he possesses. No one is permitted, however, to sacrifice his own life. How, then, can we adore God and make return to Him? God in His goodness permits man to offer a substitute. We may use sacrifice to acknowledge God's infinite excellence and His lordship over us. The sacrifices of Cain and Abel were such a substitute. In a sacrifice man takes some visible object which belongs to him and he makes it represent himself. He gives it up, lets it be consumed or destroyed in some way so as to represent the sacrifice of himself to God. In doing this he acknowledges God's supreme right over him and over all that he possesses.

Consider the need of sacrifice after the fall of man. Besides having to render worship to God for His excellence and making return for His gifts, man now had to make atonement for his many actual sins. Our Redeemer took upon Himself our sins and suffered and died for us, offering a sacrifice to God for us.

### The New Sacrifice

For this new and perfect sacrifice, God the Father did not commission an Aaron. He sent the greatest priest of all, His Son, the High Priest Jesus Christ. For this sacrifice to Himself He wanted no animal offered as a victim, but perfection itself, Jesus Christ, His Son made flesh. The sacrifices of the Old Law were a shadow of what was to come; here was the reality. They were but an imperfect figure; here finally was perfection in person and deed.

At the Last Supper Jesus Christ offered Himself under the appearance of bread and wine. He took bread, blessed and broke it, and gave it to His disciples, saying: "Take ye and eat. This is My body": and then took wine, blessed it, and gave to His disciples, saying: "Drink ye all of this. This is My blood which shall be shed for the remission of sins. Do this for a commemoration of Me." On the following day Jesus made the supreme sacrifice of His life when He offered it in a bloody manner on the cross.

These two acts, one unbloody, the other bloody, were components of the one great sacrifice of Christ to His heavenly Father. After the first act Christ turned to His Apostles and said:

"Do this for a commemoration of Me." By that He meant that they should do what He had just done, namely, sacrifice His body and blood under the appearances of bread and wine. The Apostles carried out His injunction. They repeated the sacrifice until they died, and their successors, the bishops and priests of the Catholic Church, daily carry out the same command.

In the Mass we offer the life of Christ as a substitute for our own life. We call this action the Holy Sacrifice of the Mass. Thus the *Mass is the sacrifice of the New Law in which Christ, through the ministry of the priest, offers Himself to God in an unbloody manner under the appearances of bread and wine.* Thus too, *the principal priest in every Mass is Jesus Christ, who offers to His heavenly Father, through the ministry of His ordained priest, His body and blood which were sacrificed on the cross.*

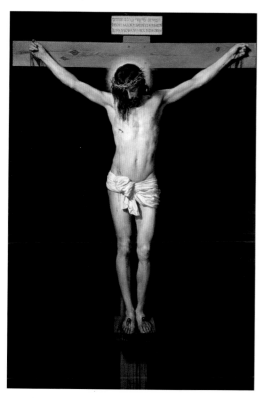

At the Last Supper we find the necessary elements of sacrifice as we also find them on Calvary and in the Sacrifice of the Mass. In all three cases the victim is one and the same: Christ, the Lord—at the Last Supper, on Calvary, in the Sacrifice of the Mass. On all three occasions Christ is the priest. He is in all three cases at the same time the Priest who offers the sacrifice and the Victim who is offered.

At Calvary and at the Last Supper He offered His life to God, and as Victim He gave it. In the Mass, He is mystically present as the Priest, acting through an earthly priest. The Mass is a sacrifice; it is the renewal of the offering of the sacrifice of the cross. Therefore *Mass is the same sacrifice as the sacrifice of the cross because in the Mass the victim is the same, and the principal priest is the same, Jesus Christ*. Accordingly, the sacrifice is of the same infinite value as Calvary was.

Have you ever given your parents or a dear friend a gift? If so, you wanted to express your love and appreciation which the gift represented. Or maybe it was an expression of gratitude for all they had done for you. Perhaps at another time you offered a gift to make your parents forget a wrong they had suffered. Again you might have given a gift in exchange for something you wanted. Your gifts express love, gratitude, sorrow, and petition.

God has done much more for us than our parents have. We want to show God our appreciation and the best way we can do it is by offering Him a sacrifice, the Holy Sacrifice of the Mass, the greatest gift we can offer. It is in fact an infinite gift. Through it we acknowledge Him as our Lord and God by adoration. Again when we thank Him for all He has done, the Mass becomes an act of thanksgiving. We also express sorrow for our many offenses

and sins. At other times we ask God to grant us what we ask, thus making the Mass an act of petition. So the Victim, Christ, is offered to God by the High Priest, Christ, in the Mass as on the cross for various purposes. These purposes are: *first, to adore God as our Creator and Lord; second, to thank God for His many favors; third, to ask God to bestow His blessings on all men; fourth, to satisfy the justice of God for the sins committed against Him.*

At this very moment Mass is being celebrated somewhere in the world. Maybe a box is being used as an altar right now in some place where the Church is being persecuted. A priest may be distributing Holy Communion to sailors somewhere on the high seas. A Mass may be just beginning in some great cathedral or some lowly church. It is not possible to be physically present at all Masses, but we can be present spiritually. Unite yourself with the Sacrifice of the Mass now being offered. Try to preserve this union throughout the day.

By this time you know that there is only one difference between the sacrifice of the cross and the Sacrifice of the Mass. *The manner in which the sacrifice is offered is different. On the cross Christ physically shed His blood and was physically slain, while in the Mass there is no physical shedding of blood nor physical death, because Christ can die no more; on the cross Christ gained merit and satisfied for us, while in the Mass He applies to us the merits and satisfaction of His death on the cross*. The sacrifice of the Mass is the same as the sacrifice of the cross. The only difference is in the manner of offering. In the sacrifice on Calvary the offering was made by Christ in His own Person, and the offering was *bloody*. At the Mass the offering is made by the priest in the name of Christ, and the offering is *unbloody*. No new graces are merited by Christ in the Mass.

Thus we see that our Mass renews the sacrifice of Calvary, and applies the merits of that one bloody sacrifice. Compare Calvary with a reservoir which has existed for two thousand years. Today it sends its waters through subterranean channels to spring forth in beautiful fountains many miles away. The water is the same water as that in the reservoir. The new fountains are the Masses.

A famous bishop once said that there is only one intelligent way of attending Mass: by consciously and deliberately imitating what the priest does. However, before we can really "Pray the Mass" intelligently, let us make sure that we understand the Mass. Do you recall the chief divisions of the Mass? How is it further divided?

Many of you have used a missal and therefore are well acquainted with it. Let us review to be sure. The structure of the Mass is made up of two parts: the Liturgy of the Word and the Liturgy of the Eucharist. The prayers of the Mass are also divided into two parts, the *Ordinary* and the *Proper*.

The Ordinary of the Mass consists of those parts which do not vary from day to day. The Proper of the Mass consists of those parts which vary according to the feast and seasons of the Church year.

## The Liturgy of the Word

Let us consider what is called in the ordinary form, the Liturgy of the Word, or as it is referred to in the extraordinary form, the Mass of the Catechumens. In the early Church, converts who were studying the Christian religion were allowed to stay until a certain part of the Mass. Accordingly this portion of the Mass was called the Mass of the Catechumens. During this part of the Mass, we hear the opening prayers, the readings, the Gospel, and the homily.

*"In regard to the divine and holy mysteries of the faith, not the least part may be handed on without the Holy Scriptures. Do not be led astray by winning words and clever arguments. Even to me, who tell you these things, do not give ready belief, unless you receive from the Holy Scriptures the proof of the things which I announce. The salvation in which we believe is not proved from clever reasoning, but from the Holy Scriptures."*

—*St. Cyril of Jerusalem*

## We Speak to God

When a town crier had important news to announce from the king, he would start out by saying, "In the name of the king I read . . ." So, too, the Holy Mass begins: "In the name of the Father, and of the Son, and of the Holy Spirit." The priest signs himself with the sign of the cross, the sign of our redemption. With him, we, too, make the sign of the cross. By doing this we dedicate ourselves to the Blessed Trinity and unite ourselves with the unbloody sacrifice of the cross.

In the extraordinary form, the priest's next prayer is one of joy: "I will go unto the altar of God, unto God, who giveth joy to my youth. . . ." Then realizing his unworthiness to offer the great sacrifice, he prays the *Judica Me*: "Judge me, O God, and distinguish my cause from the nation that is not holy; deliver me from the unjust and deceitful man" (Ps. 42).

This psalm recalls the story of David who was forced to flee from Jerusalem and as a result was unable to take part in the sacrifice in the Temple. His heart was heavy because he was far from the altar of God. He yearned to go to the altar and play on his harp, showing his confidence in God his Creator who gives life. God granted his request. We, too, are exiles on this earth, waiting for a better life. We should lift our eyes to the altar and with the priest approach God, our Hope. When we take part in the Mass we unite ourselves with Christ.

In order to approach God, we must be clean of heart. With the priest and servers we acknowl-

edge that we have often sinned "through our fault, through our fault, through our most grievous fault," and beg the heavenly court to intercede for us in the *Confiteor*. If we really intend to take part in the Mass, we must be willing to forego sin.

Do you realize that each time you recite the *Confiteor* you make a public confession of your sins and pray for their pardon? Can you select the phrases which show this? True sorrow is shown only when we are determined not to sin again, for sin keeps us from God. God, we know, will forgive us our sins if we are sorry and repent.

As the prophet says, "A contrite and humble heart God will not despise." What do you do when you hurt a good friend? By sin you hurt your best Friend and therefore you have even more reason to be sorry. We bow our head, bend our body, and strike our breast while asking God for mercy and pardon.

In the extraordinary form, the priest continues the prayers of purification while going up to the altar. He sounds the keynote of the day's feast in the *Introit*, which consists of a verse of a psalm and the Glory be to the Father.

Then we recite the *Kyrie*. This is a plea for mercy addressed three times to each Person of the Blessed Trinity. With the priest, we earnestly beg, "Lord, have mercy on us, etc." and then we join him in the hymn of praise, "Glory to God in the highest." What event in the life of our Lord does this recall? What feeling does it express?

Before the *Collect*, the priest turns to the people with the greeting, "*Dominus Vobiscum*," "The Lord be with you." We answer, "And with your spirit." The priest wants God to be with us, not only in church, but everywhere. We know the Lord will not leave unless we sin grievously.

The Collect, which follows, is the official prayer of the day. In it the priest gathers the prayers of the faithful to present them to the Lord with the gifts of bread and wine at the Offertory. It has

three distinct parts: (1) Invocation; (2) Petition; (3) Conclusion.
The chief purpose of the Collect is petition. Prayer is necessary.
Take prayer out of your life and heaven will be hard to reach. The
Collect usually ends with the words: "Through our Lord Jesus
Christ." This shows our faith in Jesus Christ as our Mediator and
acknowledges that all graces come to us through His sacrifice.
Remember that at one time Christ said, "If you ask the Father
anything in My Name, He will give it to you."

**God Speaks to Us**

Up to this point the Mass has consisted of man's prayer to God.
We saw how we ascend to God by four steps of prayer: *contrition*
(Confiteor); *longing* (Kyrie); *praise* (Gloria); *petition* (Collect). This
service of prayer has been a preparation for the service of instruction which we shall now consider.

After the *Collect in the ordinary form*, we hear the first
reading, the responsorial Psalm, and a second reading. Like the
*Introit*, the readings change from day to day. At the end of the
reading we hear the exchange: "The Word of the Lord." "Thanks
be to God." Why?

In the extraordinary form, there is one reading called the
*Epistle*, which is followed by a short chant called the *Gradual*.
The *Gradual* is a psalm, which together with the *Collect* and the
readings expresses the spirit of the Mass and the sentiments
we should feel. The word "Gradual" means a step. It is so called
because it was formerly sung from the step of the altar. (*Grad-
ually* means step by step; *graduating* means stepping higher.)
The Gradual chant of the day is sometimes called the "echo of
the Epistle," because it recalls the thoughts of the readings. It is a
brief meditation on the readings.

In the course of time, the *Alleluia* verse was added; it looks
forward to the joyful news about Christ that the Gospel will bring.
In some Masses from Septuagesima to Easter (or during Lent
in the ordinary form) and on some special feasts, a penitential

psalm called a *Tract* replaces *the Alleluia*. Tract means to go "straight on," that is, without stopping for a response.

In addition to these three chants (Gradual, Alleluia, Tract) there is sometimes another song or poem before the Gospel. It is known as the Sequence. *Sequence* means "a following of" the Gregorian notes of the Alleluia. The Alleluias sung in the Gradual had very many notes for each syllable. In order to help remember them, the people of the Middle Ages composed religious poems to be sung on the notes. About nine hundred of these were found. Since most did not fit the spirit of the Mass, Pope Pius V rejected all except five that are still in use today. How many do you know? Perhaps the best known is the *Stabat Mater*. The choir or congregation often sing some of the words of the *Stabat Mater* when the Stations of the Cross are said publicly. Do you remember the opening words? "At the Cross her station keeping, stood the mournful Mother weeping, etc." The other Sequences are the *Dies Irae*, said in some masses for the dead; *Victimae Paschali Laudes*, on Easter; *Lauda Sion*, on Corpus Christi; and *Veni Sancte Spiritus* on Pentecost.

The most important part of the Liturgy of the Word (Mass of Catechumens) is the *Gospel*. It is the word of God taken from one of the four evangelists: Matthew, Mark, Luke, and John. Before reading the Gospel,

The traditional symbols for the four evangelists.

the priest says the prayer of Isaiah: "Cleanse my heart and my lips." He begs God to purify him that he might worthily proclaim the Gospel. Then he makes the sign of the cross on the Missal, on his forehead, lips, and breast. To show our reverence and our readiness to accept God's teaching, we stand during the reading of the Gospel. With the priest we make the sign of the cross on our forehead, lips, and breast and pray to God that He may enlighten our minds to understand His teachings, guard our lips so as to speak only what is right, and protect our hearts from all harm. At the conclusion of the Gospel the priest kisses the book and the people praise God for what they have heard: "*Glory to You, O Lord*" ("Gloria tibi, Domine").

If a sermon is to be preached, it follows the Gospel. It is also designed to give instruction. Together with the readings and Gospel it is a preparation for the actual celebration of the Sacrifice of the Mass.

The Liturgy of the Word (the Mass of the Catechumens) ends with the *Creed*, or *Credo*, which is a summary of the chief truths of our faith. It is said only on Sundays and on special feasts. The Creed said at Mass is called the Nicene-Constantinopolitan Creed. Part of it was drawn up at the Council of Nicea in 325, and later on, in 381, it was given more definite form by the Council of Constantinople. We stand during the Creed, and in the extraordinary form we kneel at the words *Et incarnatus est* to venerate the mystery of the Incarnation. Examine the Creed to see what it tells about each Person of the Blessed Trinity.

In the ordinary form, we then offer the Prayers of the Faithful for various needs: for the Church, for public authorities and the salvation of the world, for those burdened by difficulties, and for the local community.

## The Liturgy of the Eucharist

We have now concluded the first part of the Mass. We saw how we prayed to God in the prayers at the foot of the altar, the Introit, the Kyrie, Gloria, and Collect. In turn, we received God's instruction in the Readings, Gradual, Gospel, and Sermon (or Homily). Then the truths of faith were professed in the Nicene Creed. Now we begin our study of the Liturgy of the Eucharist (or in the extraordinary form, the Mass of the Faithful). It is to this part that the phrase "the holy sacrifice of the Mass" truly belongs.

### We Offer Christ and Ourselves

In early times, Christians brought their gifts in an Offertory procession during which they sang a Psalm. Today, we have a remembrance of this in the *Offertory*. The priest takes the paten containing the host and offers it to the heavenly Father. Now is the time for us to place ourselves with all that we are and have upon the paten. Since we make an offering of ourselves at this part of the Mass, we should not take back anything of our self-offering during the day. At the altar, the priest then pours wine and

When the priest takes the paten containing the host and offers it to the heavenly Father, we should place ourselves with all that we are and have upon the paten.

water into the chalice. The wine, you probably know, represents Christ's divinity, and the water represents His humanity. By the mingling of the water and wine we hope to share in Christ's divinity as He humbly shared in our humanity.

The priest washes his hands. The washing signifies purity and should encourage us not only to purify our bodies but also our minds and souls when we approach the Great Sacrifice of God's love.

In the extraordinary form, the priest recites a prayer to the Holy Trinity after washing his hands: "Accept most Holy Trinity . . ."

The priest then says: "*Orate Fratres*," "Pray Brethren." Notice that the Mass is an offering in which the people take part. You should not only hear Mass; you should also participate in it.

In the extraordinary form the priest then says the *Secret* or the prayers of special petition. There may be several. They are called the Secret prayers because they are said over the gifts which have been set aside for consecration.

Now we approach the central part of the Mass, the Eucharistic Prayer, also known as the Canon, from a Greek word meaning a measuring stick. It is our "ruler" for the act of Consecration. The Canon extends from the Preface to the Doxology, the prayer just before the "Our Father."

### The Sacrifice

The priest begins the Preface, which is a prayer of preparation for the Eucharistic Prayer (Canon) of the Mass, or, at times, an invitation to praise, glorify, and give thanks to God in union with the heavenly hosts.

Examining the Preface in detail we find that it begins with an opening dialog, recited by the priest and people. This starts with the familiar *Dominus Vobiscum ("The Lord be with you")*. The priest then urges all present to lift up their hearts from things of

## The Three Essential Parts of the Mass

- Offertory
- Consecration
- Holy Communion

*"Our Lord does not come down from Heaven every day to lie in a golden ciborium. He comes to find another heaven which is infinitely dearer to him – the heaven of our souls, created in His Image, the living temples of the Adorable Trinity."*

—*St. Therese of Lisieux*

earth to the things of God. The words, *Sursum Corda*, "Lift up your hearts," invite us to think about our heavenly Father. The priest then invites all to unite with him in the prayer of thanksgiving: *Gratias agamus Domino Deo nostro*, "Let us give thanks to the Lord our God." After this, the priest sings or recites the Preface commencing with the words, "it is truly right and just, always and everywhere to give thanks" to God for His blessings. The Preface ends with the priest uniting our prayer to that of the angelic hosts; with them we say without end, "Holy, Holy, Holy," praising God the Father, God the Son, and God the Holy Spirit.

As the priest ends the *Sanctus*, praying "Holy, Holy, Holy," he turns to the Canon in the missal. The Canon begins with three mementos, or remembrances: Of the Church, of the living, and of the saints. In the first we ask God to look on our gifts as acceptable and to bless them, through Jesus Christ, His Son, our Lord. We pray also that He will protect His Church in peace and give it unity.

After a few more prayers the bell rings. There is a hushed silence, for soon Christ will be present on the altar. As the priest places his hands over the bread and wine, he offers these gifts to God in the name of the whole Church. In ancient times the Jewish priest spread his hands over a lamb that lay on the altar (Lev. 1:10–13). He meant, by this act, to show God that each person around the altar was represented by the lamb. Then the lamb was slain and given back to God, its Creator. Here in the Mass the Lamb of God will soon offer Himself to the Father and us with Him. The priest calls attention to the gifts which we are returning to God so that He can give us back His Son. At the same time we beg God for peace, the salvation of our souls, and final perseverance. In the second offering prayer, the priest begs God to make our offerings the Body and Blood of Christ. God is requested to bless, approve, and ratify our oblation, and render it reasonable and acceptable.

Now the priest takes the host into his hands, bends low over the altar, and re-enacts the sacrifice of Christ at the Last Supper. "Who, on the day before He suffered, took bread into His holy and venerable hands, and with His eyes lifted up to heaven, unto Thee, His almighty Father, giving thanks to Thee, He blessed, broke and gave it to His disciples, saying: 'Take and eat ye all of this, For this is My body.'" The priest raises the Host so that all may see It. Then he lowers It and genuflects in adoration. What should we say as we look up at the Sacred Host?

The priest has the power to change bread and wine and uses that power. Christ, who promised to come down at the priest's words, obeys. He is really present in the Host. We should adore Him.

The priest, then, holding the chalice in both hands, bows low and says: "In like manner, after He had supped, taking also this excellent chalice into His holy and venerable hands, and giving thanks to Thee, He blessed and gave it to His disciples, saying: 'Take and drink ye all of this, for this is the chalice of My blood, of the new and eternal testament: the mystery of faith, which shall be shed for you and for many unto the remission of sins. As often as ye shall do these things, ye shall do them in remembrance of Me.'"

The words of the twofold Consecration are like a mystical sword separating the blood from the body of Christ. They remind us of Christ's death on Calvary on the first Good Friday. We cannot understand this mystical separation because Christ is whole and entire under the appearances of both bread and wine.

Why does Christ renew His bloody Sacrifice of Calvary in this unbloody manner? He wants us to share in the graces He merited by His death on the cross. Each time we assist at Mass, He applies these graces to us. Also, He wants to give us a gift worthy to be offered to the Father—a perfect Sacrifice. As God-Man, Christ can perfectly adore His Father and please Him in the name of all men.

This change of the bread and wine, you remember, is called *Transubstantiation*. No longer is the substance the same, for the substance of the bread has become the body of Christ and the substance of the wine, the blood of Christ. All that remains is the appearance. Is not God's almighty power shown here again? At the Consecration our gifts are changed into the substance of the body and blood of Christ. Our human offerings have also become more holy. Like a drop of water cast into the sea, our little acts of love have become entirely lost in the infinite ocean of God's love and goodness. God the Father no longer sees our littleness but only the holiness and infinite sacrifice of His divine Son.

St. Francis Solano, the great song maker, said, "At the Consecration when the bread and wine are changed into the body and blood of Christ, I also am changed. I become holier, more pleasing to the heavenly Father, because now He sees His Son in me."

Immediately after the Consecration we offer God thanksgiving for our redemption. In the prayer which follows, the sacrifices of Abel, Abraham, and Melchizedek are recalled.

In the Eucharistic Prayer (the Canon), before the Consecra-

He was praying in a certain place, and when he ceased, one of his disciples said to him, "Lord, teach us to pray, as John taught his disciples." And he said to them, "When you pray, say:

'Father, hallowed be your name, Your kingdom come. Give us each day our daily bread; and forgive us our sins, for we ourselves forgive every one who is indebted to us; and lead us not into temptation.'"

tion, there were three mementos. Do you know them? After the Consecration the dead, sinners, and all of nature are remembered. "Be mindful, O Lord, also of Thy servants, who have gone before us with the sign of Faith," that is, the character imprinted by the sacrament of Baptism, "and rest in the sleep of peace." Having prayed for the dead we beg that we poor sinners may also come to the blessed company of the saints. The final Remembrance Prayer begs God's blessings on all created things. Giving honor and glory to the Blessed Trinity, the priest then concludes the Eucharistic Prayer (Canon).

**We Receive**

The Communion of the Mass opens with the *Our Father*. It is like grace before meals. In it we say, "Give us this day our daily bread." If our bodies stand in need of nourishment, how much more do our immortal souls! At the conclusion of the Lord's Prayer, the priest recites the *Libera ("Deliver us")*, a prayer for deliverance from past, present, and future evils. Could you name what some of these evils might be?

In the ordinary form, we then pray for peace and unity for the Church. In the extraordinary form, this is said after the Agnus Dei. The priest the recites the *Pax Domini* (Peace of the Lord). Christ came at a time when the whole world was at peace. In the Mass, the nearer the time Christ will come into our hearts, the more prayers we say for peace. Again, when Christ appeared to His Apostles after the Resurrection, His greeting was, "Peace be with you!" Do you see the similarity between Christ's prayer and the priest's? What we all need today is peace within our souls. When especially are we at peace? When our Lord was born in Bethlehem, the angels sang, "Peace on earth to men of good will."

You recall that at the Last Supper, Christ took the bread and broke it. Now the priest takes the consecrated Host, breaks It into three parts and drops one particle into the consecrated wine. In the extraordinary form, the priest does this while reciting the Pax Domini.

The words *Agnus Dei* (Lamb of God) remind us of an event that took place in Christ's life. What happened at the banks of the Jordan when John the Baptist saw Christ approaching? If you had been with St. John, what would you have done? You would certainly have asked Christ to take away your sins and have mercy on you. Let us join with the priest in saying the *Agnus Dei* (Lamb of God).

In the extraordinary form, three prayers follow. In the first prayer we ask for peace and unity for the Church. In the second we ask to be freed from our sins. In the third we ask that Communion may help us and not lead to our condemnation. Then the priest genuflects, takes the body of our Lord in his hands and before receiving Holy Communion says three times, "*Domine, non sum dignus. . . .*" Of what New Testament incident do these words, "O Lord, I am not worthy," remind you? Read Matthew 8:5–13 if you do not know. If we have faith and humility like the centurion then we can be assured that we will receive Christ worthily.

It is rare that there is a Mass when no one receives Holy Communion. At least the priest receives the body and blood of Christ, which he has offered and consecrated. However, if we wish to participate fully in the Mass, we, too, must receive Holy Communion. Should it be impossible to receive sacramentally, what else could we do?

Facing the communicants, the priest holds the Sacred Host above the ciborium and says, "Behold the Lamb of God. . . ." Then he says, "Lord, I am not worthy. . . ." In the extraordinary form of the Mass, as the priest places the Sacred Host on the tongue of each person he says, "May the body of Our Lord Jesus Christ preserve your soul unto life everlasting. Amen." In the ordinary form, the priest simply says, "The Body of

## TERMS TO KNOW

- Kyrie
- Consecration
- Secret
- Agnus Dei
- satisfy
- Gloria
- Dominus Vobiscum
- worship
- Gospel
- Orate Fratres
- Credo
- Transubstantiation
- Confiteor
- Gradual
- Ite, Missa Est
- Offertory
- Sequence
- New Law
- Pater Noster
- Amen
- sacrifice
- Alleluia
- Canon
- Collect
- Deo Gratias
- Communion
- Remembrances
- Introit
- ministry
- ordinary form
- extraordinary form

Christ," to which we respond "Amen." Those who receive Christ in Holy Communion complete the sacrifice by receiving the Gift which God gives us in return for our own.

After the Holy Eucharist has been distributed, the priest puts the ciborium away, purifies the chalice with wine and then cleanses his fingers with water and wine, saying the Ablution prayers.

In the extraordinary form, the Communion Verse is then said by the priest. It asks for union with Christ.

It is followed by the Postcommunion, or Prayer after Communion, the official prayer of thanksgiving to God for Holy Communion. These last two prayers belong to the Proper of the Mass.

Facing the people the priest says *Dominus Vobiscum, "The Lord be with you."* He then turns to the congregation and gives the blessing, "May God almighty bless you: The Father, the Son, and the Holy Spirit." He adds, *Ite, Missa Est, "*Go, the Mass is ended." (In the extraordinary form, this precedes the blessing.) We should go forth from Mass and live the Mass in our daily actions, giving ourselves for others as our Lord has given Himself for us.

In the extraordinary form of the Mass, after giving the blessing, the priest goes to the gospel side of the altar, and reads the Last Gospel, which is from the first chapter of the Gospel of St. John. When the priest has completed the reading, the server says *"Deo Gratias"* (Thanks be to God).

## We Should Live the Mass

*We should assist at Mass with reverence, attention and devotion. The best method of assisting at Mass is to unite with the priest in offering the Holy Sacrifice, and to receive Holy Communion.* We have offered ourselves to God. He has accepted our offering and taken possession of us through Christ.

When you drop a stone into a pool of still water what happens to the water? At first the ripple around the stone is very small, but it keeps getting bigger and bigger until finally it reaches all around the pool. That is the way the Mass should affect us. It should start a ripple of graces in our own soul and we should take those graces and attempt to carry them to others until they reach all around the world.

Pope Pius XII said that "one demonstrates the true love for the Church by participating devoutly every day, if possible, in the Eucharistic Sacrifice. . . . The Divine Redeemer offers not only Himself as Head of the Church to the heavenly Father, but in Himself, His Mystical members as well." And so, we members of the Mystical Body of Christ have a share in Holy Mass. There is no surer way to God than by attending Mass daily and devoutly receiving Communion.

## Summary

A sacrifice is the offering of a victim by a priest to God alone, and the destruction of it in some way to acknowledge that God is the Creator and Lord of all things. The Mass is the sacrifice of the New Law. Jesus said the first Mass at the Last Supper, the night before He died. In the Mass Christ, through the ministry of the priest, offers Himself to God in an unbloody manner, under the appearances of bread and wine. *The principal priest in every Mass is Jesus Christ who offers to His heavenly Father, through the ministry of His ordained priest, His body and blood which were sacrificed on the cross.*

The Mass is offered for the following purposes: (1) to adore God as our Creator and Lord; (2) to thank God for His many favors; (3) to ask God to bestow His blessings on all men; (4) to satisfy the justice of God for the sins committed against Him.

We should assist at Mass with reverence, attention, and devotion. The best method of assisting at Mass is to unite with the priest in offering the Holy Sacrifice, and to receive Holy Communion.

## Prayer

*Per ipsum, et cum ipso, et in ipso, est tibi Deo Patri omnipotenti, in unitate Spiritus Sancti, omnis honor et gloria.*

Through him, with him, in him, in the unity of the Holy Spirit, all glory and honor is yours almighty Father, forever and ever Amen.

## FOR ME TO REVIEW

*Catechism Lesson*

917. **Q. What is the Mass?**

   A. The Mass is the unbloody sacrifice of the body and blood of Christ.

919. **Q. What is a sacrifice?**

   A. A sacrifice is the offering of an object by a priest to God alone, and the consuming of it to acknowledge that He is the Creator and Lord of all things.

921. **Q. How is the Mass the same sacrifice as that of the cross?**

   A. The Mass is the same sacrifice as that of the cross because the offering and the priest are the same— Christ our Blessed Lord; and the ends for which the sacrifice of the Mass is offered are the same as those of the sacrifice of the cross.

922. **Q. What were the ends for which the sacrifice of the cross was offered?**

   A. The ends for which the sacrifice of the cross was offered were: 1st, To honor and glorify God; 2nd, To thank Him for all the graces bestowed on the whole world; 3rd, To satisfy God's justice for the sins of men; 4th, To obtain all graces and blessings.

931. Q. Is there any difference between the sacrifice of the cross and the sacrifice of the Mass?

A. Yes; the manner in which the sacrifice is offered is different. On the cross Christ really shed His blood and was really slain; in the Mass there is no real shedding of blood nor real death, because Christ can die no more; but the sacrifice of the Mass, through the separate Consecration of the bread and the wine, represents His death on the cross.

946. Q. How should we assist at Mass?

A. We should assist at Mass with great interior recollection and piety and with every outward mark of respect and devotion.

947. Q. Which is the best manner of hearing Mass?

A. The best manner of hearing Mass is to offer it to God with the priest for the same purpose for which it is said, to meditate on Christ's sufferings and death, and to go to Holy Communion.

*Questions and Exercises*

## Part 1: Matching

**COLUMN A**

1. Introit
2. Kyrie
3. Credo
4. Gloria
5. Epistle
6. Collect
7. Dominus Vobiscum
8. Confiteor

9. Gospel

**COLUMN B**

A. Confession of sins

B. The Lord be with you

C. Follows the Confiteor

D. The story of our Lord's life

E. An act of Faith

F. A letter from an Apostle

G. A prayer of praise

H. A prayer which asks God for special help

I. A prayer for mercy

## Part 2: Yes or No

1. Is the Consecration the most important part of the Mass?
2. Do we, in a certain sense, offer the Mass with the priest?
3. Is the *Credo* an act of Love?
4. Is the *Collect* also known as a *Reading*?
5. Is the *Secret* the same for every Mass?
6. Could the sacrifices of the Old Law forgive sin?
7. Do the prayers of the Ordinary of the Mass change from day to day?
8. Is the Mass today the same sacrifice as the Sacrifice of the Cross?
9. Does the word *Gospel* mean "good news"?

## Part 3: Matching

**COLUMN A**

1. The Last Supper, the Sacrifice of the Cross, and the Mass today are the same sacrifice

2. The priest kisses the altar stone

3. The best method of assisting at Mass is to unite with the priest

4. We stand during the Gospel

5. The water is blessed before it is poured into the chalice but the wine is not

6. The priest washes his fingers

7. A sacrifice is the offering of a victim by a priest to God alone

8. The *Credo* is like the Act of Faith and the Apostles' Creed

**COLUMN B**

A. because he wants to remind us that our souls should be pure and clean before Christ comes down upon the altar.

B. in offering the Holy Sacrifice, and to receive Holy Communion.

C. and the destruction of it in some way to acknowledge that He is the Creator and Lord of all things.

D. because it represents Christ.

E. because in each of them Christ offers Himself to adore God, to thank God, to petition God's help, to ask God's pardon.

F. because we want to show God that we honor and love His word.

G. because the wine represents Christ's divinity.

H. because in each of them we tell God we believe in Him.

## ✅ FOR ME TO DO

1. Keep a "Mass Vocabulary."

2. Draw a "Mass Clock" to show where the Mass is being offered at every hour of the day and night.

3. Find prayers in the Mass which show the four ends of sacrifice.

4. Make a Mass chart divided into three columns: (1) What the priest does; (2) What the priest says; (3) What we might think about.

5. Show how the Church honors the Blessed Virgin and the saints by preparing special Masses for their feasts.

6. Conduct a Missal hunt for the following: The Sign of the Cross; the *Dominus Vobiscum* and its response; the ceremonial kissing of the altar by the priest.

7. Prepare an individual Mass booklet with diagrams, pictures, prayers, vestments, vessels, etc.

8. Make original drawings of scenes or events suggested by various parts of the Mass.

9. Prepare a classroom "movie" of original drawings which illustrate scenes or events suggested by various parts of the Mass.

10. Study and sing Mass Chants. Listen to recordings for greater appreciation.

11. Observe and discuss some symbols which are used to represent certain parts of the Mass.

12. Draw original symbols to interpret the prayers and actions of the Mass.

13. Consult the biblical stories which are correlated with parts of the Mass, such as the Prodigal Son.

14. Dramatize biblical events and other stories and comparisons which are correlated with parts of the Mass.

15. Make a crossword puzzle, "bingo" game, etc., based on your study of the Mass.

16. Make a study of the saints in the Canon of the Mass.

17. Find various prayers in the Mass that teach us to be humble and unselfish, to have love for one another, and to practice other virtues.

18. Draw symbols of the Holy Eucharist.

19. Compose a prayer to show your love for Christ in the Holy Eucharist.

20. Learn the anthem: "O Sacred Banquet" from the Office of Corpus Christi to use for spiritual communion. Write a meditation on the truths which it contains.

## Tantum Ergo

*Down in adoration falling,*
*Lo! the sacred Host we hail,*
*Lo! o'er ancient forms departing*
*Newer rites of grace prevail;*
*Faith for all defects supplying,*
*Where the feeble senses fail.*
*To the Everlasting Father,*
*And the Son Who reigns on high*
*With the Holy Ghost proceeding*
*Forth from Each eternally,*
*Be salvation, honour, blessing,*
*Might, and endless majesty.*

*Amen.*

# Holy Communion— God's Gift to Us

You understand how important food is to the natural life of the body. It serves to strengthen and nourish it. Similarly the supernatural life of sanctifying grace, which you possess by reason of your Baptism, requires spiritual, supernatural food. That is the reason why our Lord instituted the sacrament of the Holy Eucharist. In our study of the Eucharist we have learned that the Holy Eucharist is both a sacrifice and a sacrament. In the Holy Sacrifice of the Mass, we saw how the bread and wine are changed into the body and blood of Christ to be received by the faithful in Holy Communion.

*Holy Communion*, we know, *is the receiving of Jesus Christ in the sacrament of the Holy Eucharist*. In certain sacrifices of the Old Law, the worshipers partook of the victim after it had been sacrificed to God. It was understood that God had accepted the sacrifice and that He showed His pleasure by inviting those present to the feast. This was a sign of union with God. Holy Communion is a sign of union with God, a sign which produces the effect it signifies.

## Holy Communion Should Be Received Worthily

For many years you have been receiving Christ in Holy Communion. Has your heart always been well prepared, or do you go out of habit? Do you know what is necessary to receive Holy Communion worthily? Of course. *To receive Holy Communion worthily it is necessary to be free from mortal sin, to have a right intention, and to obey the Church's laws on the fast required before Holy Communion out of reverence for the body and blood of our divine Lord. However, there are some cases in which Holy Communion may be received without fasting.* A first requirement for a worthy Communion is freedom from mortal sin. Do you recall the parable of the wedding garment? Why was the man in the parable considered unworthy to attend the wedding feast? Similarly when a person goes to Communion when in mortal sin, a sacrilege is committed. As the catechism puts it, *He who knowingly receives Holy Communion in mortal sin receives the body and blood of Christ; but he does not receive His graces and he commits a grave sin of sacrilege.* You remember that a sacrilege is an abuse or wrong use of a sacred person, place, or thing.

> "The holy Eucharist completes Christian initiation. Those who have been raised to the dignity of the royal priesthood by Baptism and configured more deeply to Christ by Confirmation participate with the whole community in the Lord's own sacrifice by means of the Eucharist."
>
> —*Catechism of the Catholic Church*, 1322

Freedom from mortal sin is the minimum requirement. *To receive more abundantly the graces of Holy Communion we should strive to be most fervent and to free ourselves from deliberate venial sin.* You want Christ to come into a heart filled with love for Him. In what ways can you free yourself from venial sin?

Another requirement for receiving Holy Communion worthily is the fast. *The Church asks that we fast for one hour before receiving the Holy Eucharist.* (1) *Water may be taken at any time before Holy Communion without breaking the fast.* (2) *Sick persons, though not confined to bed, may receive Holy Communion after taking medicine or nonalcoholic drinks. A priest's permission is not necessary.* (3) *All Catholics (in good standing with the Church) may receive Holy Communion after fasting one hour from food and drink.*

*Holy Communion may be received without fasting when one is in danger of death, or when it is necessary to save the Blessed Sacrament from insult or injury.* Do you know of any cases of persons receiving without fasting? What about those suffering persecution? A Maryknoll priest in China wrote in his life story how he consumed the Sacred Host in order to save It from the insults of his persecutors.

Many persons in former times had to make real sacrifices in order to receive Holy Communion. Today Holy Mother Church, more anxious than ever for her children's spiritual welfare, has done much to promote frequent Communion.

## Holy Communion Makes Us More Christlike

When we go to Holy Communion, we receive Christ's body, blood, soul, and divinity. He is wholly and entirely present under the appearance of bread and wine.

Before receiving, *we should prepare ourselves for Holy Communion by thinking of our divine Redeemer whom we are about to receive, and by making fervent acts of faith, hope, love, and contrition.* As you approach the communion rail, what should your actions and your sentiments be? Recall the words of the centurion who said, "Lord, I am not worthy that Thou should enter under my roof, but only say the word and my servant will be healed." Perhaps it would be well to re-read the entire account in Matthew 8:5–9.

When the priest places the Sacred Host on your tongue, say with him, "May the body of our Lord Jesus Christ preserve my soul unto life everlasting." Then what about thanksgiving? Christ

**TERMS TO KNOW**

- Holy Eucharist
- Viaticum
- dispositions
- Holy Communion
- fasting
- sacrilegious

has entered your heart. These moments are the most precious moments of your life. Love, adore, cherish Him! Be intimate with Christ. The catechism summarizes what we should do. *After Holy Communion we should spend some time adoring our Lord, thanking Him, renewing our promises of love and of obedience to Him, and asking Him for blessings for ourselves and others.*

Holy Communion produces certain effects. You know some of them. *The chief effects of a worthy Holy Communion are: first, a closer union with our Lord and a more fervent love of God and of our neighbor; second, an increase of sanctifying grace; third, preservation from mortal sin and the remission of venial sin; fourth, the less-*

*ening of our inclinations to sin and the help to practice good works.*

Let us consider these effects. When Christ said, "Except you eat the flesh of the Son of Man and drink his blood, you shall not have life in you" (Jn. 6:54), He meant it. At another time He said, "He who eats My flesh, and drinks My blood, abides in Me and I in him" (Jn. 6:57). How plainly Christ spoke! He tells us outright that He dwells in the one who communicates.

As long as the sacramental species remain (which is ordinarily about fifteen minutes), Christ remains physically with us. When you eat food, what happens to it? Yes, it becomes part of you. But a more wonderful thing happens when you receive the Sacred Host. Holy Communion transforms us into Christ. He brings to us His graces and virtues so that we might become more like Him. Do you see why your life should be Christlike? Our love of God will spread to all those around us. We can say with St. Paul, "I live now, not I, but Christ lives in me."

You learned that the Holy Eucharist is a sacrament of the living. Since this is so, what happens to the grace in you? Our Lord compared Himself to a Vine and us to the branches. If He gives us His grace, we will have the same life that He has. You will bear fruit because He will help you do good works. Hold a piece of iron in a hot fire. What happens? It takes on the nature of fire. In a much greater degree does sanctifying grace fill you with the light and holiness of God.

Holy Communion preserves you from mortal sin and remits venial sin. One mortal sin can destroy the life of grace in you. Holy Communion helps you avoid such a tragedy.

Through Holy Communion you obtain actual graces which give you the necessary strength to overcome temptations. A brilliant aviator of World War I was asked where he derived his strength and courage. He pointed to the tabernacle and replied that he went to Communion daily whenever possible. Can you tell of other outstanding men and women who were, or are, frequent communicants?

*"Just as by melting two candles together you get one piece of wax, so, I think, one who receives the flesh and blood of Jesus is fused together with him, and the soul finds that he is in Christ, and Christ is in him."*

—*St. Cyril of Jerusalem*

*We are obliged to receive Holy Communion during Easter time each year*, and we should also take care to receive Holy Communion in Viaticum when we are in danger of death. We should go more often than simply at Eastertime however. St. Pius X, the Pope of the Eucharist, said, "All the faithful, married or single, young or old, even children from the time of their first Communion are invited to go to Holy Communion frequently; yes, daily." Think of all the saints who ardently desired to receive our Lord.

*It is well to receive Holy Communion often, even daily, because this intimate union with Jesus Christ, the Source of all holiness and the Giver of all graces, is the greatest aid to a holy life.* You know the old saying, "Tell me with whom you go, and I'll tell you what you are." A person often becomes like the people with whom he associates. Could anything be more wonderful than to become like Christ? Frequent, devout, daily Communion makes one more Christlike. No matter how great our weakness or how many difficulties or troubles we have, we shall find that frequent, devout Communion makes it possible for us to serve God faithfully.

If we cannot receive Jesus sacramentally, we can beg Him to come spiritually to us. A spiritual communion is an act of faith and love joined to an ardent desire to receive Christ sacramentally in Holy Communion. This act, which we can make as often as we wish, is very pleasing and meritorious.

Let us remember the words of our Lord: "I am the living bread that has come down from heaven. If anyone eat of this bread he shall live forever; and the bread that I will give is My flesh for the life of the world" (Jn. 6:51–52). If we wish to live forever, with Christ, let us be grateful to Him for the Holy Eucharist. *We should show our gratitude to our Lord for remaining always on our altars in the Holy Eucharist, by visiting Him often, by reverence in church, by assisting every day at Mass when this is possible, by attending parish devotions, and by being present at Benediction of the Blessed Sacrament.*

## Summary

Holy Communion is the receiving of Jesus Christ in the sacrament of the Holy Eucharist. The chief effects of a worthy Holy Communion are: (1) a closer union with our Lord and a more fervent love of God and of our neighbor; (2) an increase of sanctifying grace; (3) preservation from mortal sin and the remission of venial sin; (4) the lessening of our inclinations to sin, and the help needed to practice good works.

To receive Holy Communion worthily it is necessary to be free from mortal sin, and to fast one hour from solid foods and liquids except water, which we may drink any time. We should prepare ourselves for Holy Communion by thinking of our divine Redeemer whom we are about to receive. We should also make fervent acts of faith, hope, love, and contrition. After Holy Communion we should spend some time adoring our Lord, thanking Him, renewing our promises of love and obedience to Him, and asking Him for blessings for ourselves and others.

We are obliged to receive Holy Communion during the Easter time each year and when in danger of death. It is well to receive Holy Communion frequently, even daily. If this is not possible, spiritual communion daily is possible for everyone.

 **FOR ME TO REVIEW**

*Catechism Lesson*

898. **Q. What is Holy Communion?**
   A. Holy Communion is the receiving of the body and blood of Christ.

901. **Q. What is necessary to make a good Communion?**
   A. To make a good Communion it is necessary to be in the state of sanctifying grace and to fast according to the laws of the Church.

903. **Q. Does he who receives Communion in mortal sin receive the body and blood of Christ?**
   A. He who receives Communion in mortal sin receives the body and blood of Christ, but does not receive His grace, and he commits a great sacrilege.

907. **Q. Is anyone ever allowed to receive Holy Communion when not fasting?**
   A. To protect the Blessed Sacrament from insult or injury, or when in danger of death, Holy Communion may be received without fasting.

913. **Q. What should we do after Holy Communion?**
   A. After Holy Communion we should spend some time in adoring our Lord, in thanking Him for the grace we have received, and in asking Him for the blessings we need.

912. Q. **What is a spiritual communion?**
     A. A spiritual communion is an earnest desire to receive Communion in reality, by which desire we make all preparations and thanksgivings that we would make in case we really received the Holy Eucharist. Spiritual communion is an act of devotion that must be pleasing to God and bring us blessings from Him.

*Questions and Exercises*

## Completion

1. We are obliged to receive Holy Communion during_____.

2. One who receives Holy Communion in the state of mortal sin commits a_____.

3. One of the requisites for a worthy Holy Communion is to fast_____hour from solid foods.

4. _____sin prevents us from receiving Holy Communion worthily.

5. The pope who granted privileges in regard to the Eucharistic fast is_____.

6. The drinking of_____does not break the Eucharistic fast.

7. Before receiving Holy Communion we should make acts of faith, hope,_____, and contrition.

8. We should try to free ourselves from every stain of_____ before receiving.

9. The initials of the sacrament which is both a sacrament and a sacrifice are_____.

## Act of Love

*O my God, I love you above all things, with my whole heart and soul, because you are all-good and worthy of all love. I love my neighbor as myself for the love of you. I forgive all who have injured me, and I ask pardon of all whom I have injured.*

*Amen.*

# CHAPTER 9

# Christ Restores or Increases the Life of Grace in Our Soul

## LESSON 15

# Penance and Reconciliation and Examination of Conscience

The sacrament of Penance and Reconciliation is a God-given gift which takes away our sins, whether mortal or venial, so that we can enjoy union with God. It is one of the sacraments that we are privileged to receive frequently during life. This sacrament purifies us from sin and its consequences; it also increases divine life in us. Every Catholic should grow in the knowledge and appreciation of it.

## What the Sacrament of Penance and Reconciliation Is

By this time we all know that *Penance and Reconciliation is the sacrament by which sins committed after baptism are forgiven through the absolution of the priest*. Penance and Reconciliation, to the sick soul, is like medicine to the sick body. Our Blessed Lord realized the frailty of human nature. He knew our inclination to sin and He knew the effects of sin on the supernatural life of the soul.

Mortal sin, we know, results in death to our supernatural life because it deprives us of sanctifying grace. It is beyond the power of any medicine to restore a dead person to life. The sacrament

The Tears of
St. Peter

"[The sacrament of confession] is called the sacrament of conversion because it makes sacramentally present Jesus' call to conversion, the first step in returning to the Father5 from whom one has strayed by sin."

—*Catechism of the Catholic Church, 1423*

of Penance and Reconciliation, however, can restore the supernatural life of grace no matter how many or grievous our sins.

Notice that it is "through the absolution of the priest" that our sins are forgiven. It is through the absolution of the priest that the great purpose of the sacrament of Penance and Reconciliation is achieved. "Absolution" means "a loosing," "a freeing," a "getting rid of." It refers to the words the priest says at the time he forgives the sins.

To appreciate the sacrament of Penance and Reconciliation, it is necessary to understand the sacrament of Holy Orders. Holy Orders, like Baptism and Confirmation, confers a character on the soul. The character of Holy Orders makes the priest Christ's special representative. It gives to him the power and authority to speak in Christ's name. For example, when the priest says the words "This is My body," at Mass, he is speaking for Christ. The bread does not become the body of the priest, but the body of Christ. Likewise, when he says, "I absolve you from your sins" in the confessional, he speaks for Christ. The priest, in other words, does not forgive sins on his own authority. Only Christ forgives sins, addressing us through His priests.

**Penance and Reconciliation Was Instituted by Christ**
On the first Easter Sunday night, the very day of the Resurrection, Christ instituted the sacrament of Penance and Reconciliation as He promised. He appeared to the Apostles gathered together and gave to them and their successors in the priesthood the power to forgive sins. So if you are ever questioned as to the source of the power the priest has to forgive sins, here is your answer. *The priest has the power to forgive sins from Jesus Christ, who said to His Apostles and to their successors in the priesthood: "Receive the Holy Spirit; whose sins you shall forgive, they are forgiven them;*

*and whose sins you shall retain, they are retained."*

## Power to Forgive Sins Was Conferred on the Apostles and Their Successors

We know that our Lord Himself had power to forgive sins:

Christ sending out the Apostles

*a)* because He was God.

*b)* because He worked miracles during His life on earth to prove that He personally had the power to forgive sins.

Do you recall how He cured the man who was sick of the palsy? This man pleaded with our Lord to heal him. Our Blessed Lord cured him both in body and soul simply by telling him that his sins were forgiven, and by ordering him to rise and walk. Can you think of any other incident in which Christ showed this power?

Since our Lord had the power Himself, He could give it to the Apostles. Holy Scripture reveals that the infallible Church has the power to loose and bind the bonds of sin.

It is somewhat difficult for those who desire to embrace the Catholic faith to understand why our sins must be confessed to a priest. They say that it is really Christ Himself who forgives our sins. And so they ask why a person cannot kneel down in private and confess his sins.

In the Old Testament God laid down certain regulations for a person who was cured of a disease such as leprosy. After his cure, the leper was obliged to show himself to the priest and perform certain other acts. Similarly, in the New Law, one condition laid down by our Lord for the forgiveness of sins is that we confess our sins to the priest.

Our Divine Lord could have decreed that we would receive the pardon of our sins by confessing them directly to God with sincere sorrow. But He ordained that the sacrament be administered by men in the name of God. This is a more effective means of obtaining repentance. We need the humility which confessing our sins to a priest demands. We need the advice which a priest can give us in sacramental confession, and the assurance that our sins are forgiven through the words of absolution.

The priest does not forgive sins by his own power as man, but by the authority he receives as the minister of God. We should be grateful to Christ for having given His priests this power. Think what it would mean here and hereafter if, after we had sinned, there was no way to have our sins forgiven. Imagine how terrible it must be to have no hope of forgiveness, like the fallen angels.

### Sins Are Forgiven Through the Absolution of the Priest

The formula for administering this sacrament is found in the words of absolution. *The priest forgives sins with the words: "I absolve you from your sins in the name of the Father, and of the Son, and of the Holy Spirit. Amen."* By the omnipotence of God and the power of Redemption, sin is remitted by these words. How often we have heard the priest say the words of absolution after we have sincerely and contritely confessed our sins in the sacred tribunal of penance.

The priest can, and sometimes does, refuse absolution when he thinks the penitent is not rightly disposed for the sacrament. If, in his opinion, the penitent is not truly sorry for his sins or not resolved to avoid sin and its occasions in the future, he is obliged to refuse absolution.

There are occasions, too, when the priest has no authority to forgive sins. He has the power which he received at ordination, but he may never have been authorized by the bishop to use that power. Thus, besides the power of orders received at ordination, the priest needs also what is called "the power of jurisdiction,"

*"In the life of the body a man is sometimes sick, and unless he takes medicine, he will die. Even so in the spiritual life a man is sick on account of sin. For that reason he needs medicine so that he may be restored to health; and this grace is bestowed in the Sacrament of Penance."*

—St. Thomas Aquinas

that is, authority over those whom he absolves. This power is ordinarily given to the priest by the bishop of the diocese in which the sacrament is administered.

There are also some very serious sins which the priest has no authority to absolve. In order to have such a sin forgiven, the priest must obtain special authority from the bishop or the pope to forgive this sin. Such sins are called "reserved" sins.

It is consoling, however, to know that any priest has the authority to absolve a dying person from any and every sin he may have had the misfortune to commit, provided he is sorry.

## Penance and Reconciliation Produces Wonderful Effects in the Soul

All the sacraments worthily received produce certain effects in us. *The effects of the sacrament of Penance and Reconciliation worthily received, are: first, the restoration or increase of sanctifying grace; second, the forgiveness of sins; third, the remission of the eternal punishment, if necessary, and also of part, at least, of the temporal punishment, due to our sins; fourth, the help to avoid sin in future; fifth, the restoration of the merits of our good works if they have been lost by mortal sin.*

## Effects of the Sacrament of Penance and Reconciliation

- Restoration or increase of sanctifying grace

- Forgiveness of sins

- Remission of punishment for sins

- Help to avoid sin

- Restoration of merits lost by sin

### Restores or Increases Sanctifying Grace

If the supernatural life of grace has been destroyed by mortal sin, Christ restores that life to us through the sacrament of Penance and Reconciliation. If we have not lost the life of grace through serious sin, He increases sanctifying grace in us.

It is told that St. Catherine of Siena was often favored with holy visions. On one occasion God showed her the splendor of a person in the state of grace. The sight was so beautiful that it dazzled her. "Oh my God," she cried out, "if I did not know that there is only one God, I should think that this is one." Difficult as it is for us to realize the startling beauty of one in sanctifying grace, so likewise is it hard for us to picture a person who has lost it. We can take comfort from this thought: however hideous and revolting the condition of such a person may be, the sacrament of Penance and Reconciliation, worthily received, restores him to his original beauty.

### Forgives Sins

Holy Scripture abounds with instances in which our Blessed Saviour Himself forgave sinners. We remember His words of pardon to Mary Magdalen and to the penitent thief at His right on Calvary. Can you mention others? We may be tempted to envy these people because they received this assurance of forgiveness from the lips of Christ Himself. Our assurance is equally as great when after we have made a worthy confession we hear the words: "Go in peace, your sins are forgiven." It is really Jesus Christ Himself who says these words to us through the mouth of the priest.

## Remits Punishment Due to Sins

If you hurt a friend, you try in every way possible to make up for it, even after he has forgiven you. So, too, if we have offended God, we should make some amends for the injury we have inflicted through our infidelity. God forgives our sins when we are sorry, but He demands temporal punishment for every sin we commit. This temporal punishment is not always entirely removed by the sacrament. We can pay the debt of the temporal punishment due to our sins either in this life by prayer, fasting, almsgiving, works of mercy, patient endurance of suffering, and the gaining of indulgences. If we fail to do this we must pay it by suffering in purgatory. If we are wise, we will try to pay the debt of the temporal punishment due to our sins here in this life rather than suffer in purgatory.

## Helps to Avoid Sin

Not only are our sins forgiven in the sacrament of Penance and Reconciliation, but we also receive the necessary strength to resist sin in the future. How much help or strength we receive depends upon the earnestness with which we make each confession. Even though we confess frequently, it should never

When we hear the words: "Go in peace, your sins are forgiven," we can be assured it is really Jesus Christ Himself who says these words to us through the mouth of the priest.

become a routine performance, but should always be accompanied by a genuine and sincere sorrow and a firm determination to avoid sin in the future.

### Restores Merits Lost by Mortal Sin

By committing mortal sin, a person deprives himself of the merits of any good works he has performed in the past or may perform in the future. After he receives the sacrament of Penance and Reconciliation worthily, the merits of his past good works are restored to him.

### Other Effects of the Sacrament of Penance and Reconciliation

*The sacrament of Penance and Reconciliation also gives us the opportunity to receive spiritual advice and instruction from our confessor.* The role of the priest in confession is not merely to impart absolution. He has other duties to perform—those of teacher, judge, doctor of souls. It is advisable to have a regular confessor who knows our spiritual condition, just as it is wise to have a regular doctor who knows our physical condition. Never fear to bring your spiritual problems to the priest either in the confessional or out of it. He is only too willing to give you the advice and instruction that you need to lead a good and holy life.

## Acts Required For Worthy Reception of Penance and Reconciliation

By this time certainly everyone knows by heart that to receive the sacrament of Penance and Reconciliation worthily we must do five things:

1.  We must examine our conscience.

2.  We must have sorrow for our sins.

3.  We must make a firm resolution never more to offend God.

4.  We must confess our sins to the priest.

5.  We must accept the penance which the priest gives us.

**Examination of Conscience**

*An examination of conscience is a sincere effort to call to mind all the sins we have committed since our last worthy confession.* In the examination of conscience we throw a spotlight, as it were, on our spiritual condition to determine what sins we have committed and the number of times we have committed them. All mortal sins committed since our last worthy confession must be recalled and confessed.

There is something which should precede the examination of conscience. *Before our examination of conscience we should ask God's help to know our sins and to confess them with sincere sorrow.* Before every important act in our life, we should invoke God's guidance and help. In our preparation for the worthy reception of the sacrament of Penance and Reconciliation we should ask God to refresh our memory and help us to be sorry for the sins we are about to confess.

> "The reception of this sacrament ought to be prepared for by an *examination of conscience* made in the light of the Word of God. The passages best suited to this can be found in the Ten Commandments, the moral catechesis of the Gospels and the apostolic Letters, such as the Sermon on the Mount and the apostolic teachings."
>
> —*Catechism of the Catholic Church,* 1454

*We can make a good examination of conscience by calling to mind the commandments of God and the precepts of the Church, and the particular duties of our state of life, and by asking ourselves how we may have sinned with regard to them.* In most prayer books you will find a table of sins, or examination of conscience which follows the plan mentioned above. If one goes to confession frequently, it is not necessary to follow this plan every time. It is important that we should examine our conscience carefully, and, having remembered our sins, be truly sorry for having offended so good a God. Do not, however, make the mistake of considering as sins things which are really not sins.

By the particular duties of our state of life we mean that we have duties binding us which are not binding on others. For example, the duties of religious differ from those of lay persons; the duties of children from those of adults; the duties of doctors from those of newspaper reporters. Could you name some differences?

In your present state of life you have an obligation to obey your parents. You must examine your conscience as to how you fulfill this obligation. Your spiritual and physical well-being is the responsibility of your parents. They must examine their conscience on the manner in which they discharge this trust or responsibility.

## Summary

The sacrament of Penance and Reconciliation is the sacrament by which sins committed after Baptism are forgiven through the absolution of the priest. The priest has the power to forgive sins from Jesus Christ. Our Lord said to the Apostles and to their successors in the priesthood: "Receive the Holy Spirit; whose sins you shall forgive, they are forgiven them; and whose sins you shall retain, they are retained." The effects of the sacrament of Penance and Reconciliation, worthily received, are: (1) sanctifying grace; (2) the forgiveness of sins; (3) the remission of the eternal punishment, if necessary, and also, of part at least, of the temporal punishment due to our sins; (4) the help to avoid sin in future; (5) the restoration of the merits of our good works if they have been lost by mortal sin.

To receive the sacrament of Penance and Reconciliation worthily, we must: (1) examine our conscience; (2) be sorry for our sins; (3) have the firm purpose of not sinning again; (4) confess our sins to the priest; (5) be willing to perform the penance the priest gives us.

**TERMS TO KNOW**

- achieved
- frailty
- ratified
- routine
- conferred
- incite
- remission
- sanctions
- decreed
- laden
- remitting
- discharge
- omnipotence
- restoration

**FOR ME TO REVIEW**

*Catechism Lesson*

**721. Q. What is the sacrament of Penance and Reconciliation?**

   A. Penance and Reconciliation is a sacrament in which the sins committed after Baptism are forgiven.

**722. Q. Has the word penance any other meaning?**

   A. The word penance has other meanings. It means also those punishments we inflict upon ourselves as a means of atoning for our past sins; it means likewise that disposition of the heart in which we detest and bewail our sins because they were offensive to God.

**723. Q. How does the institution of the sacrament of Penance and Reconciliation show the goodness of our Lord?**

   A. The institution of the sacrament of Penance and Reconciliation shows the goodness of our Lord, because having once saved us through Baptism, He might have left us to perish if we again committed sin.

**726. Q. What is absolution?**

   A. Absolution is the form of prayer or words the priest pronounces over us with uplifted hand when he forgives the sins we have confessed. It is given while we are saying the Act of Contrition after receiving our penance.

**733. Q. How do you know that the priest has the power of absolving from the sins committed after Baptism?**

   A. I know that the priest has the power of absolving from the sins committed after Baptism, because Jesus Christ granted that power to the priests of His Church when He said: "Receive ye the Holy Spirit. Whose sins you shall forgive, they are forgiven them; whose sins you shall retain, they are retained."

**741.** Q. **What must we do to receive the sacrament of Penance and Reconciliation worthily?**

A. To receive the sacrament of Penance and Reconciliation worthily we must do five things:

1. We must examine our conscience.

2. We must have sorrow for our sins.

3. We must make a firm resolution never more to offend God.

4. We must confess our sins to the priest.

5. We must accept the penance which the priest gives us.

**749.** Q. **What is the examination of conscience?**

A. The examination of conscience is an earnest effort to recall to mind all the sins we have committed since our last worthy confession.

**751.** Q. **How can we make a good examination of conscience?**

A. We can make a good examination of conscience by calling to memory the commandments of God, the precepts of the Church, the seven capital sins, and the particular duties of our state in life, to find out the sins we have committed.

**752.** Q. **What should we do before beginning the examination of conscience?**

A. Before beginning the examination of conscience we should pray to God to give us light to know our sins and grace to detest them.

*Questions and Exercises*

## Part 1: Short Answer

1. What punishment is entirely taken away by the sacrament of Penance and Reconciliation, worthily received?

2. What punishment is not always taken away by the sacrament of Penance and Reconciliation?

3. What kind of punishment do we satisfy for either in this life or in purgatory?

4. From whom does the priest have the power to forgive sins?

5. Who is the minister of the sacrament of Penance and Reconciliation?

## Part 2: Completion

1. We should ask God's help to_____(a)_____, our sins and to_____(b)_____them with sincere sorrow.

2. The sacrament of Penance and Reconciliation, worthily received, restores the_____of our good works when they are lost by mortal sin.

3. An_____is a sincere effort to call to mind all the sins we have committed since our last worthy confession.

4. The sacrament of Penance and Reconciliation, worthily received, gives_____grace.

5. Jesus said to the Apostles and their successors in the priesthood: "Receive the Holy Spirit; whose sins you shall _____(a)_____they are_____(b)_____them; whose sins you shall_____(c)_____they are_____(d)_____."

**FOR ME TO DO**

2.  Discuss the topic: The sacrament of Penance and Reconciliation as the Medicine of the Soul.

3.  Find New Testament passages which tell of Christ's forgiveness of sins.

4.  Compose a prayer to thank Christ for instituting the sacrament of Penance and Reconciliation.

5.  Write from memory the words which our Lord spoke Easter Sunday evening when He conferred on the Apostles the power to forgive sins.

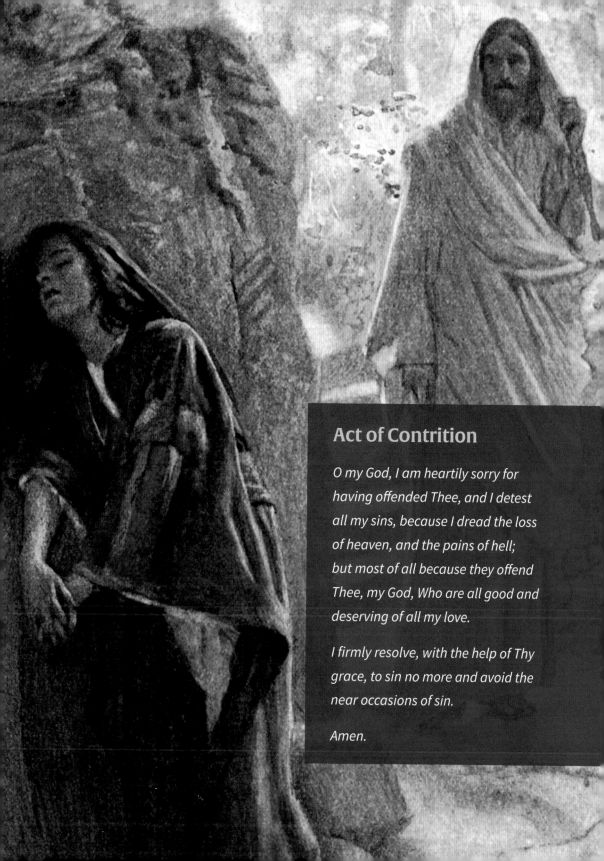

## Act of Contrition

*O my God, I am heartily sorry for having offended Thee, and I detest all my sins, because I dread the loss of heaven, and the pains of hell; but most of all because they offend Thee, my God, Who are all good and deserving of all my love.*

*I firmly resolve, with the help of Thy grace, to sin no more and avoid the near occasions of sin.*

*Amen.*

LESSON 16

# Contrition and Firm Purpose of Amendment

No one who has turned away from God by sin can hope to be pardoned unless he turns back to his heavenly Father by contrition. Our catechism, we can recall, tells us that *contrition is sincere sorrow for having offended God, and hatred for the sins we have committed with a firm purpose of sinning no more*. The word contrition is derived from the Latin and means the "breaking to pieces of anything solid or hard." Sin hardens the heart; sorrow softens it. Sorrow for sin is so necessary that *God will not forgive us any sin, whether mortal or venial, unless we have true contrition for it.*

## Qualities of True Contrition

Can you mention any persons in the Bible who were sorry for their sins? No doubt you recall the story of the publican who accused himself in the Temple of his sins and of whom Christ said, "I say to you, this man went down to his house justified." Who was the person who felt such deep sorrow that his tears made deep furrows in his cheeks? Surely he had true contrition.

Do you know the four things required to make our sorrow true contrition? *Sorrow for sin is true contrition when it is interior, supernatural, supreme, and universal*. In order to have this sorrow you will need to know what is meant by each of these qualities.

### Sorrow Should Be Interior

*Our sorrow is interior when it comes from the heart, and not merely from our lips*. This sorrow need not bring tears as it did to St. Peter. God does not require that of us. However, it should be an act of the will by which one detests one's own sins and resolves to avoid them in the future. This sorrow must be joined with a firm purpose of amendment. This is not a feeble, half-hearted wish to avoid sin, but a strong, wholehearted determination to shun the persons, places, or things that in the past have been occasions of sin for us. We must also intend to use all the means necessary to lead a new life. Some of these are to pray more fervently, to examine our conscience daily, to think often of the four Last Things, to go more frequently to confession and Holy Communion, and to use all the means of grace.

**Sorrow Should Be Supernatural**

The second quality of our sorrow is that it must be supernatural. *Our sorrow is supernatural when, with the help of God's grace, it arises from motives which spring from faith and not merely from natural motives.* This means that our sorrow must come not from just a natural source such as that of a man who is sorry because he is caught in his wrongdoing. Such sorrow is purely natural. If our sorrow arises from the fear of hell, or loss of heaven, or for the highest motive, the love of God, then our sorrow is truly supernatural. Most of us need the fear of hell to keep us from sin. Many who are in heaven today would never have reached there but for fear of hell. While the fear of hell is sufficient motive for supernatural sorrow, the loss of heaven is a higher motive for sorrow. "Eye hath not seen, ear hath not heard, what God has prepared there for those who love Him." We all want to be happy but unless we seek our happiness in God we will never attain it. St. Augustine,

*"They that are whole, need not the physician: but they that are sick. I came not to call the just, but sinners to penance."*

*—Luke 5:31–32*

after having searched in vain for happiness in created objects, said, "For thyself thou hast made us, O Lord, and our hearts are restless till they rest in thee." Earthly happiness passes quickly; the happiness of heaven alone satisfies the soul and is eternal.

The last and highest motive for sorrow is the love of God. Sin offends God who is infinitely good. Love of God brings perfect sorrow. Such sorrow obtains pardon of our sin even before we confess it to the priest. Of course, we know that we are still obliged to tell the sin in confession even though its guilt has been erased. Thinking of the price our divine Lord paid for sin should make us realize how much He loves us, and how much we should love Him in return.

## Sorrow Should Be Supreme

In addition to being interior and supernatural, our sorrow should be supreme. *Our sorrow is supreme when we hate sin above every other evil, and are willing to endure any suffering rather than offend God in the future by sin.* We can readily see by now that sin is the greatest of all evils. Mortal sin takes from us our right to heaven. If we lose heaven, we have lost everything.

While we should consider the evil caused by sin more serious than any other evil, it does not mean that our emotions or feelings are always more deeply affected. For instance, a mother who has lost her child may shed bitter tears at the grave whereas she may never shed tears for her sins. Still her sorrow for sin may be greater. True contrition is not a matter of feeling or emotion, but a matter of conscience and reason—a matter of our wills.

## Sorrow Should Be Universal

Lastly our sorrow should be universal. *Our sorrow is universal when we are sorry for every mortal sin which we may have had the misfortune to commit.* We cannot be sorry for some of our mortal sins while at the same time we are not sorry for others. Every mortal sin takes away supernatural life, and we must be sorry for all our mortal sins before that life is restored. It is like the man who drank two fatal poisons. The doctor was able to draw off the one but the second poison that still remained caused his death. In like manner, a man who has two mortal sins on his soul and is sorry for only one is dead spiritually because he must be sorry for both in order to have them forgiven. It is impious to hope for half a pardon. If all the locks on a prison are unfastened except one, the prison cannot be opened. A mortal sin may be compared to a lock of the soul. We must be sorry for all if we want to open the door to sanctifying grace.

We must also realize that God will not forgive even a venial sin unless we have true contrition for it. Therefore, *we should try to have sorrow for all our venial sins when receiving the sacrament*

Contrition is sincere sorrow for having offended God, and hatred for the sins we have committed with a firm purpose of sinning no more.

"Among the penitent's acts contrition occupies first place. Contrition is 'sorrow of the soul and detestation for the sin committed, together with the resolution not to sin again.'

"When it arises from a love by which God is loved above all else, contrition is called 'perfect' (contrition of charity). Such contrition remits venial sins; it also obtains forgiveness of mortal sins if it includes the firm resolution to have recourse to sacramental confession as soon as possible.

"The contrition called 'imperfect' (or 'attrition') is also a gift of God, a prompting of the Holy Spirit. It is born of the consideration of sin's ugliness or the fear of eternal damnation and the other penalties threatening the sinner (contrition of fear). Such a stirring of conscience can initiate an interior process which, under the prompting of grace, will be brought to completion by sacramental absolution. By itself however, imperfect contrition cannot obtain the forgiveness of grave sins, but it disposes one to obtain forgiveness in the sacrament of Penance."

—*Catechism of the Catholic Church, 1451-53*

of Penance and Reconciliation, and, when we have only venial sins to confess, we must have sorrow for at least one of them or for some sin of our past life which we confess. In such a case we should conclude our confession by saying, "I accuse myself of all the sins of my past life, and especially lies, or sins of pride, etc.," mentioning some particular sin of the past which we had previously confessed.

How do you consider mortal sin? As a great evil?

When St. Jane Frances de Chantal was nursing a leper, a friend warned her that she might catch that hideous disease. The saint replied, "I fear no leprosy but the leprosy of sin." Do we feel that way about mortal sin? It is the only thing that is really evil in itself because it robs us of the presence of God and lets the devil take His place. As our catechism tells us, *We should have contrition for mortal sin because it is the greatest of all evils, gravely offends God, keeps us out of heaven, and condemns us forever to hell.* The greatest loss is the loss of God, our highest Good. Imagine how you will feel when your mother dies. Multiply by a million your lonesomeness and your sadness and you will still have no idea what it means to lose God forever. Suppose an atom bomb exploded where you live. Describe the destruction. Is one mortal sin worse? Yes!

Mortal sin requires contrition; but we must be sorry for venial sin, too. That also offends God and deserves His just punishment. *We should have contrition for venial sin because it is displeasing*

*to God, merits temporal punishment, and may lead to mortal sin.*
Venial sin does not separate us entirely from God. Grace can still
operate, but the sinner shows ingratitude to God who has done
so much for him.

## Kinds of Contrition

How many kinds of contrition are there? *There are two kinds
of contrition: perfect contrition and imperfect contrition.*
We shall first consider perfect contrition, which is motivated
by the love of God.

### Perfect Contrition

How do you know when your contrition is perfect? For the purpose of review we can say *our contrition is perfect when we are
sorry for our sins because sin offends God, whom we love above all
things for His own sake.* A child can have an unselfish love for his
mother and grieve over a fault just because it offends her who is
so good and loving. So, too, a penitent who has perfect contrition
loves God because He is all-good, all-holy, and infinitely lovable.
Do you know the story of King David and his sorrow? What person mentioned in the account of Christ's Passion showed perfect
contrition for his sins? Can you prove that he had perfect contrition? What about non-Catholics? May they also be sorry for their
sins because of their love for God? It may be easy to think of sin
solely in terms of the punishments and rewards we will receive
after death. But heaven and hell can become a reality for us even
on earth. When we sin mortally, we become separated from God.
This is the state of a soul in hell: eternal separation from God.

While venial sin is a lesser offense against God, this does not
mean that our sorrow for it should be any less sincere. We should
have contrition for venial sin because it is displeasing to God and
damages our relationship with Him. Even venial sins greatly dis-
figure our souls. These sins blind us to the Truth who is Christ and
prevent us from experiencing the joy of a good and holy life on

earth and in heaven. Friendship with others and God becomes very difficult. Sin separates us from ourselves, from other people, and from God. To be sorrowful for our sins because we so value our friendship with God is the essence of perfect contrition.

## Imperfect Contrition

The second kind of contrition is called imperfect contrition. If someone asked you to explain what you mean by imperfect contrition, what would you say? *Our contrition is imperfect when we are sorry for our sins because they are hateful in themselves or because we fear God's punishment.*

We already know that *to receive the sacrament of Penance and Reconciliation worthily, imperfect contrition is sufficient.* Imperfect contrition of itself never takes away mortal sin, but it is sufficient for forgiveness in the sacrament of Penance and Reconciliation. Nevertheless, *we should always try to have perfect contrition in the sacrament of Penance and Reconciliation because perfect contrition is more pleasing to God and because with His help we can always have it.*

When we have perfect contrition we show that we are thinking of God and not of ourselves, in other words, our sorrow is unselfish. Naturally God values that kind of sorrow more, so if we ask Him for it and make an effort to obtain it, He will give it to us. St. Thomas Aquinas tells us that the least degree of perfect contrition suffices instantly to cancel the guilt of sin. What does this mean?

Perhaps it may be our misfortune to be in mortal sin and unable to go to confession. What must we do then? A *person in mortal sin can regain the state of grace before receiving the sacrament of Penance and Reconciliation by making an act of perfect*

### TERMS TO KNOW

- emotionally
- impious
- specific
- justified
- exclusion
- attrition
- intensity
- derives
- suffices
- motivated

*contrition with the sincere purpose of going to confession*.

Many years ago the father of a family was found dying. Someone was sent immediately to call the priest. The youngest son, seeing that death was very near, held a crucifix before his father's eyes and recited aloud an act of perfect contrition. Perfect sorrow filled the man as he thought of the suffering of Christ. The priest arrived before he died and heard his confession. But even if the priest had been late the perfect contrition would have saved him. What lesson does this teach us about the value of perfect contrition? It teaches us that *if we have the misfortune to commit a mortal sin, we should ask God's pardon and grace at once, make an act of perfect contrition, and go to confession as soon as we can.*

Prudent Catholics make an act of perfect sorrow every night before going to bed so that they will be prepared to meet their Judge in case of sudden death. Does that mean that they may receive Holy Communion? Why may we not receive Holy Communion? Our catechism tells us that *we may not receive Holy Communion after committing a mortal sin if we merely make an act of perfect contrition; one who has sinned grievously must go to confession before receiving Holy Communion.* But venial sins do not deprive us of sanctifying grace; worthy reception of Holy Communion, in fact, blots out any venial sins we may have committed.

## Firm Purpose of Amendment

In explaining the qualities of contrition, we mentioned a firm purpose of amendment. Do you understand what that means? *The firm purpose of sinning no more is the sincere resolve not only to avoid sin but to avoid as far as possible the near occasions of sin.* This purpose of amendment is an essential part of true contrition. As long as the will remains attached to sin, there is no sorrow and the sin cannot be forgiven.

Bob attended an indecent movie and planned to attend a similar one next week. Did he have a firm purpose of sinning no more? What should have been his resolution? We are striving to reach heaven. Therefore, it is very important that we make and keep our resolutions to avoid sin.

How about the near occasions of sin? Must we avoid them also? Yes. Occasions of sin include persons, places, or things that can easily lead us into sin. You would call a person foolish who continually swept away the cobwebs but would never kill the spiders. Or another who would cut the weeds in his garden but never dig up their roots. A person is more foolish who makes an act of contrition but does not keep away from the occasions of sin.

Our resolution should not only be a general one such as, "I am going to keep away from all sin," but it should also be very specific. It should include the one fault we are most likely to commit, such as being disobedient to our parents, or speaking unkindly of our neighbor, or immodest talk.

Many times, thanks to the grace of God, a person has no mortal sins to confess. *If a person has only venial sins to confess, he must have the purpose of avoiding at least one of them*.

Tom thought he had the ability to become a great athlete. In preparing for the interscholastic meet, he practiced for five different events. On the day of the races he got so tired that any sixth grader could have beaten him. That taught him a lesson. For the next contest he practiced for only one type of race. His intensity of effort won him the prize for his school.

## Summary

Contrition is sincere sorrow for having offended God, and hatred for the sins we have committed, with a firm purpose of sinning no more. God will not forgive us any sin, whether mortal or venial, unless we have true contrition for it. This means: (1) our sorrow must come from the heart, and not merely from our lips; (2) with the help of God's grace we must be sorry because we have offended God; (3) we must hate sin above every other evil and be willing to endure anything rather than offend God by sin in the future; (4) we must be sorry for every mortal sin which we may have had the misfortune to commit.

There are two kinds of contrition; perfect contrition and imperfect contrition. Our contrition is perfect when we are sorry for our sins because sin offends God, whom we love above all things for His own sake. Our contrition is imperfect when, with God's grace, we are sorry for offending Him because our sins are so hateful in themselves or because we fear God's punishment.

To receive the sacrament of Penance and Reconciliation worthily, imperfect contrition is sufficient. But since perfect contrition is more pleasing to God, and because with His help we can always have it, we should always try to have perfect contrition.

A firm purpose of sinning no more is the sincere resolve not to sin, and to avoid as far as possible the near occasions of sin. If a person has only venial sins to confess, he must have the purpose of avoiding at least one of them.

 **FOR ME TO REVIEW**

*Catechism Lesson*

753. Q. **What is contrition, or sorrow for sin?**
     A. Contrition, or sorrow for sin, is a hatred of sin and a true grief of the soul for having offended God, with a firm purpose of sinning no more.

755. Q. **What kind of sorrow should we have for our sins?**
     A. The sorrow we should have for our sins should be interior, supernatural, supreme, and universal.

756. Q. **What do you mean by saying that our sorrow should be interior?**
     A. When I say that our sorrow should be interior, I mean that it should come from the heart, and not merely from the lips.

757. Q. What do you mean by saying that our sorrow should
be supernatural?

A. When I say that our sorrow should be supernatural, I
mean that it should be prompted by the grace of God,
and excited by motives which spring from faith, and
not by merely natural motives.

759. Q. What do you mean by saying that our sorrow should
be universal?

A. When I say that our sorrow should be universal, I mean
that we should be sorry for all our mortal sins without
exception.

761. Q. What do you mean when you say that our sorrow
should be supreme?

A. When I say that our sorrow should be supreme, I mean
that we should grieve more for having offended God
than for any other evil that can befall us.

764. Q. How many kinds of contrition are there?

A. There are two kinds of contrition: perfect contrition
and imperfect contrition.

765. Q. What is perfect contrition?

A. Perfect contrition is that which fills us with sorrow and
hatred for sin, because it offends God, who is infinitely
good in Himself and worthy of all love.

767. Q. What is imperfect contrition?

A. Imperfect contrition is that by which we hate what
offends God because by it we lose heaven and deserve
hell; or because sin is so hateful in itself.

770. Q. What do you mean by a firm purpose of sinning
no more?

A. By a firm purpose of sinning no more I mean a fixed
resolve not only to avoid all mortal sin, but also its near
occasions.

771. Q. What do you mean by the near occasions of sin?
   A. By the near occasions of sin I mean all the persons, places and things that may easily lead us into sin.

772. Q. Why are we bound to avoid occasions of sin?
   A. We are bound to avoid occasions of sin because our Lord has said: "He who loves the danger will perish in it"; and as we are bound to avoid the loss of our souls, so we are bound to avoid the danger of their loss. The occasion is the cause of sin, and you cannot take away the evil without removing its cause.

*Questions and Exercises*

## Part 1: Completion

1. "When love of God comes, sin leaves." This is the effect of _____ contrition.

2. Confession and a firm purpose of amendment must be added to imperfect contrition before we can obtain forgiveness of_____.

3. Mary Magdalen's sorrow was_____because it was prompted by love of God.

4. _____is the most important part of the sacrament of Penance and Reconciliation.

5. Being sorry for sin because it means the loss of heaven is _____sorrow.

6. The motives for both perfect and imperfect contrition are found in the_____.

7. If I were to be seriously hurt in an accident, I should immediately_____.

8. In preparing for confession more time should be given to _____than other points.

9. If your sorrow includes all your sins without exception, your sorrow is_____.

10. If a person refuses to give up_____he is not truly sorry for his sins.

## Part 2: True or False

1. Because perfect contrition gains for us immediate forgiveness of sins, we do not need to confess those sins unless we wish to.

2. Any kind of sorrow is sufficient for the sacrament of Penance and Reconciliation.

3. Mary Magdalen's sorrow was interior.

4. A girl who was sorry she told a lie because her friends were so surprised had supernatural sorrow.

5. The fear of hell is a good, though imperfect, motive for contrition.

6. The fear of hell is insufficient for perfect contrition.

7. After committing a mortal sin, a person should not receive Holy Communion if he has merely made an act of perfect contrition.

8. A person can refuse to give up an occasion of sin and still have true sorrow for his sins.

9. It is possible to have perfect sorrow for sin because God will give this grace to us if we ask for it and make an effort to obtain it.

10. The Good Thief's sorrow was perfect because it was motivated by the love of God.

## After Confession

*O Lord! I abandon my past to Thy mercy, my present to Thy Love, and my future to Thy Providence!*

*Amen.*

LESSON 17

# Confession and Penance

Let us review and expand our knowledge of confession. Every-one knows that *confession is the telling of our sins to a priest for the purpose of obtaining forgiveness*. What a great grace this sacrament is! Even while it is possible for God to forgive our sins without the sacrament of Penance and Reconciliation (through perfect contrition), the sacrament puts us back in union with the Church, the Body of Christ. Additionally, the sacrament helps remove some of the punishment due to sin and provides graces to the penitent in his battle against temptation. Truly the sacra-ment of Penance and Reconciliation is no burden to the soul that loves God; it is a gift.

In order to exercise the power of forgiving or retaining, the priest must know the sins the penitent has committed and what his dispositions are at the time. As the quotation from St. John indicates (*"Whose sins you shall forgive, they are forgiven them; and whose sins you shall retain, they are retained"*), the priest

> *"Sorrow for sin is indeed necessary, but it should not be an endless preoccupation. You must dwell also on the glad remembrance of God's loving-kindness; otherwise, sadness will harden the heart and lead it more deeply into despair."*
>
> —*St. Bernard*

must know what evil the penitent has done and his intentions about his future conduct. *These words of Christ oblige us to confess our sins because the priest cannot know whether he should forgive or retain our sins unless we tell them to him.*

A judge does not condemn or acquit a person before hearing his case. A doctor does not pass verdict on a person's condition unless he has examined him and considered well all the symptoms of the disease. You, too, are like a sick person when you go to confession. You are spiritually sick, and in order to apply the proper remedy the priest must know what ails you.

Must you confess all the sins you have committed? *It is necessary to confess every mortal sin which has not yet been confessed and forgiven; it is not necessary to confess our venial sins, but it is better to do so.* Why must mortal sin be confessed? Why should we also confess our venial sins? If you want to remain close to Christ, you should keep yourself spiritually spotless and pure.

Confessing venial sins helps remove the temporal punishment due to them and makes one more pleasing in God's sight. A penitent once came to the Curé of Ars inquiring how one should go to God. The Curé replied, "Go straight." In other words, don't put off telling any of your sins and you will stay on God's path.

## Qualities of Confession

*The chief qualities of a good confession are three: it must be humble, sincere, and entire.* Let us examine each.

### Humble

*Our confession is humble when we accuse ourselves of our sins with a conviction of guilt for having offended God.* You know the story of the Prodigal Son. He left his father's house and lived riotously for a time. After a while he came to his senses, and, realizing the wrong he had done, in all humility returned to his father saying, "I am no longer worthy to be called thy son" (Lk. 15:19).

Pause for a moment and consider how much like the Prodigal Son you are. You, too, may have left your Father's house through sin. If so, He is anxiously awaiting your return to Him.

When we recall the greatness and goodness of God and the insignificant creatures we are, the realization that we have dared to offend God should help us to be truly humble. Why make an effort to hide our sins so as to appear better than we really are? *God sees me.* Three little words; yet how powerfully they remind us of what we are in the sight of God.

### Sincere

*Our confession is sincere when we tell our sins honestly and frankly.* Since God knows all things, He knows the sins we have committed. What folly to conceal a sin or to make a mortal sin sound like a venial sin. If we do this, we increase our guilt. We have committed a sacrilege in making a bad confession. Should you ever be tempted to conceal a mortal sin, think of what hap-

The Prodigal
Son

pened to Ananias and Sapphira who tried to deceive Peter. Do
you know the story?

### Entire

*Our confession is entire when we confess at least all our mortal
sins, telling their kind, the number of times we have committed
each sin, and any circumstances changing their nature.* When
there is question of a mortal sin, we must be careful to tell
just what particular kind of sin was committed. It would not

be enough to confess "I used improper words." Why not? The improper words used might have been angry, blasphemous, uncharitable, impure, or profane words which differ as far as kind is concerned. If we cannot remember the exact number of times, we should tell about how many times a day, a week, or a month we have committed each sin.

It is also important to tell the circumstances of a sin if they change its nature or seriousness. One man may strike a priest, or his neighbor. There is a big difference between the two cases. Moreover, we know stealing is a sin against the seventh commandment. Whether a person steals a great amount or a small amount, whether from a rich man or a poor man, will affect the gravity of the sin. Do you now see why it is necessary to tell the circumstances connected with the sin? To deliberately conceal a circumstance which greatly affects the gravity of a sin (and would make a mortal sin sound like a venial sin) is the same as concealing a mortal sin in confession.

## Forgotten Mortal Sin

*If without our fault we forget to confess a mortal sin, we may receive Holy Communion, because we have made a good confession and the sin is forgiven; but we must tell the sin in confession if it again comes to our mind.* When a person recalls a mortal sin which he forgot, he can wait until his next regular confession to tell it. In the meantime, he does not have to remain away from Holy Communion.

*If we knowingly conceal a mortal sin in confession, the sins we confess are not forgiven; moreover, we commit a mortal sin of sacrilege.* You remember what a sacrilege is. To omit a mortal sin in confession makes the next confession more difficult. It is better not to go to confession than to make a bad confession. Why?

*A person who has knowingly concealed a mortal sin in confession must confess that he has made a bad confession, tell the sin he has concealed, mention the sacraments he has received since that time, and confess all the other mortal sins he has committed since his last good confession.* One who is ashamed to confess a mortal sin should remember that he cannot obtain pardon for his sins unless he confesses them. When a little child breaks a vase he will run to his mother and tell her. Why? Because he loves her and wants her to know he is sorry for what he did.

God expects us to act the same way with Him. Maybe we did offend Him by mortal sin, but being a forgiving Father, He awaits

*"Just as an animal becomes a stronger beast of burden and more beautiful to behold the more often and better it is fed, so too confession—the more often it is used and the more carefully it is made as to both lesser and greater sins—conveys the soul increasingly forward and is so pleasing to God that it leads the soul to God's very heart."*

—*St. Bridget*

our humble confession. A good practice when going to confession is to tell any grievous sins first.

*A sense of shame and fear of telling our sins to the priest should never lead us to conceal a mortal sin in confession because this is a grave sacrilege, and also because the priest, who represents Christ Himself, is bound by the seal of the sacrament of Penance and Reconciliation never to reveal anything that has been confessed to him.* When we studied the eighth commandment, we saw how St. John Nepomucene suffered death rather than reveal what the queen had told him in the confessional. Another martyr who died in Mexico in 1927 was Don Matteo Correa. He was brought, with a number of Catholics, to General Ortiz. The next morning the general told the priest to hear their confessions. The old priest did. When he was finished the general mockingly cried: "And now you will tell me what these people told you!" "Never," replied the priest. "Then I will have you shot together with them." And the priest accepted death rather than break the seal of confession. Every priest is bound in conscience never to reveal any sin a person has confessed to him. Neither must he allow his conduct toward a penitent outside the confessional to be influenced in any way by what he has heard in confession.

Someone once said that a priest has the longest and strongest arm in the world. In what sense is this true? Other persons may be able to write, swing a bat, build a magnificent monument, draw a superb picture, but it is only the priest with his arm raised in absolution who can open the gates of heaven for us. Remember this if you should run into a priest who has had a long session in the confessional.

## Penance

Before forgiving our sins the priest gives us a penance to perform. Why? *The priest gives us a penance after confession that we may make some atonement to God for our sins, receive help to avoid them in the future, and make some satisfaction for the temporal punishment due to them*. Ordinarily this penance is light and we should take care of it immediately after confession. We must remember that even though this penance is easy to fulfill it has special value and power as part of the sacrament because of the merits of Christ.

Can you recall how sometimes after having offended your mother you tried to make up for your misdeed by doing some

A sense of shame and fear of telling our sins to the priest should never lead us to conceal a mortal sin in confession.

helpful chore? So, too, by performing the penance which we receive in confession we are in some small way making up to God for our sin. There is no question of making things even, but at least there is the effort to make some atonement. Christ's merits, not our efforts alone, give to our penances their full value.

In the early days of the Church the penances given in confession were much more severe and lasted longer than the penances we receive today. Since the Church is now far more lenient in the matter of imposing penances, we should perform voluntary deeds of self-denial. Extraordinary penances may be good. But ordinary acts of self-denial are an easy and a valuable means of satisfying for the punishment due to our sins.

**Temporal and Eternal Punishment**

The penance which the priest gives us satisfies in some measure for the temporal punishment due to our sins. That brings us to the kinds of punishment due to sin. Our catechism tells us: *Two kinds of punishment are due to sin: the eternal punishment of hell, due to unforgiven mortal sins, and temporal punishment, lasting only for a time, due to venial sins and also to mortal sins after they have been forgiven.*

Let us consider the eternal punishment due to unforgiven mortal sin. We know that mortal sin deprives us of supernatural life and makes us enemies of God. Mortal sin is a choice against union with God. Dying in a state of mortal sin means choosing separation from God forever. This is the state of a soul in hell—eternal separation from God. Hell is the continuation of the soul's choices on earth.

Temporal punishment refers to that punishment which lasts only for a certain length of time either here or hereafter. Although our sins are forgiven by a good confession, yet a debt of temporal punishment for forgiven sins, both mortal and venial, is naturally expected. Just as repairs must be made to a broken window even after we've been forgiven for breaking it, so too our sins have lasting damage that must be repaired, even after we are forgiven them. Some of this temporal punishment, or even all of it, may be taken away in the very reception of the sacrament, depending on how sorry we are. Usually, however, some remains to be remitted later. Let us remember, then, *that the sacrament of Penance and Reconciliation, worthily received, always takes away all eternal punishment; but it does not always take away all temporal punishment.* It follows that *we pay the debt of our temporal punishment either in this life or in purgatory.* Temporal punishment is the only debt that remains after a good confession.

In the time of our Lord people looked upon physical handicaps, such as blindness, lameness, and deafness as punishments either for their own sins or the sins of their parents. They considered the bearing of such afflictions as a payment of the debt of temporal punishment in this life. We, too, look upon the patient enduring of sufferings as a valuable means of satisfying in some measure for the temporal punishment due to our sins. What is not paid here must be paid hereafter.

**Why Temporal Punishment?**

Perhaps you have wondered why God exacts temporal punishment for sins already forgiven. *God requires temporal punishment for sin to satisfy His justice, to teach us the great evil of sin, and to warn us not to sin again.*

Do you recall how, in the course of the wanderings of the Israelites, God commanded Moses to strike a rock with his staff that water might come forth? Remember how Moses doubted for an instant? Even though God forgave him, what punishment did He impose upon him for the momentary doubt? Let us go back to the story of our first parents. God forgave Adam and Eve for their act of disobedience, but their punishment was very great. Can wars and all the sufferings they bring be considered the results of sin? Sins of greed and injustice?

A glance at the crucifix will help us realize better than anything else the great evil of sin and the reason why God requires temporal punishment for it. Can you think of any examples of punishment following the committing of sin? How does the punishment serve as a warning not to sin again?

The penance given us in confession is not the only means of satisfying for temporal punishment due to sins. *Besides the penance imposed after confession, the chief means of satisfying the debt of our temporal punishment are: prayer, attending Mass, fasting, almsgiving, the works of mercy, the patient endurance of sufferings, and indulgences.* Do you make use of any of these means?

### ✓ FOR ME TO REVIEW

*Catechism Lesson*

**776. Q. What is confession?**
   A. Confession is the telling of our sins to a priest, for the purpose of obtaining forgiveness.

**780. Q. What sins are we bound to confess?**
   A. We are bound to confess all our mortal sins, but it is well also to confess our venial sins.

**781. Q. Why is it well to confess also the venial sins we remember?**
   A. It is well to confess also the venial sins we remember 1) because it shows our hatred of all sin, and 2) because it is sometimes difficult to determine just when a sin is venial and when mortal.

**785. Q. Which are the chief qualities of a good confession?**
   A. The chief qualities of a good confession are three: it must be humble, sincere, and entire.

786. Q. When is our confession humble?

A. Our confession is humble when we accuse ourselves of our sins, with a deep sense of shame and sorrow for having offended God.

787. Q. When is our confession sincere?

A. Our confession is sincere when we tell our sins honestly and truthfully, neither exaggerating nor excusing them.

789. Q. When is our confession entire?

A. Our confession is entire when we tell the number and kinds of our sins and the circumstances which change their nature.

793. Q. Is our confession worthy if, without our fault, we forget to confess a mortal sin?

A. If without our fault we forget to confess a mortal sin, our confession is worthy, and the sin is forgiven; but it must be told in confession if it again comes to our mind.

795. Q. Is it a grievous offense willfully to conceal a mortal sin in confession?

A. It is a grievous offense willfully to conceal a mortal sin in confession, because we thereby tell a lie to the Holy Spirit, and make our confession worthless.

797. Q. Why is it foolish to conceal sins in confession?

A. It is foolish to conceal sins in confession: 1) Because we thereby make our spiritual condition worse; 2) We must tell the sin sometime if we ever hope to be saved; 3) It will be made known on the Day of Judgment, before the world, whether we conceal it now or confess it.

LESSON 18

# Making a Good Confession

We have learned that we must do penance for the sins that we have committed. We do not want, however, to add to our guilt by any carelessness in our preparation for confession. How do we prepare ourselves for a worthy confession?

## Before Confession

*Before entering the confessional, we should prepare ourselves for a good confession by taking sufficient time not only to examine our conscience but, especially, to excite in our hearts sincere sorrow for our sins and a firm purpose not to commit them again.*

To make a worthy confession we should:

Examine our conscience and incite in our heart true sorrow for sin and a firm purpose of amendment.

Confess our sins.

Answer the questions of the priest.

When the priest is giving absolution, say the act of contrition.

Thank God and say our penance.

We must guard against preparing for confession in a hasty manner, but in the confessional we should not waste the priest's time. Many people want to go to confession. The discovering of our sins is important; the telling of sins to the priest is important; but having the necessary sorrow for our sins is the most important of all. Have you ever heard the saying, "Without contrition, no remission"? True contrition and a firm purpose of amendment are required for the forgiveness of sins.

We are sometimes obliged to wait for our turn to enter the confessional. How should we spend this time of waiting? This time should not be spent in distraction or idleness but in prayer and devotion. Everyone should take his proper turn.

Jack dashed into the confessional ahead of a woman. She was in a hurry to get home to start supper. Jack wanted to go and play ball. What do you think of Jack?

## In Confession

*We should begin our confession in this manner: Entering the confessional, we kneel, and making the sign of the cross we say to the priest: "Bless me, Father, for I have sinned"; and then we tell how long it has been since our last confession.* When we confess we should speak clearly, distinctly, and loudly enough to be heard by the confessor but not by persons outside the confessional.

*After telling the time of our last confession, if we have committed any mortal sins since that time we must confess them, and also any that we have forgotten in previous confessions, telling the nature and number of each; we may also confess any venial sins we wish to mention.* Telling the time of our last confession helps the priest to know and to understand our spiritual condition. Do you think that a penitent who has not been to confession for a year or more would need different direction than one who confesses every two weeks?

It is not necessary to confess venial sins. Why? May we do so? There are many good people who never commit a mortal sin. They tell the priest whatever venial sins they have committed and how many times they have committed them. They are as sorry for their venial sins as others are for mortal sins.

We know that we must say exactly how many times we have sinned grievously. *If we cannot remember the exact number of our mortal sins, we should tell the number as nearly as possible, or say how often we have committed the sins in a day, a week, a month, or a year.* Telling the number of times is necessary; it gives the priest a definite idea of our condition and lets him know whether a certain sin is habitual or not.

Perhaps you recall that there must be matter for absolution. This can be supplied by recalling our venial sins. *When we have*

*committed no mortal sin since our last confession, we should con-
fess our venial sins in order that the priest may give us absolution.*
If we mention no sin since our last confession the priest cannot
give us absolution but only a blessing.

## After Telling Our Sins

After confessing our sins *we should end our confession by saying:
"I am sorry for these and all the sins of my past life."* It may be necessary for the confessor to question the penitent. The penitent
must answer the priest's questions plainly and truthfully. We are
instructed that *after confessing our sins, we should answer truthfully any question the priest asks, seek advice if we feel that we
need any, listen carefully to the spiritual instruction and counsel
of the priest, and accept the penance he gives us.* As we have previously mentioned this spiritual counsel is a valuable part of the
sacrament. If, at any time, you are in doubt whether something is
sinful or not, ask the priest in confession.

Finally, there comes the most important part of the sacrament of Penance and Reconciliation. It is sorrow for sins. You
have already learned that we express that sorrow by our act of
contrition. *When the priest is giving us absolution, we should say
from our heart the act of contrition in a tone to be heard by him.*

In the parable of the Ten Lepers Christ showed that He
expected thanks for this miracle of curing a bodily disease.
Should He expect even more gratitude for curing us of our spiritual illness in the sacrament of Penance and Reconciliation?

## After Confession

*After leaving the confessional we should return thanks to God for
the sacrament we have received, beg our Lord to supply for the
imperfections of our confession, and promptly and devoutly perform our penance.* We should thank God after confession for His
mercy in granting us pardon for all the offenses we have committed against Him. This gratitude should make it easier for us to

> *"If we confess our sins, he is faithful and just, to forgive us our sins, and to cleanse us from all iniquity."*
>
> —1 John 1:9

perform the penance we have been given. In a court of justice the guilty person receives a sentence which he must serve. In confession we are the guilty ones and we must satisfy for our offenses.

## Summary

We should take sufficient time to prepare ourselves to make a good confession. We should carefully examine our conscience, and especially we should arouse in our hearts sincere sorrow for our sins and a firm purpose never to commit them again.

We should begin our confession by making the sign of the cross and saying to the priest: "Bless me, Father, for I have sinned." We then should tell how long it has been since our last confession.

Next, if we have committed any mortal sins since our last confession, we confess them and also any that we may have forgotten in previous confessions. We must tell the nature and number of each of them. We may also confess any venial sins we wish to mention, and it is good to do so. When we have committed no mortal sin since our last confession, we should confess our venial sins. This is necessary that the priest may give us absolution.

We should end our confession by saying: "I am sorry for these and all the sins of my past life." It is well to tell one or several of the sins which we have previously confessed and for which we are particularly sorry.

After confessing our sins, we should answer truthfully any

question the priest asks. We should ask for advice if we feel that we need it. We should listen carefully to the instruction of the priest and accept the penance he gives us. While the priest is giving us absolution we should say again from our heart the act of contrition.

When we leave the confessional we should thank God for the sacrament we have received. Then we should promptly and with devotion perform our penance. God is so very merciful to us. The gift of this sacrament cannot be measured. So often we feel the weight of sin and the desire to be forgiven so as to begin again. As we come to face our sin, we can be sure that God's mercy is there to greet us with open arms. Remember his words in Psalm 81: "I freed your shoulder from the burden; your hands were freed from the load. You called in distress and I saved you" (Psalm 81). There is no sin too great for God's mercy. Like the father of the prodigal son, God yearns for our return. So long as we desire His grace and mercy, God will always give us the strength we need to begin again.

 **FOR ME TO REVIEW**

*Catechism Lesson*

798. Q. **What must he do who has will-fully concealed a mortal sin in confession?**

A. He who has willfully concealed a mortal sin in confession must not

## TERMS TO KNOW

- Absolution
- conscience
- Sincere
- penitent
- Penance
- examination
- Indulgence
- detest
- Sacrilege
- contrition
- Repentant
- spiritual life
- Temporal
- inspiration
- resolve
- infinite majesty
- Partial
- mortal
- Mystical Body
- mercy
- Iniquities
- supernatural
- absolution
- forgiveness
- Satisfaction
- amendment
- plenary

only confess it, but must also repeat all the sins he has committed since his last worthy confession.

800. Q. **Why does the priest give us a penance after confession?**

A. The priest gives us a penance after confession, that we may satisfy God for the temporal punishment due to our sins.

801. Q. **Why should we have to satisfy for our sins if Christ has fully satisfied for them?**

A. Christ has fully satisfied for our sins and after our Baptism we were free from all guilt and had no satisfaction to make. But when we willfully sinned after Baptism, it is but just that we should be obliged to make some satisfaction.

802. Q. **Is the slight penance the priest gives us sufficient to satisfy for all the sins confessed?**

A. The slight penance the priest gives us is not sufficient to satisfy for all the sins confessed: 1) Because there is no real equality between the slight penance given and the punishment deserved for sin; 2) Because we are all obliged to do penance for sins committed, and this would not be necessary if the penance given in confession satisfied for all. The penance is given and accepted in confession chiefly to show our willingness to do penance and make amends for our sins.

803. Q. **Does not the sacrament of Penance and Reconciliation remit all punishment due to sin?**

A. The sacrament of Penance and Reconciliation remits the eternal punishment due to sin, but it does not always remit the temporal punishment which God requires as satisfaction for our sins.

804. **Q. Why does God require a temporal punishment as a satisfaction for sin?**

A. God requires a temporal punishment as a satisfaction for sin to teach us the great evil of sin and to prevent us from falling again.

805. **Q. Which are the chief means by which we satisfy God for the temporal punishment due to sin?**

A. The chief means by which we satisfy God for the temporal punishment due to sin are: prayer, fasting, almsgiving; all spiritual and corporal works of mercy, and the patient suffering of the ills of life.

*Questions and Exercises*

## **Part 1**: Yes or No

1. Are sins forgiven through the merits of our Blessed Mother and the Apostles?

2. When the priest speaks the words of absolution, is it Christ Himself who absolves?

3. May we receive Holy Communion if, unintentionally, we forgot to tell a mortal sin in confession?

4. Is our contrition perfect when we are sorry for our sins because they are hateful in themselves or because we fear God's punishment?

5. Does the sacrament of Penance and Reconciliation take away all temporal punishments?

6. Is it sufficient to make the Act of Contrition only mentally as the priest imparts his absolution?

7. Are we seriously obliged to examine our conscience?

8. Is contrition the most important part of the sacrament of Penance and Reconciliation?

9. If a person will not give up the occasions of sin, is he truly sorry for his sins?

10. Should we stay away from confession if we find that we easily fall back into sin?

11. Does a sinner's relapse into sin always prove that his purpose of amendment was not firm and sincere?

12. Ronald is not sure he committed a sin. Must a doubtful sin be confessed?

13. Can we of ourselves ever repair the damage done by our sins?

14. Did Christ do penance for our sins?

15. Does the sacrament of Penance and Reconciliation prevent sin as well as remedy sins?

16. Is it a sin to neglect your penance?

17. Would you think it proper to tell others the advice the priest has given you in confession?

18. Is the confessor bound to keep secret the sins we have confessed?

19. Does the law of secrecy bind all those who in any way become aware of anything derived from confession?

20. May the confessor refuse to absolve us from our sins?

21. After our sins are forgiven, do we still have to do penance?

22. Is it a very good practice to examine one's conscience each night before going to bed?

23. Is imperfect contrition sufficient when you go to confession?

24. Does confession make us better Christians?

## Part 2: Matching

**COLUMN A**

1. Sorrow for sin through fear of the loss of heaven

2. The telling of our sins to a priest for the purpose of obtaining forgiveness

3. Reasons for acts

4. To give back

5. The sacrament we receive when we go to confession to have our sins forgiven

6. The power of our mind to judge what we should do as good or avoid as evil

7. God's pardon for our sins

8. Sorrow for sin because sin offends God who is infinitely good

9. Refuse to forgive

10. A sincere effort to call to mind all the sins we have committed since our last worthy confession

**COLUMN B**

A. Absolution

B. Penance and Reconciliation

C. Imperfect Contrition

D. Examination of Conscience

E. Confession

F. Perfect Contrition

G. Restore

H. Firm purpose of amendment

I. Retain

J. Motives

K. Conscience

## Part 3: Recognition Exercise

*Number the following in their correct order*

A.　Confess our sins to the priest.

B.　Be willing to perform the penance the priest gives us.

C. Examine our conscience.

D. Have a firm purpose of not sinning again.

E. Be sorry for our sins.

F. Ask God's help to know our sins and to confess them with sincere sorrow.

## ✓ FOR ME TO DO

1. Discuss the topic: "The Sacrament of Penance and Reconciliation as the Medicine of the Soul."

2. Compose a prayer to thank Christ for instituting the sacrament of Penance and Reconciliation.

3. List the particular duties at home and in school concerning which children must examine their conscience.

4. Write the Confiteor and underline the different persons to whom you confess that you have sinned.

5. Write a paragraph explaining how the tribunal of penance is like a court. Include the judge, the accused, the evidence, the decision, and the sentence imposed on the defendant. But also explain how the judge shows mercy on the truly repentant.

6. Make a list of the various ways you can pay some of the temporal punishment due to your sins besides the penance the priest gives you.

7. Find New Testament passages which tell of Christ's forgiveness of sin. Dramatize one.

8. Study symbols of this sacrament and explain them.

LESSON 19

# Indulgences

## Indulgences Help Us on Our Way to Heaven

Every sin leaves a debt of temporal punishment on the soul. This debt of punishment remains even after the sins have been forgiven. You can readily imagine how much temporal punishment there will be if many sins are committed. This punishment must be undergone either here on earth or else in purgatory. It is here that indulgences are important. You will probably recall that *indulgence is the remission granted by the Church of the temporal punishment due to sins already forgiven.*

### How We Gain Indulgences

We must:

Be in the state of grace.

Have at least a general intention of gaining the indulgence.

Perform the required works.

When we gain an indulgence all or part of the temporal punishment is removed. In other words we lessen or eliminate entirely the time we shall have to spend in purgatory and thus hasten our entrance into heaven. Indulgences are not a pardon for sin, as some people falsely think; neither are they a permission to commit sin. On the contrary, a person is unable to gain an indulgence for himself if he is not in the state of grace.

*"An indulgence is a remission before God of the temporal punishment due to sins whose guilt has already been forgiven, which the faithful Christian who is duly disposed gains under certain prescribed conditions through the action of the Church which, as the minister of redemption, dispenses and applies with authority the treasury of the satisfactions of Christ and the saints."*

—Catechism of the Catholic Church, 1471

## Indulgences Are of Two Kinds

Do you remember the number and kinds of indulgences? Yes, *there are two kinds of indulgences, plenary and partial.* What do you understand by a plenary indulgence? *A plenary indulgence is the remission of all the temporal punishment due to our sins.* What do we mean by a partial indulgence? *A partial indulgence is the remission of part of the temporal punishment due to our sins.*

An indulgence might be compared to a bonus added to your regular pay. God has agreed to reward good deeds performed in the state of grace. The Church adds more merit to deeds when she attaches indulgences to them. For example, a prayer said without the intention to gain the indulgence attached to it has a merit of its own; if the intention to gain the indulgence is added, the prayer will have a greater merit.

## Indulgences Remit Temporal Punishment

From what source do we draw this special "bonus" on our prayers and good deeds? From the same source whence all graces come to us, the spiritual treasury of the Church. *The Church by means of indulgences remits the temporal punishment due to sin by applying to us from her spiritual treasury part of the infinite satisfaction of Jesus Christ and of the superabundant satisfaction of the Blessed Virgin Mary and of the saints.*

What do you understand by the spiritual treasury of the Church? We know that it is not something material like the trea-

sury of a bank. We can compare it to the bank
account of a family made up of a mother and
three sons. The eldest receives a very large
salary, the second enough to support himself,
and the youngest very little. They give their
earnings to their mother who provides for
all. She can draw on the large salary of the
eldest to supply the needs of the youngest. In
this way the one who has less is, through his
mother, aided by the one who has more than
he needs.

**TERMS TO KNOW**

- plenary
- superabundant
- immediate
- beneficial
- remission
- partial
- utterly
- satisfaction

Now the Church is our mother and she has an inexhaustible
treasury at her disposal. She can draw on the merits earned by
Christ, His Blessed Mother, and the saints. By His Passion and
death our Lord gained an infinite number of graces. Our Blessed
Lady acquired so much merit by her heroic life that a superabundant supply still remains. In addition the saints earned more than
enough to gain heaven. All these merits gained by Christ, His
Blessed Mother, and the saints make up the spiritual treasury of
the Church.

*The superabundant satisfaction of the Blessed Virgin Mary
and of the saints is that which they gained during the lifetime
but did not need, and which the Church applies to their fellow
members of the communion of saints.* So the Church like a loving mother draws upon the abundant spiritual satisfaction of
her richer children to help her poorer ones. When you gain an
indulgence, the Church draws on her treasury and gives you the
means to pay part or all of the temporal punishment you owe for
your sins.

## What We Can Do to Gain Indulgences

Now that we understand the great value of indulgences, we should make certain that we know how to gain them. *To gain an indulgence for ourselves we must be in the state of grace, have at least a general intention of gaining the indulgence, and perform the works required by the Church.*

The first part of this answer shows that indulgences are not a pardon for sin nor are they a permission to commit sin. You will remember that we must be free from mortal sin before we can gain any indulgences.

It is not only for ourselves that we are able to gain indulgences, we can gain them for others also. However, *we cannot gam indulgences for other living persons, but we can gain them for the souls in purgatory, since the Church makes most indulgences applicable to them.* By "applicable" we mean capable of being applied or given to them.

## Summary

An indulgence is the remission or pardon of the temporal punishment due to sins already forgiven. This remission is granted by the Church. The Church applies to its members part of the infinite satisfaction of Jesus Christ and of the more than sufficient satisfaction of the Blessed Virgin and the saints.

There are two kinds of indulgences: plenary and partial. A plenary indulgence is the remission of all the temporal punishment due to our sins. A partial indulgence is the remission of part of the temporal punishment due to our sins.

To gain any indulgence for ourselves we must be in the state of grace. We must also have at least the general intention to gain the indulgence, and we must perform the works required by the Church. We cannot gain indulgences for other living persons. The Church, however, permits most indulgences to be applied to the souls in purgatory.

**FOR ME TO REVIEW**

*Catechism Lesson*

839. **Q. What is an indulgence?**

A. An indulgence is the remission in whole or in part of the temporal punishment due to sin.

843. **Q. How many kinds of indulgences are there?**

A. There are two kinds of Indulgences—plenary and partial.

844. **Q. What is a plenary indulgence?**

A. A plenary indulgence is the full remission of the temporal punishment due to sin.

845. **Q. Is it easy to gain a plenary indulgence?**

A. It is not easy to gain a plenary indulgence, as we may understand from its great privilege. To gain a plenary indulgence, we must hate sin, be heartily sorry for even our venial sins, and have no desire for even the slightest sin. Though we may not gain entirely each plenary indulgence we seek, we always gain a part of each; that is, a partial indulgence, greater or less in proportion to our good dispositions.

847. **Q. What is a partial indulgence?**

A. A partial indulgence is the remission of part of the temporal punishment due to sin.

849. **Q. How do we show that the Church has the power to grant indulgences?**

A. We show that the Church has the power to grant indulgences, because Christ has given it power to remit all guilt without restriction, and if the Church has power, in the sacrament of Penance and Reconciliation, to remit the eternal punishment—which is the greatest—it must have power to remit the temporal or lesser punishment, even outside the sacrament of Penance and Reconciliation.

850. Q. How do we know that these indulgences have their effect?

A. We know that these indulgences have their effect, because the Church, through her councils, declares indulgences useful, and if they have no effect they would be useless, and the Church would teach error in spite of Christ's promise to guide it.

851. Q. Have there ever existed abuses among the faithful in the manner of using indulgences?

A. There have existed, in past ages, some abuses among the faithful in the manner of using indulgences, and the Church has always labored to correct such abuses as soon as possible. In the use of pious practices we must be always guided by our lawful superiors.

853. Q. How does the Church by means of indulgences remit the temporal punishment due to sin?

A. The Church, by means of indulgences, remits the temporal punishment due to sin by applying to us the merits of Jesus Christ, and the superabundant satisfactions of the Blessed Virgin Mary and of the saints; which merits and satisfactions are its spiritual treasury.

854. Q. What do we mean by the "superabundant satisfaction of the Blessed Virgin and the saints"?

A. By the superabundant satisfaction of the Blessed Virgin and the saints, we mean all the satisfaction over and above what was necessary to satisfy for their own sins. As their good works were many and their sins few—the Blessed Virgin being sinless—the satisfaction not needed for themselves is kept by the Church in a spiritual treasury to be used for our benefit.

855. Q. **Does the Church, by granting indulgences, free us from doing penance?**

A. The Church, by granting indulgences, does not free us from doing penance, but simply makes our penance lighter that we may more easily satisfy for our sins and escape the punishments they deserve.

*Questions and Exercises*

## Part 1: True or False

1. Only a plenary indulgence forgives mortal sin.

2. Indulgences shorten the time to be spent in purgatory.

3. The remission of all the temporal punishment due to sin is a plenary indulgence.

4. One must be in the state of grace to gain an indulgence for himself.

5. By saying prayers and performing good works, we can gain many indulgences for other living persons.

6. It is only in purgatory that we can atone for temporal punishment.

7. The spiritual treasury of the Catholic Church is inexhaustible.

8. We profit from the infinite satisfaction of Christ and the merits of the Blessed Virgin Mary and of the saints.

9. Temporal punishment is the result of sin.

10. An indulgence does not free us from the eternal punishment due to sin.

**Part 2**: Problems for Discussion

1. Margaret attends Mass as often as she can. She knows it is the best act she can offer for the relief of the poor souls. Prepare a two-minute talk suggesting additional helps for the members of the Church Suffering.

2. Mary and Jean were great friends. Each of them promises to say the rosary and offer the indulgences gained for the other. If Mary and Jean are still attached to certain sinful bad habits (and therefore are not in the state of grace), can they still receive indulgences? Discuss.

LESSON 20

# Anointing of the Sick

As Christ has provided the sacrament of Penance and Reconciliation for the forgiveness of actual sins, so He has instituted Anointing of the Sick not only to strengthen us at the moment of death but also to remit venial sins and the remains of sin. As the immediate preparation for death, confession and the reception of Holy Communion are followed by the sacrament of Anointing of the Sick. Christ guards the close of life with a most firm defense, the sacrament of Anointing of the Sick. This we shall now study in detail.

## Anointing of the Sick Gives Health and Strength to the Soul and Sometimes to the Body

Your knowledge of this sacrament is perhaps very limited. You know that it is one of the seven sacraments instituted by Christ. We learn this from the command given to the Apostles contained in the Epistle of St. James 5:14. It reads: "Is any one among you sick? Let him bring in the presbyters of the Church, and let them pray over him, anointing him with oil in the name of the Lord. And the prayer of faith will save the sick man, and the Lord will raise him up, and if he be in sins, they shall be forgiven him."

When and how Christ instituted the sacrament of Anointing of the Sick is not mentioned in Holy Scripture, but the words of St. James prove that it was instituted by Christ as a sacrament.

Jesus healing
in the land of
Gennesaret.

The Church invariably taught this doctrine. Anointing of the Sick has been administered by the Church in all ages. Pope Innocent I, in the fourth century, expressly declared that these words of St. James referred to the sacrament of Anointing of the Sick.

Let us now study Anointing of the Sick in more detail.

*Anointing of the Sick is the sacrament which, through the anointing with blessed oil by the priest, and through his prayer, gives health and strength to the soul and sometimes to the body when we are sick or in danger of death.*

Did you notice in the statement above that it is through the anointing with blessed oil by the priest and through his prayer, that the sacrament of Anointing of the Sick brings health to the soul and sometimes to the body? The oil used is the oil of the sick, which is olive oil, blessed every year by the bishop on Holy Thursday. The prayers said by the priest during the anointing have been prescribed by the Church.

The first time you were anointed with blessed oil was at baptism. Your second anointing took place when you were confirmed. Those of you who may become priests will be anointed when you receive the sacrament of Holy Orders. If you are fortunate enough, you will be anointed with blessed oil for the last time as death draws near.

Oil, as you know, has healing properties. This explains the use of oil in the external sign of this sacrament. Do you recall the story about the man who fell among robbers? His wounds were healed by the pouring in of oil. Oil heals the wounds of the body, so oil is used as a symbol of the healing of the soul. Remember, however, that it is not only through the anointing with oil, but also through the prayers of the priest that health of the soul and health of the body are restored.

> *"Illness can lead to anguish, self-absorption, sometimes even despair and revolt against God. It can also make a person more mature, helping him discern in his life what is not essential so that he can turn toward that which is. Very often illness provokes a search for God and a return to him."*
>
> —Catechism of the Catholic Church, 1501

## Anointing of the Sick Should Be Received by Those Who Are Sick or in Danger of Death

You may wonder who can receive this sacrament. *All Catholics who have reached the use of reason and are sick or in danger of death should receive Anointing of the Sick*. Only Catholics who have reached the use of reason may receive this sacrament. It may not be given to those who have not reached the use of reason and are not capable of sin. Infants or persons feeble-minded from birth could never have committed actual sin. It would be impossible for them, therefore, to receive the effects of this sacrament.

Anointing of the Sick is administered only to those who are sick or in danger of death. It is fitting to receive the sacrament, for instance, just prior to a serious operation.

Perhaps you have been present when this sacrament was administered to one of your loved ones who was seriously sick. Did you ever witness a train wreck, an automobile accident, or an airplane crash? You may have observed in what a surprisingly

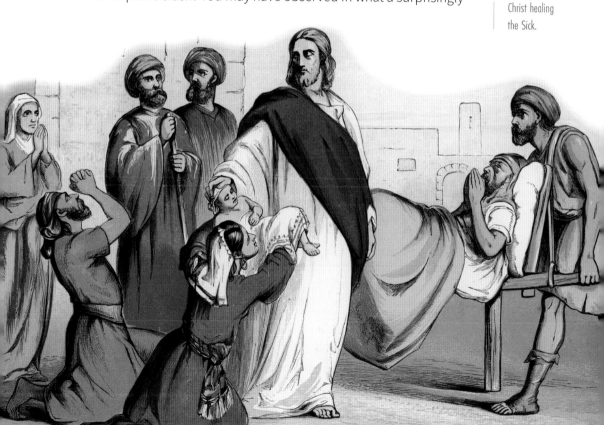

Christ healing the Sick.

> *"Is any of you sad? Let him pray. Is he cheerful in mind? Let him sing. Is any man sick among you? Let him bring in the priests of the church, and let them pray over him, anointing him with oil in the name of the Lord. And the prayer of faith shall save the sick man: and the Lord shall raise him up: and if he be in sins, they shall be forgiven him."*

*—James 5:13–15*

short time a priest or priests arrived to administer Anointing of the Sick to those who were in danger of death. Maybe you witnessed the anointing of your grandmother or grandfather. What prayers did the priest say? What actions did he perform?

If you were present on any such occasion, and if it were not an emergency, you saw the priest anoint the sense organs, namely: the eyes, ears, nostrils, lips, hands. You heard him say this prayer over each in turn. "Through this holy anointing and his most tender mercy, may the Lord forgive whatever wrong thou hast done through sight" (hearing, smell, taste, speech, and touch). It is through the senses that evil enters the heart. If there is not sufficient time to anoint all the senses, the priest may use a short formula and anoint only the forehead.

## The Effects of Anointing of the Sick

*The effects of the sacrament of Anointing of the Sick are: first, an increase of sanctifying grace; second, comfort in sickness and strength against temptation; third, preparation for entrance into heaven by the remission of our venial sins and the cleansing of our souls from the remains of sin; fourth, health of body when it is good for the soul.*

Anointing of the Sick, as you know, is a sacrament of the living. You may remember that to receive a sacrament of the living worthily, one must ordinarily be in the state of grace. The first effect of a sacrament of the living is an increase of sanctifying grace. Anointing of the Sick increases sanctifying grace, but, as we shall see, it may restore grace to a person in serious sin.

The second effect is the comfort and strength it gives to the dying person. He may be in severe pain and sorely tempted by the devil, who is making his final efforts to bring about eternal ruin to the sick person. The devil tries to fill his mind with despairing thoughts and doubts about the mercy of God. Anointing of the Sick is a spiritual remedy, giving the dying or sick person strength to fight the devil.

The third effect of this sacrament is "preparation for entrance into heaven by the remission of our venial sins and the cleansing of our souls from the remains of sin." You know that when we go to confession we have an obligation to confess our mortal sins. We may or may not tell our venial sins. Unconfessed venial sins are remitted through the sacrament of Anointing of the Sick. St. James says, "and if he be in sins, they shall be forgiven him." This anointing must be a sacrament, or it could not take away sins.

One of the chief punishments of Adam which we inherit through original sin is a strong inclination to sin. The oftener we commit sin, the weaker our will becomes. The inclination to evil and the weakness of the will are what is meant by the "remains of sin." These remain in us after our sins have been forgiven. Through the sacrament of Anointing of the Sick we are cleansed from the remains of sin.

The fourth effect of Anointing of the Sick is "health of body when it is good for the soul." God does all things for the best. He alone knows why He restores health to one person and not to another.

An old lady had a touch of pneumonia and a very weak heart. As she was seventy-nine and lived a great distance from the church, the priest wanted to anoint her. But she said: "No, what makes you think I'm dying? Bring me Holy Communion if you like, but I don't want to be anointed yet." Who knows the answer the priest might make to her? He would tell her that her age and condition justified his giving her Anointing of the Sick. What is more, the anointing is intended to make one better if it is God's will.

## Anointing of the Sick in Certain Circumstances Takes Away Mortal Sin

As indicated, Anointing of the Sick may remove mortal sin from a person. When does this happen? *Anointing of the Sick takes away mortal sin when the sick person is unconscious or otherwise unaware that he is not properly disposed, but has made an act of imperfect contrition.*

Now that you have considered the benefits derived from the reception of this sacrament, you can understand how important it is to send for the priest while the sick person is still conscious. Do not make the mistake, however, of neglecting to send for a priest if the person has become unconscious or even if the person is found dead.

### TERMS TO KNOW

- apparent
- instruments
- prescribed
- unaware
- conditionally
- justified
- remitted
- eligible
- unconscious
- resignation
- formula
- lapses
- tolerable

You just learned that Anointing of the Sick takes away mortal sin when the sick person is unconscious and has made an act of imperfect contrition. Who but God knows what takes place in the last conscious moments of a dying person? None of us knows what change of heart may come to those who, in spite of very sinful lives, may, like the good thief on the cross, still win pardon from our merciful Saviour by one last act of fervent sorrow. If the person during his last conscious moments, however, had the intention of continuing in mortal sin, he would not receive any benefit from the sacrament.

What is meant by "the sick person is otherwise unaware that he is not properly disposed"? It means that he is in the state of mortal sin, but is not aware of the fact. He may have completely forgotten that he committed a serious sin or sins since his last worthy confession. If he has, however, made an act of imperfect contrition before becoming unconscious, and the sacrament of Anointing of the Sick is administered to him, mortal sin will be taken away.

## Anointing of the Sick Should Be Preceded by a Suitable Preparation

*We should prepare ourselves to receive Anointing of the Sick worthily by a good confession, by acts of faith, hope, charity, and, especially, by resignation to the will of God.* We should be in the

*"I do not desire to die soon, because in Heaven there is no suffering. I desire to live a long time because I yearn to suffer much for the love of my Spouse."*

—*St. Mary Magdalene de Pazzi*

state of grace when we receive the sacrament of Anointing of the Sick. Does this make you understand the importance of being fully conscious and of preparing ourselves by making a good confession? We read in Holy Scripture, these words: "My son, in thy sickness, neglect not thyself; but pray to the Lord and he shall heal thee. Turn away from sin and order thy hands aright; and cleanse thy heart from all offense" (Sir. 38:9–10). Look up the following passages in the New Testament (Lk. 22:41–42; and Jn. 21:15–17). Can you explain them?

In addition to a good confession, it is recommended that we prepare ourselves to receive Anointing of the Sick by reciting the acts of faith, hope, and love. The words contained in these acts tell you why they are considered a good preparation. The Act of Faith is a profession of our belief in revealed truths proposed by the Catholic Church. The Act of Hope is an expression of our trust in the power and mercy of God to keep His promise to pardon our sins and give us life everlasting. The Act of Love is an out-pouring of love for God, above all things, for His own sake and for our neighbor as ourselves out of love for Him. We conclude the

All Catholics who have reached the use of reason and are sick or in danger of death should receive Anointing of the Sick.

308

prayer by saying that we forgive all who have injured us, and ask pardon of all whom we have injured.

One of our Lord's last words as He was hanging on the cross was a prayer of forgiveness. Remember? "Father, forgive them, for they know not what they do."

We should prepare ourselves "especially, by resignation to the will of God." This means that we should put ourselves in the hands of God to dispose of us as He sees fit. If He wishes to restore us to health, we will it also; if not, His holy will be done. Does this remind you of our Lord's prayer during his agony in the Garden of Olives? "Father, not My will, but Thine be done." It is a perfect prayer of resignation to God's will.

The external preparation that should be made for the administration of the last sacraments is as follows: A table covered with a white cloth, a crucifix, two lighted blessed wax candles, and holy water in a small container. Out of respect for the sacraments, and in particular for the presence of our Lord, everything about the sickroom and the sick person should be as neat and clean as possible.

## The Priest Is the Minister of the Sacrament of Anointing of the Sick

*Only a priest can administer Anointing of the Sick.* It is expressly stated in the Epistle of St. James, "bring in the presbyters of the Church." Also you will remember in his epistle that priests are asked to pray for the sick man and to anoint him in the name of the Lord, that through this prayer and anointing, his sins are to be forgiven. From this it is clear that only priests can administer this sacrament.

## The Priest Should Be Asked to Visit the Sick in Any Serious Illness

Many people have the mistaken notion that a priest should not be asked to visit the sick unless there is danger of death. On the contrary, *it is advisable to call the priest to visit the sick in any serious illness, even though there be no apparent danger of death, as it is the duty of the priest to visit the sick and to administer to them the sacraments they need, including Anointing of the Sick.*

On many occasions when our Lord was on earth, He manifested His great sympathy for the sick and ailing. He comforted them by His words, and in some instances worked miracles to effect their cure. The priest is another Christ. His comforting words can prove a source of great consolation to the sick. There is a special blessing he can give and appropriate prayers he can read over the sick person. Also, those who are seriously sick should receive the sacraments of Penance and Reconciliation and Holy Eucharist regularly. Try to help the priest to fulfill this duty he has to visit the sick and administer to them the sacraments they need by notifying him promptly of any sick you may have in your home.

## The Priest Should Be Called in Case of Sudden or Unexpected Death

No one is absolutely certain of the moment when death occurs. It is possible that the person may be still alive even after he appears to be dead. Penance and Reconciliation and Anointing of the Sick can be administered conditionally for several hours after the person has ceased to give any signs of life, because it is possible that he may still be alive. It is very important, therefore, that *in case of sudden or unexpected death a priest should be called always, because absolution and Anointing of the Sick can be given conditionally for some time after apparent death.*

The grace to die in the friendship of almighty God is the greatest blessing that can ever come to us. We should beg God daily for this grace and remember to pray for those who are dying that they may die a happy death. St. Joseph is the patron of a happy death. Ask him to obtain for you the grace to receive Anointing of the Sick with the most perfect disposition possible before you die. It will prepare you for the vision of God for all eternity. Do you know any prayers for a happy death?

## Summary

Anointing of the Sick is the sacrament which, through the anointing with blessed oil by the priest, and through his prayers, gives health and strength to the soul and sometimes to the body. All Catholics who have reached the use of reason and are sick or in danger of death should receive Anointing of the Sick.

The effects of the sacrament of Anointing of the Sick are: (1) an increase of sanctifying grace; (2) comfort in sickness and strength against temptation; (3) preparation for entrance into heaven by the remission of our venial sins and the cleansing of our soul from the remains of sin; (4) health of body when it is good for the soul.

Anointing of the Sick takes away mortal sin when the sick person is unconscious or otherwise unaware that he is not properly disposed, but has made an act of imperfect contrition.

We should prepare ourselves to receive Anointing of the Sick by a good confession, by acts of faith, hope, charity, and especially, by resignation to the will of God.

Only a priest can administer Anointing of the Sick. It is advisable to call the priest to visit the sick in any serious illness even though there be no apparent danger of death. It is the duty of the priest to visit the sick and to administer to them the sacraments they need. In case of sudden or unexpected death a priest should be called always, because absolution and Anointing of the Sick can be given conditionally for some time after apparent death.

##  FOR ME TO REVIEW

*Catechism Lesson*

**956.** **Q. What is the sacrament of Anointing of the Sick?**

A. Anointing of the Sick is the sacrament which, through the anointing and prayer of the priest, gives health and strength to the soul, and sometimes to the body, when we are sick or in danger of death.

**959.** **Q. To whom may Anointing of the Sick be given?**

A. Anointing of the Sick may be given to all Christians who are ill, who have ever been capable of committing sin after Baptism and who have the right dispositions for the sacrament. Hence it is never given to children who have not reached the use of reason, nor to persons who have always been insane.

**962.** **Q. When should we receive Anointing of the Sick?**

A. We should receive Anointing of the Sick when we are sick or in danger of death.

**969.** **Q. Which are the effects of the sacrament of Anointing of the Sick?**

A. The effects of Anointing of the Sick are: 1st, To comfort us in the pains of sickness and to strengthen us against temptations; 2nd, To remit venial sins and to cleanse our soul from the remains of sin; 3rd, To restore us to health, when God sees fit.

970. **Q. Will Anointing of the Sick take away mortal sin if the dying person is no longer able to confess?**

A. Anointing of the Sick will take away mortal sin if the dying person is no longer able to confess, provided he has the sorrow for his sins that would be necessary for the worthy reception of the sacrament of Penance and Reconciliation.

974. **Q. How should we receive the sacrament of Anointing of the Sick?**

A. We should receive the sacrament of Anointing of the Sick in the state of grace, and with lively faith and resignation to the will of God.

975. **Q. Who is the minister of the sacrament of Anointing of the Sick?**

A. The priest is the minister of the sacrament of Anointing of the Sick.

*Questions and Exercises*

## **Part 1**: Problems

1. Agnes says that Father Augustine anointed her grandmother today. She is 81 but there doesn't seem to be anything physically wrong with her. She seldom leaves the house, but is not confined to bed. She reads a good deal, sews, and does some of the housework. Agnes seems surprised by what Father did. How would you explain the case to her?

2. Four Catholic boys go for a swim in the lake. One of them, Ralph, is drowned. The boys recover his body two hours later. They immediately begin first-aid efforts to revive him. Someone goes to get a doctor. Should they bother about getting a priest? Why?

3. Can dead people receive any sacrament? Explain your answer.

4. As a rule, what is the first anointing we receive? The second? The last?

5. Jimmy, an eighth-grade student, is seriously ill. He has the desire to receive the Last Sacraments. His request frightens his mother, who doesn't know her religion very well, and she agrees to his request, when he says he wants to go to confession and receive Holy Communion. She makes him promise he won't mention being anointed. What is your opinion of her attitude?

## Part 2: True or False

1. In case of necessity, the sacrament of Anointing of the Sick may be administered by anyone who has the use of reason.

2. A person should not be anointed if there is any chance of recovery because he might become frightened and become worse.

3. Those who have the care of sick persons should not allow them to die, if possible, without the Last Sacraments.

4. Anointing of the Sick takes away mortal sin when the sick person is unaware that he is not properly disposed but has made an act of imperfect contrition.

5. To receive Anointing of the Sick a person must certainly be dying.

6. The sacrament of Anointing of the Sick was instituted by Jesus Christ.

7. The sacrament of Anointing of the Sick increases sanctifying grace in the soul.

## Part 3: Matching

**COLUMN A**

1. Anointing of the Sick

2. Holy Oils

3. Minister of Anointing of the Sick

4. A Sacrament of the Living

5. The senses

6. Last Sacraments

7. Proper preparation for Anointing of the Sick

8. St. Joseph

**COLUMN B**

A. Reconciliation, Holy Communion

B. Confession, Communion, Anointing of the Sick

C. Sight, hearing, taste, smell, and touch

D. The Patron of a happy death

E. Used for the anointing

F. Last anointing

G. Anointing of the Sick

H. Priest

 **FOR ME TO DO**

1. Find examples in the New Testament of Christ healing the sick.

2. Prepare a talk on the benefits of Anointing of the Sick.

3. Discuss the other anointing a Catholic receives in life.

4. Prepare a table with the necessary items for Anointing of the Sick.

5. Read the prayers used by the priest in administering the sacrament.

6. Make a chart illustrating the things needed in the home for Anointing of the Sick.

7. Write a story about how Johnny convinced his neighbors to call the priest for their dying father.

# Achievement Test

*Write your answers on a separate sheet of paper*

 **I. Multiple Choice**

1. When a person is sorry for his sins because they offend God, his sorrow is:
   A. universal.
   B. supreme.
   C. interior.
   D. supernatural.

2. The sacrament of Anointing of the Sick should normally be administered:
   A. only when a person becomes unconscious.
   B. after the person is dead.
   C. when a person is sick or in danger of death.
   D. whenever a baby is sick.

3. An indulgence takes away:
   A. sin.
   B. grace.
   C. temporal punishment.
   D. eternal punishment.

4. We are obliged to receive Holy Communion within the:
   A. Christmas octave.
   B. Pentecost season.
   C. Advent season.
   D. Easter season.

5.   Christ's sufferings and death are renewed in the:
A. Sorrowful mysteries of the rosary.
B. Mass.
C. Stations of the Cross.

6.   Comfort in sickness and strength against temptation is an effect of:
A. Confirmation.
B. Penance and Reconciliation.
C. Anointing of the Sick.
D. Holy Eucharist.

7.   Easter time in the United States is from:
A. Ash Wednesday to Holy Saturday.
B. the second Sunday of Lent to Pentecost.
C. Holy Saturday to Low Sunday.
D. First Sunday of Lent to Trinity Sunday.

8.   Sins are forgiven through the:
A. merits of Jesus Christ.
B. merits of the saints.
C. merits of the priest.
D. indulgences.

9.   The sacrament which contains the body and blood, soul and divinity of our Saviour Jesus Christ is:
A. Holy Orders.
B. Baptism.
C. Holy Eucharist.
D. Penance and Reconciliation.

10. The chief reason we do penance is to:
    A. satisfy for the punishment due for our sins.
    B. resist temptation.
    C. make ourselves strong.
    D. imitate the saints.

11. Christ gave the Apostles the power to forgive sins:
    A. before His Ascension.
    B. at the Last Supper.
    C. on Pentecost.
    D. on the evening of His resurrection.

 **II. Completion**

1. The sacrifice of Christ on Calvary is continued each day in the
   _____.

2. The principal ways of obtaining grace are____(a)____ and the
   ____(b)____ .

3. The sin committed by receiving a sacrament of the living when
   one is in the state of mortal sin is called_____.

4. _____is the telling of our sins to an authorized priest for the
   purpose of obtaining forgiveness.

5. The most important part of the sacrament of Penance and
   Reconciliation is_____.

6. The chief punishment remitted by the sacrament of Penance
   and Reconciliation is called_____.

7. We pay the debt of our temporal punishment either in this ___(a)___ or in the state of punishment called___(b)___.

8. The obligation on the priest to keep absolute silence about knowledge gained in confession is called the_____of confession.

9. The first Mass was celebrated at the_____.

10. Anointing of the Sick sometimes restores_____to the body.

11. From the sufferings and death of Christ we learn that_____ is the worst evil in the world.

12. The benefits which we receive from assisting at Mass depend chiefly on our_____.

13. The change of the entire substance of the bread and wine into the body and blood of Christ is called_____.

14. The principal priest in every Mass is_____.

15. _____is the receiving of Jesus Christ in the sacrament of the Holy Eucharist.

16. The sacrament of Penance and Reconciliation___(a)___ sanctifying grace if it was lost or___(b)___ it, if it was not lost.

17. Holy Communion received by a person in danger of death is called_____.

**III.** Matching

| COLUMN A | COLUMN B |
|---|---|
| 1. The most important part of the Mass | A. Kyrie |
| 2. The highest form of public worship in the Catholic Church | B. Credo |
| 3. The part of the Mass in which the bread and wine are offered up to God in anticipation of their change into the body and blood of Christ | C. Agnus Dei |
| 4. A ninefold plea addressed to the Three Divine Persons | D. Gloria |
| 5. The homage we give to God | E. Collect |
| 6. A hymn of praise to Christ. | F. Sacrifice of the Mass |
| 7. An act of faith | G. Consecration |
| 8. A symbol of our redemption | H. Offertory |
| 9. Reminds us of John the Baptist's introduction of Christ | I. Adoration |
| 10. The prayer of the day's Mass | J. The sign of the Cross |

## IV. Matching

**COLUMN A**

1. A prayer of praise to God opening the Canon

2. A prayer which asks God to give us what we need in order to serve Him better

3. Usually an inspired letter written by one of the Apostles and contained in the New Testament

4. Chiefly an act of contrition

5. The victim of sacrifice in the Mass

6. The prayers before and after the consecration which gather the whole Church around the sacrifice of Christ

7. Said at the foot of the altar and reminds us that sin makes us exiles from God like King David

8. Recalls the centurion who knew that Jesus could cure his servant

9. The most important part in the Mass of preparation; the Word of God

10. A greeting said eight times during the Mass

**COLUMN B**

A. Preface

B. Confiteor

C. Dominus Vobiscum

D. Pater Noster

E. Remembrances

F. Epistle

G. Gospel

H. The 42nd Psalm

I. Jesus Christ

J. The "Domine non sum dignus" ("Lord I am not worthy . . .")

UNIT

# 3

Christ Works
Through Us

# CHAPTER 11

# Christ Has Work for Each of Us to Do

*We have studied the first five sacraments in unit 2. There are two more—often referred to as the social sacraments. They were intended by God to provide for the continuation of physical life (Matrimony) and spiritual life (Holy Orders). A careful study of them will help you choose the state of life in which you can best serve God and reach heaven.*

# Vocations in General and Holy Orders

## What a Vocation Is

Have you ever heard a man remark, "I think I have a vocation to the priesthood," or perhaps you've witnessed the marriage of a young couple? You may have wondered, "What is a vocation?" A vocation is a calling from God which can only be heard in the innermost recesses of our souls. This calling is more than simply a state of life--such as marriage or consecrated celibacy. It is a calling to *be* a certain *kind* of person, filled with a burning love for Christ and His Church. We can enter a specific state of life without this love; to do so is to reject the grace God wishes to bestow upon us. Many marriages fail, and many priests and nuns also fail in living the Gospel. What does this tell us about the nature of a vocation? It is not enough to enter a specific state of life. We must actively seek to live holy and virtuous lives within our married or celebrate states, taking care to receive all the graces God wishes to bestow upon us. When it is time for us to make a decision as to whether we will marry or consecrate our lives to God and His Church, the question we should consider is, "what state of life will help me know, love, and serve God to the best of my abilities?"

## Different Types of Vocations

By nature, God designed men and women with an inclination toward the married state of life. Unless we feel a strong desire for the priesthood or consecrated life, we will most likely enter the married state. Others choose to remain single and strive for perfection in their ordinary daily life. While many people may exhibit certain qualities of the priesthood, marriage, or consecrated life, only the individual can know and discern for himself his vocation. Even the choice to remain single, while it may seem to some as the avoidance of commitment, can truly be the means of salvation for particular people. Think of St. Joan of Arc or Blessed Pier Giorgio Frassati; they became perfected in holiness as single people in the world. Some priests are diocesan priests, that is, they are attached to a certain diocese. They are sometimes called secular priests because they work for Christ in the world. Other priests have entered consecrated life by taking the three vows of poverty, chastity, and obedience. Religious brothers and sisters also take these vows.

In considering the religious or consecrated life it is well to remember that Christ does not command, but He does extend a loving invitation to a chosen few to live for Him in a consecrated state. Those who receive and accept this call often become members of some community of their choice. They live a common life, engage in the particular work undertaken by the community and give themselves to a life of perfection through the observance of the evangelical counsels (poverty, chastity, and obedience).

"The very differences which the Lord has willed to put between the members of his body serve its unity and mission. For 'in the Church there is diversity of ministry but unity of mission. To the apostles and their successors Christ has entrusted the office of teaching, sanctifying and governing in his name and by his power. But the laity are made to share in the priestly, prophetical, and kingly office of Christ; they have therefore, in the Church and in the world, their own assignment in the mission of the whole People of God.' Finally, 'from both groups [hierarchy and laity] there exist Christian faithful who are consecrated to God in their own special manner and serve the salvific mission of the Church through the profession of the evangelical counsels.'"

—Catechism of the Catholic Church, 873

## Certain Qualifications Are Required for Each State

Every vocation, whether it be the married, single, or consecrated state, has definite requirements. Moral fitness are certainly necessary qualifications. Another is perfect freedom in making a choice of a particular state of life. A person's motives must also be worthy.

Perhaps you have given considerable thought to what you might like to do when you are old enough to make a definite choice. Before making such an important decision, you should understand the necessity for living a virtuous life, quiet prayer, frequent reception of the sacraments, and competent guidance. Given that all these things are in place, we should not be afraid to choose what

St. Augustine had a vocation to the sacrament of Holy Orders.

we desire. God speaks to the heart; when our hearts are steeped in prayer and virtue, our desires reveal to us what it is God wants of us. "Love and do what you will," says St. Augustine. In his book *The Confessions*, St. Augustine often spoke of his love as being the motivating factor of all his actions: "My weight is my love, by it am I borne wherever I am borne." What does this tell us about the discernment of our desires? By living a virtuous life of prayer and holiness, we learn to love the things of God. When the time comes for us to choose a state in life we may, with St. Augustine "love and do what we will." The will of a good Christian is the will of God. External factors will help us in our discernment as well, such as particular needs in the community, gifts and talents we may have, as well as the advice and council of mentors and spiritual directors.

# Holy Orders

### Christ Acts in and Through His Priests

In our study of vocations we will begin with the greatest of all vocations, the call to the priesthood or Holy Orders. *Holy Orders is the sacrament through which men receive the power and grace to perform the sacred duties of bishops, priests, and deacons of the Church.* The powers received by the priest in Holy Orders are the same as those conferred by Christ on His Apostles.

In establishing His Church, Christ intended that the work which He had begun should be carried on by His Apostles and their successors to the end of time. As Christ went about teaching, He was preparing His Apostles for the work they were to accomplish in preaching the truths He had taught them and in dispensing His graces. Not only did Christ give them the power to teach but also the power to sanctify. This work of sanctification is accomplished by administering the sacraments. Christ also governed His little flock, thereby showing His Apostles and their successors how to guide men. Just as Christ taught, sanctified, and governed, so do His Apostles and their successors perform these same functions. Thus the bishop, through his assistants, the priests, exercises the same offices that Christ exercised.

### The Requirements for Admission to the Priesthood

Your catechism tells you that in order *that a man may receive Holy Orders worthily it is necessary to be in the state of grace, to have the necessary knowledge, and a divine call to this sacred office.*

Let us consider some of the requirements for admission to the priesthood. First, there must be an inclination for the particular life and work of the priesthood. If, even after much prayer and discernment, a young man expressed his dislike for the work of a parish priest, you would hardly recommend him as a possible candidate for the priesthood. Physical and psychological fitness

is also very necessary to carry on day after day the many and arduous tasks of a priest. In your own parish you probably have had occasion to observe the priest spending long hours in the confessional, in caring for the sick, and in handling the many difficult and often emotional problems of those who come to him. Can you appreciate how important physical and mental fitness would be?

The prospective priest has great need for mental fitness also. The long years of study and his task of solving intricate problems as a priest make it necessary that he be well equipped mentally. But don't get the idea that one must be a genius in order to prepare for the priesthood. A young man with average ability and a will to study hard could be sufficiently well equipped.

An indispensable qualification is moral fitness. By this is meant a firm character and virtuous conduct on the part of the candidate. You can understand how necessary this moral fitness would be in one who is to represent Christ. The catechism states that the man be of "excellent character."

*"The priesthood is the love of the heart of Jesus. When you see a priest, think of our Lord Jesus Christ."*

—St. Jean Vianney

### The Steps That Lead to the Priesthood

Only after years of study and preparation is the candidate ready for the actual reception of the priesthood. A year prior to his ordination to the priesthood, the candidate is ordained to the deaconate. Some married men stay permanent deacons. Those preparing for the fullness of the priesthood are ordained *transitional* deacons.

### The Effects of the Sacrament of Holy Orders

The rite of ordination is long and detailed and can be best appreciated by attendance at an ordination ceremony.

*The bishop is the minister of the sacrament of Holy Orders.* In administering the sacrament the bishop places his hands upon the candidates, calls down the Holy Spirit upon them, anoints their hands and presents them with the sacred vessels they are to use.

*The effects of ordination to the priesthood are: first, an increase of sanctifying grace; second, sacramental grace, through which the priest has God's constant help in his sacred ministry; third, a character, lasting forever, which is a special sharing in the priesthood of Christ and which gives the priest special supernatural powers.*

Let us consider the graces and powers mentioned as effects of ordination. In your study of the sacraments in general you learned that Holy Orders is one of the sacraments of the living. With the reception of this sacrament, then, there is an increase of sanctifying grace. In other words, the individual receiving the sacrament of Holy Orders receives an increase of that supernatural life first received in Baptism.

Holy Orders is the sacrament through which men receive the power and grace to perform the sacred duties of bishops, priests, and deacons of the Church.

The priest also receives the right to sacramental grace in Holy Orders. This sacramental grace is intended to help him to carry out the purpose for which the sacrament was instituted. In the sacrament of Penance and Reconciliation, the sacramental grace bestowed helps the penitent to avoid sin in the future; in Confirmation the sacramental grace assists the person confirmed to live his faith loyally and profess it courageously. In Holy Orders the sacramental grace is a continuous series of actual helps or graces to assist the priest in carrying out the duties of his sacred priesthood.

In addition to this increase of sanctifying grace and to the special sacramental grace, a spiritual character is conferred on the priest. When you studied Baptism and Confirmation you learned that because these sacraments conferred a spiritual character they could be received only once. So too, in Holy Orders—once ordained, a young man remains a priest forever. Remember that spiritual mark sets him apart forever. Neither in time nor in eternity can that mark ever be erased.

In considering the effects of Holy Orders we also mentioned the special supernatural powers of the priest. *The chief supernatural powers of the priest are: to change bread and wine into the body and blood of Christ in the Holy Sacrifice of the Mass, and to forgive sins in the sacrament of Penance and Reconciliation.* Do you recall how Christ instituted the Holy Eucharist and then gave His Apostles the commission: "Do this in remembrance of Me"? By "this," Christ meant they were to do what He had just done. He had changed bread and wine into His body and blood.

This power was not to be exercised by His Apostles alone but was to be exercised in the Church by Jesus Christ through the ministry of His priests. Each time, then, that a priest offers the Holy Sacrifice of the Mass he acts in the name of Christ Himself, and does what Christ has commanded.

You recall how Christ in one of His visits after the Resurrection said to His Apostles: "Receive the Holy Spirit; whose sins you shall forgive, they are forgiven them; and whose sins you shall retain, they are retained." This power, too, was to be passed on and exercised by priests in the sacrament of Penance and Reconciliation.

We have studied some of the privileges and powers of the priest. Let us now consider briefly some of his obligations. In the first place a priest, a diocesan priest, owes obedience to his bishop.

**TERMS TO KNOW**

- ministry
- deacon
- seminary
- ordination
- breviary
- dispenser
- vocation
- qualifications
- diocesan clergy
- admonition
- celibacy

Celibacy is also required of a priest of the Latin rite. Celibacy means that the priest gives up his right to marry. This is required by the Latin Church and is of long standing. It is different in the Eastern rites.

In the Eastern rites deacons and priests who were married before ordination are allowed to remain with their wives. But unmarried men who become ordained may not marry.

St. Paul explains very well the wisdom of such a vow of celibacy. He says, "But I would have you to be without concern. He that is without a wife is concerned for the things that belong to the Lord: how he may please God. But he that is with a wife is concerned for the things of the world: how he may please his wife. And he is divided" (1 Cor. 7:32–33). Can you see now how this vow of celibacy is a help to the priest in fulfilling the obligation of giving his undivided service to his people?

The priest is obliged to pray the Divine Office each day from his breviary. It is part of the public worship of God by the Church.

### What Our Attitude Toward the Priest Should Be

What should be our attitude toward priests? The catechism tells us that *Catholics should show reverence and honor to the priest because he is the representative of Christ Himself and the dispenser of His mysteries.* This point was clearly emphasized in a little incident told about St. Francis of Assisi. One day when the saint was conversing with some of his brothers on the respect due to priests, he said, "If I should happen to meet on the way an angel and a priest walking together I would salute the priest in the first place and then the angel." Noticing the surprise of those who listened, he continued, "I would salute the priest first because he is the representative of Jesus Christ Himself, whereas the angel, great as he is, is only His servant."

## Summary

Holy Orders is the sacrament through which men receive the power and grace to perform the sacred duties of bishops, priests, and other lesser ministers of the Church. The effects of ordination to the priesthood are: (1) an increase of sanctifying grace; (2) sacramental grace through which the priest has God's constant help in his sacred ministry; (3) a character, lasting forever, which bestows a special participation in the priesthood of Christ and gives the priest special supernatural powers. The chief supernatural powers of the priest are: (1) to change bread and wine into the body and blood of Christ in the Holy Sacrifice of the Mass; (2) to forgive sins in the sacrament of Penance and Reconciliation.

Catholics should show reverence and honor to the priest. He is the representative of Christ Himself. In His name the priest teaches and administers the sacraments.

## ✓ FOR ME TO REVIEW

*Catechism Lesson*

**978. Q. What is the sacrament of Holy Orders?**

    A. Holy Orders is a sacrament by which bishops, priests, and other ministers of the Church are ordained and receive the power and grace to perform their sacred duties.

**992. Q. What is necessary to receive Holy Orders worthily?**

    A. To receive Holy Orders worthily it is necessary to be in the state of grace, to have the necessary knowledge, and a divine call to this sacred office.

**999. Q. Why should we show great respect to the priests and bishops of the Church?**

    A. We should show great respect to the priests and bishops of the Church: 1) Because they are the representatives of Christ upon earth, and 2) Because they administer the sacraments without which we cannot be saved.

**1000. Q. Should we do more than merely respect the ministers of God?**

    A. We should do more than merely respect the ministers of God. We should earnestly and frequently pray for them, that they may be enabled to perform the difficult and important duties of their holy state in a manner pleasing to God.

**1001. Q. Who can confer the sacrament of Holy Orders?**

    A. Bishops can confer the sacrament of Holy Orders.

*Questions and Exercises*

## Multiple Choice

1. The priest fulfills his office as mediator between God
   and man by:
   A. studying in the seminary.
   B. offering the Holy Sacrifice of the Mass.
   C. fasting and abstaining on the days appointed.

2. Christ gave the Apostles the power to forgive sins:
   A. on the evening of His resurrection.
   B. at the Last Supper.
   C. before His Ascension.
   D. on Pentecost.

3. Love, devotion, and obedience are due to our priests
   especially because:
   A. the priest is another Christ.
   B. he is good to us.
   C. he gives us the sacraments.
   D. he sacrifices much for us.

4. "Do this in commemoration of Me" marked:
   A. Christ's first ordination at the Last Supper.
   B. the giving of power to forgive sins.
   C. the end of the Old Testament.

5. The Divine Office which the priest recites daily is
   contained in the:
   A. Breviary.
   B. Missal.
   C. New Testament.
   D. Old Testament.

6.  A diocesan priest prepares for his work in the priesthood in:
    A. the cloister.
    B. the seminary.
    C. the monastery.

7.  The best way to show appreciation for the spiritual bene-
    fits we have received through Christ's priests is to:
    A. pray for them.
    B. support the parish.
    C. show reverence toward them.
    D. assist them in parish activities.

8.  Holy Orders was instituted by Christ:
    A. on Holy Thursday.
    B. on Calvary.
    C. on Easter Sunday.
    D. at the Ascension.

9.  Every boy who accepts Christ's invitation to the priesthood
    seeks in the first place:
    A. perfection for its own sake.
    B. the glory of God.
    C. the welfare of his fellow men.
    D. refuge from the spiritual dangers of the world.

**FOR ME TO DO**

1.  Ask a priest to tell you his vocation story. How did he come to know that God was calling him to the priesthood?

2.  Pray for priests all over the world, especially your pastor.

3.  Discuss how the life of grace is continued in the Church through the sacrament of Holy Orders.

4.  Ask the pastor or one of the parish priests to describe the ordination ceremony.

5.  Plan a visit to a diocesan seminary if possible.

6.  Write a composition on "What the Priest Means to Me."

## Prayer for Insight

*May the Lord Jesus touch our eyes, as he did those of the blind. Then we shall begin to see in visible things those which are invisible. May he open our eyes to gaze, not on present realities, but on the blessings to come. May he open the eyes of our heart to contemplate God in Spirit, through Jesus Christ the Lord, to whom belong power and glory through all eternity.*

*Amen.*

LESSON 22
# Matrimony

## What Matrimony Is

Marriage is the state of life to which most men and women are called. When Father Joseph Sarto first showed his mother his episcopal ring, she looked at her son, the future Pope St. Pius X, and smiled. "Yes, it is very pretty," she said, and added as she pointed to her own wedding ring, "but without this you could not have had that." She was emphasizing the fact that marriage is the foundation of society. According to God's plan men and women have a natural inclination to marry.

At Cana Christ turned water into wine. In the sacrament of Matrimony He turns human love into an image of His love for the Church.

Jesus turns water into wine at the marriage in Cana.

We can gain some idea of how Christ regarded marriage from the fact that He made Christian marriage a representation of His union with the Church. St. Paul says: "The husband is the head of the wife as Christ is the head of the Church. Therefore, as the Church is subject to Christ, so also let the wives be to their husbands in all things. Husbands, love your wives, as Christ also loved the Church, and delivered Himself up for it" (Eph. 5:22–29).

Since the sacrament of Matrimony represents the union of Christ with the Church, and because it imposes special obligations on man and wife, Christ has arranged that it also confer grace to fulfill these obligations.

*Matrimony is the sacrament by which a baptized man and a baptized woman bind themselves for life in a lawful marriage and receive the grace to discharge their duties.* A lawful marriage is one that is performed according to the laws of the Church. The sacramental grace gives the husband and wife strength and courage to fulfill their duties in marriage, to bear with each other's faults, to remain faithful to each other, and to bring up their children in the love and fear of God. Persons who are not baptized can be married, but they do not receive the sacrament of Matrimony.

> "Sacred Scripture begins with the creation of man and woman in the image and likeness of God and concludes with a vision of 'the wedding-feast of the Lamb.' Scripture speaks throughout of marriage and its 'mystery,' its institution and the meaning God has given it, its origin and its end, its various realizations throughout the history of salvation, the difficulties arising from sin and its renewal 'in the Lord' in the New Covenant of Christ and the Church."
>
> —*Catechism of the Catholic Church,* 1602

## The Duties of Matrimony

Matrimony brings with it many duties, but *the chief duties of husband and wife in the married state are to be faithful to each other, and to provide in every way for the welfare of the children God may give them.* It is a serious matter for two persons to enter a contract that they will be faithful to each other until death. Have you ever read the promises the couple make on their wedding day? They promise to take each other "for better, for worse, for richer, for poorer, in sickness and in health, till death do us part." Even if the persons change their feelings for each other, the promise still binds them.

Parents must provide for the material welfare of the children God may give them. They have the right and duty to feed, clothe, shelter, and to educate their children. These are God-given rights. The State may neither take away these rights nor interfere with them if they are properly exercised. Parents must also provide for the spiritual welfare of their children by bringing them up in the love and fear of God, and rearing them as good Christian citizens here and as future citizens of heaven. In the lives of the saints what Christian mother gives us a wonderful example of looking after the spiritual welfare of her son by praying for his conversion for thirty years? How were her prayers answered?

## Qualities of Christian Marriage

*The bond of the sacrament of Matrimony lasts until the death of husband or wife because Christ has said: "What therefore God has joined together, let no man put asunder."* God intended this, because it is so essential for the welfare both of the children and of the nation. But most importantly, it helps the two who made the promise. They receive special sacramental graces but they must also pray and receive the sacraments in order to carry out God's will. Sometimes people change or develop bad habits which make it difficult to keep their promise. God's grace is there for them if they ask for it.

One of the chief qualities of the sacrament of Matrimony is its unity. *By the unity of the sacrament of Matrimony is meant that the husband cannot during the life of his wife have another wife, nor the wife during the life of her husband have another husband.* What are Christ's works concerning this?

A true Christian marriage is a contract which cannot be broken. Marriage as a contract, or mutual agreement, differs from other contracts because it binds until the death of one of

The chief duties of husband and wife in the married state are to be faithful to each other, and to provide in every way for the welfare of the children God may give them.

the parties. No person who is married may attempt marriage with another person as long as the partner is alive. If he does, he commits a grave sin and lives in sin as long as he stays with that person. Even if the State permits divorce, it is still wrong for one who is validly married to marry someone else. This is true of non-Catholics as well as Catholics.

You read the phrase, "a true marriage." Do you understand what that means?

The Church has made certain regulations regarding the marriage of baptized persons. In order for the marriage to be lawful, the following conditions must be fulfilled:

1. The man and woman must have sufficient use of reason to know the nature and obligations of marriage.

2. Neither one may be validly married to another person.

3. Both must be free from all other impediments.

A person cannot be held responsible for something he does not understand. If he does not understand the nature of marriage and its obligations, he cannot contract a lawful marriage. If one has been truly married, the Church forbids him to marry another while his first partner is still living. Finally, the man and woman must be free from all other impediments that would keep the marriage from taking effect. Can you mention any of these obstacles that would prevent a couple from entering into a valid marriage even if they go through a marriage ceremony?

## Marriage Is Sacred

*Every true marriage between a baptized man and a baptized woman is a sacrament because Christ Himself raised every marriage of this kind to the dignity of a sacrament.* Even before the institution of the sacrament of Matrimony, marriage had always been considered sacred because of the dignity of its purpose.

What is the primary purpose of marriage? God's plan is that married people should be perfected in charity through their love for one another, they should bring children into the world, educate them and prepare them for heaven. Because Christ knew that marriage was important and that men and women were weak spiritually, He elevated marriage to the dignity of a sacrament. Unlike other sacraments, this one is administered by the

man and woman who are being married, and not by the priest who witnesses it. The bride administers it to the groom, and the groom administers it to the bride.

## Laws In General Governing Marriage

What are some of the specific Church laws regarding marriage? One law requires that a Catholic be married in the presence of his own parish priest (or a priest or deacon delegated by him) and before two witnesses. This is necessary even when there is question of a mixed marriage because this law governs the validity of marriage.

Another law says that first cousins or persons related more closely are not permitted to marry one another.

A third law states that a Catholic is forbidden to marry a non-Catholic. Sometimes, for serious reasons, the Church may permit such marriages, but she does so reluctantly. With her long years of experience the Church sees the danger to the faith of those concerned. The great number of mixed marriages constitutes a serious loss to the Catholic Church although in a few cases they may turn out well.

*The Catholic Church alone has the right to make laws regulating the marriages of baptized persons because the Church alone has authority over the sacraments and over sacred matters affecting baptized persons. Regarding the marriages of baptized persons, the State has the authority to make laws concerning their effects that are merely civil.* The State may make regulations concerning the age at which a person may marry, the property rights, and legal inheritance.

## Two Kinds of Preparation Are Required

### Remote Preparation

*To prepare for a holy and happy marriage, Catholics should: first, pray that God may direct their choice.* God is the third party to a marriage, and happiness in marriage, as in everything else, comes from fulfilling His law. You should pray often that God will enlighten you as to whom you should marry.

*Second, seek the advice of their parents and confessors.* Parents as well as priests have received special graces to instruct and guide. Ordinarily anyone who does not carefully weigh their advice is very foolish.

*Third, practice the virtues, especially chastity.* It is necessary at all times to practice virtue, and especially during the time before marriage when temptations may be very strong. Happi-

**TERMS TO KNOW**

- administered
- reluctantly
- constitute
- civil effects
- immediate
- specific
- validity
- remote

ness in marriage comes from fulfilling God's law.

*Fourth, frequently receive the sacraments of Penance and Reconciliation and Holy Eucharist.* Why is the Holy Eucharist called the holiest sacrament? Christ Himself has said, "If God be with you, who can be against you?" and St. Paul said, "I can do all things in Him who strengthens me." Truly the Bread of Life is the one sure way of living in constant union with Christ. What better way to prepare for the union of marriage?

At your parish, you may have seen announcements about pre-Cana classes. Do you know what they are? These meetings are very helpful for young people who are eager to prepare for a holy and happy marriage. What two kinds of preparation are we encouraged to make in receiving Holy Communion? There are also two kinds of preparations required before receiving the sacrament of Matrimony.

**Immediate Preparation**

The immediate preparation includes making arrangements with the bride's pastor, knowing the duties and responsibilities of the state, and receiving the sacrament of Penance and Reconciliation before the marriage. In the words of the catechism you may sum up the immediate preparation by saying that in order *to receive the sacrament of Matrimony worthily it is necessary to be in the state of grace, to know the duties of married life, and to obey the marriage laws of the Church.*

## Prayer

*Saint Joseph, father and guardian of virgins, into whose faithful keeping were entrusted Innocence itself, Christ Jesus, and Mary, the Virgin of virgins, I pray and beseech thee through Jesus and Mary, those pledges so dear to thee, to keep me from all uncleanness, and to grant that my mind may be untainted, my heart pure and my body chaste; help me always to serve Jesus and Mary in perfect chastity. Amen.*

*"Marriage and the family are the first community called to announce the Gospel to the human person during growth and to bring him or her ... to full human and Christian maturity."*

—*Pope St. John Paul II*

Do you remember any of these laws which the Church has made? One refers to the persons who must be present when a Catholic marries. *The laws of the Church require a Catholic to be married in the presence of the parish priest, or the bishop of the diocese, or a priest delegated by either of them, and before two witnesses.* Therefore, if a Catholic attempts to marry a Catholic or even a non-Catholic before a minister or a justice of the peace, such a marriage is not valid. Of course, two non-Catholics may contract a valid marriage when the ceremony is performed by a minister or a judge, but a Catholic never can, although the State may consider him legally married. Instead he is guilty of grave sin.

## The Effects of the Sacrament

*The chief effects of the sacrament of Matrimony are: first, an increase of sanctifying grace; second, the special help of God for husband and wife to love each other faithfully, to bear with each other's faults, and to bring up their children properly.* What is this special help of God called? Does a person receive it only on his wedding day? There may be many occasions when this sacramental grace will be needed by the married couple. When a difference arises between them, it may quickly disappear if a silent prayer is said to ask God's help. Strength to put up with some annoying fault may come in answer to another appeal. And in these days when the devil is using every means possible to tempt people to sin, it is the special help, to which God gave the couple the right on their wedding day, that can enable them to overcome the temptations.

## Christ's Blessing on the Marriage

*Catholics can best obtain God's blessing for their marriage by being married at a Nuptial Mass and by receiving Holy Communion devoutly.* A Nuptial Mass is one which has special prayers to beg God's blessing on the married couple. As marriage is not something to be entered into lightly, everything should be arranged in such a way that all the grace possible may be obtained. Because marriage is so holy, everything about it and any celebration that follows should be characterized by Christian dignity, modesty, and good taste. And surely the man and woman who begin married life with God's blessing can rest assured that divine assistance will accompany them through life.

## Summary

Matrimony is the sacrament by which a baptized man and a baptized woman bind themselves for life in a lawful marriage. In this sacrament they receive the grace to discharge their duties. The chief duty of husband and wife is to be faithful to each other, and to provide in every way for the welfare of the children God may give them.

The bond of the sacrament of Matrimony lasts until the death of husband or wife. Christ said: "What therefore God has joined together, let no man put asunder." A husband, during the life of his wife, cannot have another wife, nor can a wife during the life of her husband have another husband.

To receive the sacrament of Matrimony worthily it is necessary to be in the state of grace, to know the duties of married life, and to obey the marriage laws of the Church. The sacrament of Matrimony gives to those receiving it: (1) an increase of sanctifying grace; (2) the special help of God for husband and wife to love each other faithfully, to bear with each other's faults, and to bring up their children properly.

 **FOR ME TO REVIEW**

*Catechism Lesson*

**1005. Q. What is the sacrament of Matrimony?**

   A. The sacrament of Matrimony is the sacrament which unites a Christian man and woman in lawful marriage.

**1010. Q. What are the chief ends of the sacrament of Matrimony?**

   A. The chief ends of the sacrament of Matrimony are: 1) To enable the husband and wife to aid each other in securing the salvation of their souls; 2) To propagate or keep up the existence of the human race by bringing children into the world to serve God; 3) To prevent sins against the holy virtue of purity by faithfully obeying the laws of the marriage state.

**1023. Q. Can the bond of Christian marriage be dissolved by any human power?**

   A. The bond of Christian marriage cannot be dissolved by any human power.

**1034. Q. Who has the right to make laws concerning the sacrament of marriage?**

   A. The Church alone has the right to make laws concerning the sacrament of marriage, though the state also has the right to make laws concerning the civil effects of the marriage contract.

**1031. Q.** To receive the sacrament of Matrimony worthily is it necessary to be in the state of grace?

**A.** To receive the sacrament of Matrimony worthily it is necessary to be in the state of grace, and it is necessary also to comply with the laws of the Church.

**1028. Q.** Which are the effects of the sacrament of Matrimony?

**A.** The effects of the sacrament of Matrimony are: 1st, To sanctify the love of husband and wife; 2nd, To give them grace to bear with each other's weaknesses; 3rd, To enable them to bring up their children in the fear and love of God.

**1046. Q.** When are motives for marriage worthy?

**A.** Motives for marriage are worthy when persons enter it for the sake of doing God's will and fulfilling the end for which He instituted the sacrament. Whatever is opposed to the true object of the sacrament and the sanctification of the husband and wife must be an unworthy motive.

**1047. Q.** How should Christians prepare for a holy and happy marriage?

**A.** Christians should prepare for a holy and happy marriage by receiving the sacraments of Penance and Reconciliation and Holy Eucharist; by begging God to grant them a pure intention and to direct their choice; and by seeking the advice of their parents and the blessing of their pastors.

*Questions and Exercises*

## Part 1: Completion

1.  Parents who have different_____beliefs find it hard to agree regarding the training of their children.

2.  The Church obliges her children to be married in the presence of____(a)____ and____(b)____.

3.  _____is the state of life to which most men and women are called.

4.  The special blessing given for the woman being married is given only during a_____.

5.  Marriage has always been considered_____because of the dignity of its purpose.

6.  A man and woman may, with permission of the bishop, separate and obtain a civil divorce, but neither one may again_____during the lifetime of the other.

7.  The right and the duty to feed, clothe, shelter, and educate their children are given to____(a)____ by____(b)____.

8.  The sacrament of Matrimony is administered by the_____.

9.  Marriage is both a____(a)____ and a____(b)____.

10. Anyone contemplating marriage should seek the advice of his____(a)____ and____(b)____.

## Part 2: True or False

1.  Parents are obliged to take care only of the spiritual welfare of their children.

2.  God instituted marriage in the Garden of Eden.

3.  Christ elevated marriage to the dignity of a sacrament.

4.  A civil divorce has no effect on the bond of the sacrament of Matrimony.

5.  The greater number of mixed marriages constitute a loss to the Catholic Church.

6.  The State has no authority to make laws concerning marriage.

7.  The sacramental grace of Matrimony benefits only the married couple.

8.  The Catholic Church alone has the right to make laws concerning the sacrament of Matrimony.

9.  Catholics may be married during Lent or Advent.

10. The priest is the ordinary minister for the sacrament of Matrimony.

## ☑ FOR ME TO DO

1.  In her talk on the sacrament of Matrimony Jane said, "Marriage is for life, or it is no marriage at all." Can you give one proof to back up her statement?

2.  After a few years of married life Barbara and George separated and, with the bishop's consent, obtained a civil divorce. Are they free to marry again? Why or why not?

3.  Bob and Jean are planning a secret marriage. They want to surprise everyone. Bob is certain their pastor will "bless the marriage" afterward. What advice would you give the couple?

4.  Ray tries to be very "up-to-date" in his opinions. He believes that the Church is "old-fashioned" with regard to divorce and should leave all marriage regulations to the State. What two questions in this lesson should prove to him that he is incorrect in his ideas?

5.  Perhaps your vocation later on will be to the married state. What four things can you be doing now to prepare for a holy and happy marriage?

# 4 | Sanctification Through Sacramentals and Prayer

# CHAPTER 12

# Obtaining Spiritual and Temporal Favors from God

*In our introduction to the study of the sacraments, we called attention to the fact that the sacramentals and prayer were also means of grace given us by God. Let us here come to a better knowledge and appreciation of them. We might say that, in relation to the safety of our souls, they are what good safety habits are in relation to the protection of our physical life and bodily welfare.*

*In the previous units we saw that the sacraments were a source of divine life. The sacramentals, which we shall now consider, are called by this name because they resemble the sacraments in some ways. The sacramentals form an outer circle around the sacraments helping us to obtain actual grace from God.*

*Another means of grace and one of the chief acts of a Christian is prayer. It is one of the most important means of obtaining grace. Prayer is so important in our life that we cannot be saved without it. Both the sacramentals and prayer aid in our sanctification—helping us to become more like Christ.*

LESSON 23

# Sacramentals

You have learned that *sacramentals are holy things or actions of which the Church makes use to obtain for us from God, through her intercession, spiritual and temporal favors*. The sacramentals encourage good thoughts and stir up our devotion. For example, when you gaze at a crucifix, it brings to mind the thought of Christ. The sight of the wounds in His hands, feet, and side helps to make you sorry for your sins. The thought of His patient acceptance of sufferings inspires you to endure your trials and difficulties patiently. Do you see the help you obtain through the devout use of this sacramental?

## Sacramentals Obtain Favors from God in Two Ways

Perhaps you wonder how the sacramentals obtain favors from God. *The sacramentals obtain favors from God through the prayers of the Church offered for those who make use of them, and through the devotion they inspire.*

### Through the Prayers of the Church Offered for Those Who Use Them

Let us take, for example, a blessed medal which is a sacramental. When that medal was blessed, the priest prayed in the name of the Church that God would make it holy and sanctify those who would use it. A sacramental is, therefore, a twofold prayer. You

"O Mary, conceived without sin, pray for us who have recourse to thee."

pray when you use the rosary. While you use it, the whole Mystical Body of Christ, the Church, adds its prayers to yours. This applies to all the other sacramentals as well. The use of every sacramental is accompanied by prayer. In this way you dispose yourself to receive the favors that come to you from their use.

### Through the Devotion They Inspire

The sacramentals help us by making us more devout.

Recall the example of the crucifix. What help did you obtain from looking at the image of your Crucified Lord? You were inspired to feel sorrow for your sins which caused His sufferings and you resolved to bear patiently the difficulties you experience in your life. Christ set you the example of patience in sufferings. You want to imitate Him and thus become more like Him.

## Sacramentals Bestow Many Benefits

The sacramentals assist us in numerous ways.

*The chief benefits obtained by the use of the sacramentals are: first, actual graces; second, the forgiveness of venial sins; third, the remission of temporal punishment; fourth, health of body and material blessings; fifth, protection from evil spirits.*

### Actual Graces

You recall that *actual grace is a supernatural help of God which enlightens our minds and strengthens our will to do good and avoid evil.* Let us consider an example. On Ash Wednesday the priest places blessed ashes on the forehead and says, "Remember man that thou art dust and into dust thou shalt return." This ceremony is intended to make us think of death, judgment, heaven, and hell. Through the use of this sacramental a person who has been away from the sacraments for years may be inspired to return to his God.

Here is a story of a man who received an actual grace through the use of a sacramental. Alphonsus Ratisbonne, an Alsatian

Jew, was a commercial traveler. He had occasion to go to Rome on business. While there he visited a friend whom he had known since boyhood. This friend was engaged in a literary career and had become a Catholic. He gave Alphonsus a medal of our Lady as a keepsake. Alphonsus laughed at it, but kept the medal and wore it constantly on his person.

The conversion of St. Paul, depicted in this painting by Caravaggio, gave him a strong appreciation for the gift of faith.

During his stay in Rome he visited many places of interest, among them the church of St. Andrea. While there he was suddenly surrounded by a brilliant light, and beheld before him a figure resplendent with glory. This figure resembled the image of our Lady on the medal given him by his friend. The Lady smiled kindly and beckoned him to approach her. Alphonsus, overwhelmed with awe and astonishment, fell upon his knees. Tears rolled down his cheeks.

After the apparition had vanished, he remained a long time on his knees absorbed in prayer. Later he was baptized in Rome and became a zealous missionary. This wonderful conversion of a Jew reminds one of the conversion of Saul, the persecutor of the early Christians.

### The Forgiveness of Venial Sins; the Remission of Temporal Punishment

A blessed crucifix, or a picture of the crucifixion, as mentioned before, is a sacramental. If one looks at Christ and realizes the terrible sufferings our Lord endured for the sins of men, he may be moved to have real sorrow for his own sins. The sorrow for sin aroused by a sacramental can, thus, inspire the individual to make an act of contrition and obtain from God "the forgiveness of venial sins" and "the remission of temporal punishment." An act of sorrow or contrition, even though it be imperfect, remits venial sin.

### Health of Body and Material Blessings

Sacramentals may also obtain health of body as well as material blessings. These may come for instance as the result of the blessing for the sick given to sick people in their homes or in hospitals, or they may come from the blessing of a home by the priest. Were you ever present when the priest gave the blessing for the sick to any member of your family? What do you recall concerning the experience? Perhaps you were the one who received the blessing.

Can you tell us about it? Was your home ever blessed by a priest? What did the priest say on this occasion? What did he do? One of your parish priests might explain other blessings you can receive.

On February 3, the feast of St. Blaise, we go to church to get our throats blessed. As the priest is giving us the blessing of St. Blaise, he prays that God will deliver us from diseases of the throat. Do you know the origin of this ceremony?

St. Blaise was the bishop of Sebaste in Asia Minor in the early part of the fourth century. He was a physician before he became a priest. The story goes that one day a woman came to him with her boy who was choking. A fish bone had lodged in his throat. His life was in danger. She begged the bishop to do something for her child. St. Blaise lighted two candles and held them crosswise under the boys chin. At the same time he recited some prayers and then gave the boy his blessing. Almost immediately the fish bone loosened and was easily removed.

St. Blaise is the patron saint of choking, among other things, and is invoked for protection against ailments of the throat.

**Protection from Evil Spirits**

We know that the devil flees at the sign of the cross and the use of holy water. You often hear the expression, "He hates it like the devil hates holy water." The oft-repeated phrase reveals the purpose in using holy water, namely, to drive away the devil and his temptations. Good Catholics use holy water at home as well as in church.

## Sacramentals Are of Various Kinds

*The chief kinds of sacramentals are: first, blessings given by priests and bishops; second, exorcisms against evil spirits; third, blessed objects of devotion*. The first two are holy actions; the third, blessed objects of devotion, are holy things.

Some of the blessings given either by priests or by bishops are:

a) the blessings of churches

b) the blessings of sacred vessels and vestments

c) the blessings of the sick, of houses, of crops, of palms, of ashes, of holy water

## Exorcism Against Evil Spirits

Exorcism consists in commanding the devil to depart, in the name of Christ, from possessed persons or things. Christ Himself cast out many evil spirits. He also gave His Apostles power and authority over all the devils (Lk. 9:1) and declared that "in My name they shall cast out devils" (Mk. 16:17).

## Sacramentals Should Be Used With Faith and Devotion

You will recall that *the blessed objects of devotion most used by Catholics are: holy water, candles, ashes, palms, crucifixes, medals, rosaries, scapulars, and images of our Lord, the Blessed Virgin, and the saints.* How many different kinds of medals have you seen? How many different kinds of scapulars?

*We should make use of the sacramentals with faith and devotion, and never make them objects of superstition.* The effect of the sacramentals depends upon the faith and devotion of the individual who uses them. If we use them with faith and devotion we share in the prayers and blessings of the entire Church, in whose name the priest consecrates and blesses them.

> "Holy Mother Church has, moreover, instituted sacramentals. These are sacred signs which bear a resemblance to the sacraments. They signify effects, particularly of a spiritual nature, which are obtained through the intercession of the Church. By them men are disposed to receive the chief effect of the sacraments, and various occasions in life are rendered holy."
>
> —Catechism of the Catholic Church, 1667

Many people, as they grow older, forget about the sacramentals and so they lose countless graces that could easily be obtained through their use.

We should never make sacramentals objects of superstition, for example as good luck charms. Nor should we believe they produce effects apart from the prayer of the Church and from the devotion they inspire. Some people are careless about attending Sunday Mass and receiving the sacraments, but would never be without a medal or blessed palm. Could this indicate a superstitious attitude?

## Summary

Sacramentals are holy things or actions which the Church blesses and asks us to use to obtain spiritual and temporal favors. The sacramentals obtain favors from God through the prayers of the Church offered for those who make use of them and through the devotion they inspire. The chief benefits obtained by the use of the sacramentals are: (1) actual graces; (2) the forgiveness of venial sins; (3) the remission of temporal punishment; (4) health of body and material blessings; (5) protection from evil spirits.

The chief kinds of sacramentals are: (1) blessings given by priests and bishops; (2) exorcisms against evil spirits; (3) blessed objects of devotion. The blessed objects of devotion most used by Catholics are: holy water, candles, ashes, palms, crucifixes, images of our Lord, the Blessed Virgin and the saints, medals, rosaries, and scapulars. We should use the sacramentals with faith and devotion, and never make them objects of superstition.

**FOR ME TO REVIEW**

*Catechism Lesson*

**1052. Q.  What is a sacramental?**

   A.  A sacramental is anything set apart or blessed by the Church to excite good thoughts and to increase devotion, and through these movements of the heart to remit venial sin.

**1054. Q.  Do the sacramentals of themselves remit venial sins?**

   A.  The sacramentals of themselves do not remit venial sins, but they move us to truer devotion, to greater love for God and greater sorrow for our sins, and this devotion, love and sorrow bring us grace, and the grace remits venial sins.

**1063. Q.  Which is the chief sacramental used in the Church?**

   A.  The chief sacramental used in the Church is the Sign of the Cross.

**1074. Q.  Are there other sacramentals besides the Sign of the Cross and holy water?**

   A.  Beside the Sign of the Cross and holy water there are many other sacramentals, such as blessed candles, ashes, palms, crucifixes, images of the Blessed Virgin and of the saints, rosaries, and scapulars.

**1060. Q.  How may persons sin in using sacramentals?**

   A.  Persons may sin in using sacramentals by using them in a way or for a purpose prohibited by the Church; also by believing that the use of sacramentals will save us in spite of our sinful lives. We must remember that sacramentals can aid us only through the blessing the Church gives them and through the good dispositions they excite in us. They have, therefore, no power in themselves, and to put too much confidence in their use leads to superstition.

*Questions and Exercises*

## Part 1: True or False

1. Our Lord gave His Apostles power over the devils.

2. One who wears a scapular can be certain that he will not be drowned.

3. Through the use of the sacramentals we obtain the forgiveness of mortal sins.

4. The sacramentals bring to their users the benefit of the Church's prayers.

5. The use of medals and scapulars is intended only for children or uneducated persons.

6. The sacramentals are intended principally to give us spiritual blessings.

7. The blessing given by the priest is a sacramental.

8. The sacramentals are minor sacraments.

## **Part 2**: Matching

**COLUMN A**

1. How the sacramentals obtain favors from God

2. The chief kinds of sacramental

3. Blessed objects of devotion that are sacramental

4. The chief benefits obtained by the use of sacramental

5. Sacramentals

6. The manner in which we should use sacramental

**COLUMN B**

A. Holy water, candles, ashes, palms, crucifixes, medals, rosaries, scapulars, and images of our Lord, the Blessed Virgin, and the saints

B. With faith and devotion and never as an object of superstition

C. Through the prayers the Church offers for those who make use of them and through the devotion they inspire

D. Holy things or actions which the Church uses to obtain for us from God, through her intercession, spiritual and temporal favors

E. Actual graces, forgiveness of venial sins, remission of temporal punishment, health of body and material blessings

F. Blessings given by priests and bishops, exorcisms against evil spirits, blessed objects of devotion

## Part 3: Problems and Exercises

1.  Edwin has his throat blessed on February 3, the feast of St. Blaise. A week later he is absent from school with a very sore throat. Did the blessing fail to work?

2.  Have scapulars, medals, badges, and other articles of devotion any spiritual power in themselves? What gives them their power? Spiritually, is there any difference between a bronze medal of the Immaculate Conception, a silver one, and a gold one? Explain your answer.

3.  George, a basketball player at St. Martha's, fears he is going to be late for the game. He "steps on the gas," goes through a couple of red lights, passes the car ahead, and finally ends up in a serious smashup, gravely injuring himself, and killing all the people in the other car. He remarked to his sister that he counted on better luck because he had a medal of St. Christopher in the car. Did St. Christopher fail George? Explain your answer.

# CHAPTER 13
## Prayer Is Another Means of Obtaining God's Grace

LESSON 24

# Prayer

### What Prayer Is

You know what prayer is. It is part of your everyday living. For the purpose of review let us recall the answer in the catechism. *Prayer is the lifting up of our minds and hearts to God.*

When we engage in meaningful conversation with someone, we forget everything else. This is what we should do when we talk with God, that is, when we pray. It is the great privilege of angels and men to speak to God in prayer. Man alone of all God's visible creatures enjoys this privilege. St. John Chrysostom says that to be permitted to talk with his Creator and hold familiar conversation with Him, is the greatest honor and privilege mortal man can enjoy.

You know the story of St. John Vianney and the farm laborer who often remained for hours kneeling before the tabernacle. The man's lips never moved, but his eyes remained fixed on the tabernacle. The saint asked him what he said to God during the long visits. The farm hand replied, "I say nothing. I look at Him and He looks at me." The man just lifted up his heart and mind to God. He was really praying.

Prayer is not the difficult task some believe it to be. People who love one another do not need words to express their love. Heart speaks to heart.

## Prayer Has Various Purposes

Prayer is a means of fulfilling our obligations to God. *We pray: first, to adore God, expressing to Him our love and loyalty; second, to thank Him for His favors; third, to obtain from Him the pardon of our sins and the remission of their punishment; fourth, to ask for graces and blessings for ourselves and others.*

The first commandment tells us we are obliged to adore God. In the explanation of that commandment we learned that we adore God by prayer. The blessed in heaven are continually

occupied in the prayer of adoration. It is the most perfect kind of prayer. It gives the greatest glory to God. In this kind of prayer we most truly fulfill our obligation to honor, worship, and adore God. It is necessary only that we lift up our mind and heart to God and say "My God, I adore Thee." When we assist at the Holy Sacrifice of the Mass, we offer adoration in the most perfect way.

The second purpose for which we pray is to offer thanks. It is just common courtesy to thank our fellow man for favors received. How much more should we thank God for His favors? He is our first and greatest Benefactor. Do you remember what our Lord said after He cured the ten lepers and only one returned to give thanks? If you have forgotten the story, look it up in the New Testament. Why not resolve to say more "thank you" prayers to God?

*"There is no danger if our prayer is without words or reflection because the good success of prayer depends neither on words nor on study. It depends upon the simple raising of our minds to God, and the more simple and stripped of feeling it is, the surer it is."*

*—St. Jane Frances de Chantal*

Prayer can be said to offer satisfaction to an offended God. We have all sinned and need to implore God's mercy and pardon. Sin makes us understand better the power and goodness of God. How is it possible that we, miserable creatures, could offend almighty God! Let us often repeat the prayer of the publican, "O Lord, be merciful to me a sinner."

Lastly, our needs are many and various. We can ask for graces to perform supernatural deeds with which to merit life eternal. We also need temporal favors such as food, clothing, success in our undertakings. So we pray to our loving Father and ask Him for those graces and blessings needed by ourselves and others.

**The Purpose of Prayer**

- Thanksgiving
- Adoration
- Supplication
- Contrition

## Prayer Requires Certain Dispositions on Our Part

There is a great difference between the mere recitation of prayers with our lips and the still quiet prayer of the heart. Someone said: "Our prayers can be gold or silver or straw." What did he mean? That the effectiveness of our prayer depends upon its possessing certain qualities. *We pray: first, with attention; second, with a conviction of our own helplessness and our dependence upon God; third, with a great desire for the graces we beg of Him; fourth, with loving trust in His goodness; fifth, with perseverance.*

### We Should Pray With Attention

The required attention consists in fixing our minds and hearts on what we are doing and what we are saying when we pray. It requires us to remember that we are in the presence of God, and that we are speaking to Him. Recall the picture you have seen so often of our Lord's agony in the Garden of Olives. Gaze upon the countenance of our loving Saviour. How does He pray? Jesus is thinking only of God His Father. His mind, heart, and entire body are united to Him in prayer. Let us learn from Him how to pray with attention.

### We Should Pray With a Conviction of Our Own Helplessness and Our Dependence Upon God

Prayer is in itself an act of humility, for by it we acknowledge our dependence upon the Lord of heaven and earth. When we pray we act as helpless beggars knocking at the door of our Father's house, asking for His help in our miseries. If we humble ourselves when we ask another for help, why should we not humble ourselves when we pray to our Creator, our Lord, and our God? Do you remember the parable about the Pharisee and the publican who went to the Temple to pray? The proud Pharisee found no favor with God. The humble publican was very pleasing in His sight. Reread the story in Luke 18:9–14.

## We Should Pray With a Great Desire for the Graces We Beg of Him

Let us learn more from Christ's prayer in the Garden. Our Lord had a human nature like ours. He was troubled at the thought of the sufferings He was to endure on the cross. He begged His Father, if it were possible, to let the chalice of suffering pass from Him. Jesus prayed most fervently for what He wished. He did not speak to His heavenly Father in a halfhearted manner. He repeated the same prayer three times. Each time He begged His Father with great earnestness for the favor He asked.

When you want something very badly, you do not ask in a halfhearted way. You are not satisfied with a single request for what you want. No, you repeat that request over and over again especially if it is important. Finally, you beg for it as if your whole happiness depended upon your obtaining it. Why not do this in your prayers to God? Were it not for the persevering prayers of Monica, Augustine's words "You have made us for Yourself, O God, and our hearts are restless till they rest in Thee," might never have been spoken.

St. Augustine and his mother St. Monica

## We Should Pray With Loving Trust in His Goodness

Our Lord prayed with confidence. In the Garden we hear His words: "Not as I will but as Thou wilt." He trusted that His Father would remove the chalice of suffering. However, He understood perfectly, that His Father's decision in the matter would be for the best. We, too, must pray like Him; we must trust in the goodness of God.

### We Should Pray With Perseverance

There is nothing which our blessed Lord insists on more than perseverance in prayer. Parable after parable in the New Testament shows that having our petitions answered depends upon our perseverance in asking.

Do you know the story of the woman who asked Christ to cure her daughter who was grievously troubled by a devil? At first He seemed to take no notice of her. She did not give way to discouragement but continued to ask with humility and perseverance until the Saviour's heart could resist no longer. Her humility, her confidence, her perseverance made a powerful impression on our Lord. Turning to her, He said: "O woman, great is thy faith! Let it be done to thee as thou wilt." Her daughter was cured from that hour (Mt. 15:28).

When God delays granting what we ask, He wants us to continue to pray with confidence and patience. In His own good time He will hear us and either grant our request or give us something better.

### Our Prayer Should Be All-Inclusive

Holy Scripture is filled with quotations which show us what we should pray for. Here is one quotation: "Pray for one another that you may be saved. For the unceasing prayer of a just man is of great avail" (James 5:16). Can you find others? As good Christians we should pray for everyone, for the living and for the dead. The catechism expressed it this way. Remember? *We should pray especially for ourselves, for our parents, relatives, friends, and enemies, for sinners, for the souls in purgatory, for the pope, bishops, and priests of the Church, and for the officials of our country.* Should we include the officials of all countries? Even our enemies? Of course.

## Prayer Is Very Powerful

*We know that God always hears our prayers if we pray properly because our Lord has promised: "If you ask the Father anything in My name, He will give it to you."* When you recite the Act of Faith you mention certain things that you believe. You end the prayer by telling why you believe them, "because Thou hast revealed them, who canst neither deceive nor be deceived." In the Act of Hope you list the motives of hope, "relying on Thy almighty power and infinite mercy and promises." God is faithful in keeping His promises. We can trust Him as we can trust no other person. But we must pray in our Lord's name. We must pray as He prayed in the Garden, submissive to His Father's will.

God has promised to grant us the things which we ask in prayer, if they contribute to His honor and glory and to our salvation. But He has not promised to give them to us at the time, or in the manner or measure we ask for them. This might not always be best for us.

The favor we ask may not be good for us. Being our kind and loving Father, God may see fit to refuse it, but He always rewards our prayers. Sometimes we do not obtain what we pray

> *"Mental prayer is nothing else but being on terms of friendship with God, frequently conversing in secret with Him."*
>
> —*St. Teresa of Avila*

for because we do not pray properly. The catechism says: *We do not always obtain what we pray for, either because we have not prayed properly or because God sees that what we are asking would not be for our good.*

As for praying properly, how often we kneel down to pray with every intention of praying well, but no sooner than we start we find our minds wandering? It is hard to keep our thoughts free from such distractions as our work, our play, our friends, our plans. When we become aware of the fact that our thoughts have wandered and try to bring them back, God is pleased with our prayers. *Distractions in our prayers are not displeasing to God, unless they are willful.* When are distractions willful?

### The Two Kinds of Prayer

*There are two kinds of prayer: mental prayer and vocal prayer.* The first kind, *mental prayer, is that prayer by which we unite our hearts with God while thinking of His holy truths.* The second kind, *vocal prayer, is that prayer which comes from the mind and heart and is spoken by the lips.*

It is not necessary that we have a prayer book or rosary in our hands when we pray. *We may use our own words in praying to God, and it is well to do so often.* God is our Father, our Friend, our greatest Benefactor. He is pleased when we talk to Him just as we do to our father, our mother, our friends. What would you think if a friend came to visit you and everything he said came from a book? God feels the same way as you do. The next time you visit our Lord in the Blessed Sacrament try to pray to Him in your own words, for He is your friend.

Mental prayer or meditation is practiced daily by priests, religious, and any number of good lay persons who desire to become more perfect. There is nothing difficult about this kind of prayer. If vocal prayer is said very slowly with thoughtful pauses, it can be mental prayer. Do you want to try it? Suppose you begin with the "Our Father," the most perfect prayer. Take it slowly, very slowly; one word, one phrase, at a time, thinking of the meaning of the words in each phrase. You will be surprised how easy it is to practice mental prayer.

Vocal prayer makes it possible for us to say prayers in common. Prayer in common means that a group prays together as one, such as a family saying night prayers or the rosary together. Is the family rosary said daily in your home? Did you ever hear of the famous priest whose main work was getting people to say the Family Rosary daily in their homes? His favorite quotation was: "The family that prays together, stays together." What can you do about starting or continuing this practice of the daily Family Rosary?

### There Are Prayers Every Catholic Should Know by Heart

There are many beautiful prayers. You most likely have come across some of them in your prayer book. If you use a missal, you know the beauty of the prayers said by the priest during the Holy Sacrifice of the Mass. Nobody expects you to know these prayers by heart. There are some, however, that every Catholic should know from memory. *The prayers that every Catholic should know by heart are: the Our Father, the Hail Mary, the Apostles' Creed, the Confiteor, the Glory be to the Father, and the acts of faith, hope, charity, and contrition.* These are very important prayers. Maybe we could call them fundamental prayers and compare them in importance with fundamentals in arithmetic.

*We usually begin and end our prayers with the sign of the cross.* It provides as it were, a setting for the prayers we are about to say. It is also a fitting close to our prayers. Let us be very careful to make the sign of the cross with devotion and reverence. Be sure you say all the words. Do not slide over any of them. Examine yourself on this point. The custom of making the sign of the cross dates back to the earliest days of the Church. Catholics were able to recognize one another by the use of this sign. It is an act of faith. *We make the sign of the cross to express two important mysteries of the Christian religion, the Blessed Trinity and the Redemption.* By this sign we openly profess our faith in three divine Persons in one God. We call this truth the mystery of the Blessed Trinity. We also profess our belief that Christ died to redeem us and to reopen for us the gates of heaven. This mystery is called the Redemption.

Let us examine the words contained in the sign of the cross and see how these mysteries are expressed by this sign. *When we say "in the name," we express the truth that there is only one God; when we say "of the Father, and of the Son, and of the Holy Spirit," we express the truth that there are three distinct Persons in God; and when we make the form of the cross on ourselves, we express the truth that the Son of God, made man, redeemed us by His death on the cross.*

## Summary

Prayer is the lifting up of our minds and hearts to God. We pray: (1) to adore God, expressing to Him our love and loyalty; (2) to thank Him for His favors; (3) to obtain from Him the pardon of our sins and the remission of their punishment; (4) to ask for graces for ourselves and for others.

We should pray: (1) with attention; (2) with a conviction of our own helplessness and our dependence upon God; (3) with a great desire for the graces we beg of Him; (4) with loving trust in His goodness; (5) with perseverance.

There are two kinds of prayer: mental prayer and vocal prayer. Mental prayer is that prayer by which we unite our hearts with God while thinking of His holy truths. Vocal prayer is that prayer which comes from the mind and heart and is spoken by the lips. We may use our own words in praying to God; and it is well to do so often. The prayers that every Catholic should know by heart are: the Our Father, and the Hail Mary, the Apostles' Creed, the Glory Be to the Father, the Confiteor, and the acts of faith, hope, charity, and contrition.

We usually begin and end our prayers with the sign of the cross. We make the sign of the cross to express two important mysteries of the Christian religion, the Blessed Trinity and the Redemption.

 **FOR ME TO REVIEW**

*Catechism Lesson*

**1099. Q. What is prayer?**

    A. Prayer is the lifting up of our minds and hearts to God, to adore Him, to thank Him for His benefits, to ask His forgiveness, and to beg of Him all the graces we need whether for soul or body.

**1100. Q. How many kinds of prayer are there?**

    A. There are two kinds of prayer: 1) Mental prayer, called meditation, in which we spend the time thinking of God or of one or more of the truths He has revealed, that by these thoughts we may be persuaded to lead holier lives; 2) vocal prayer, in which we express these pious thoughts in words.

**1104. Q. Is prayer necessary to salvation?**

    A. Prayer is necessary to salvation, and without it no one having the use of reason can be saved.

**1106. Q. How should we pray?**

A. We should pray: 1st, With attention; 2nd, With a sense of our own helplessness and dependence upon God; 3rd, With a great desire for the graces we beg of God; 4th, With trust in God's goodness; 5th, With perseverance.

**1109. Q. What should we do that we may pray well?**

A. That we may pray well we should make a preparation before prayer: 1) By calling to mind the dignity of God, to whom we are about to speak, and our own unworthiness to appear in His presence; 2) by fixing upon the precise grace or blessing for which we intend to ask; 3) by remembering God's power and willingness to give if we truly need and earnestly, humbly, and confidently ask.

**1112. Q. Which are the prayers most recommended to us?**

A. The prayers most recommended to us are the Lord's Prayer, the Hail Mary, the Apostles' Creed, the Confiteor, and the Acts of Faith, Hope, Love, and Contrition.

**1115. Q. Do, then, the distractions which we often have at prayer deprive our prayers of all merit?**

A. The distractions which we often have at prayer do not deprive our prayers of all merit, because they are not willful when we try to keep them away, for God rewards our good intentions and the efforts we make to pray well.

**1116. Q. What, then, is a distraction?**

A. A distraction is any thought that, during prayer, enters our mind to turn our thoughts and hearts from God and from the sacred duty we are performing.

**1117. Q. What are the fruits of prayer?**

A. The fruits of prayer are: It strengthens our faith, nourishes our hope, increases our love for God, keeps us humble, merits grace and atones for sin.

**1118. Q. Why should we pray when God knows our needs?**

A. We pray not to remind God or tell Him of what we need, but to acknowledge that He is the Supreme Giver, to adore and worship Him by showing our entire dependence upon Him for every gift to soul or body.

**1066. Q. Why do we make the sign of the cross?**

A. We make the sign of the cross to show that we are Christians and to profess our belief in the chief mysteries of our religion.

**1067. Q. How is the sign of the cross a profession of faith in the chief mysteries of our religion?**

A. The sign of the cross is a profession of faith in the chief mysteries of our religion because it expresses the mysteries of the Unity and Trinity of God and of the Incarnation and death of our Lord.

**1068. Q. How does the sign of the cross express the mystery of the Unity and Trinity of God?**

A. The words, "In the name," express the Unity of God; the words that follow, "of the Father, and of the Son, and of the Holy Spirit," express the mystery of the Trinity.

**1069. Q. How does the sign of the cross express the mystery of the Incarnation and death of our Lord?**

A. The sign of the cross expresses the mystery of the Incarnation by reminding us that the Son of God, having become man, suffered death on the cross.

*Questions and Exercises*

## Part 1: Completion

1.  We pray to adore God, expressing to Him our love and_____.

2.  We pray to God to_____Him for His favors.

3.  We pray to God to obtain from Him the_____of our sins and the remission of their punishment.

4.  We pray to God to_____for graces and blessings for ourselves and others.

5.  Distractions in our prayers are displeasing to God, if they are_____.

6.  It is well to use our own_____in praying to God.

7.  The sign of the cross expresses two important mysteries of the Christian religion, the____(a)____ and ____(b)____.

8.  Prayer is the lifting up of our____(a)____ and ____(b)____ to God.

## Part 2: True or False

1. Prayer is necessary for salvation for all those who have the use of reason.

2. We should pray for our friends but not for our enemies.

3. We always obtain exactly what we pray for.

4. Willful distractions in our prayers are displeasing to God.

5. The sign of the cross expresses the mystery of the Ascension of our Lord.

6. We may use our own words when praying to God.

7. Vocal prayer is that prayer which comes from the mind and heart and is spoken by the lips.

## Part 3: Problems and Exercises

1. Find an example from the Gospel, of a prayer of perseverance; of confidence; of humility; of thanksgiving.

2. Distinguish between mental prayer and vocal prayer.

3. The Magnificat is a beautiful hymn of praise. Find it in your New Testament, Luke 1:46–55.

4. You learned that you should pray for others. How do some of the persons who should be included in our prayers link up with our study of the fourth commandment?

LESSON 25

# The Our Father

Did you notice that the Our Father was mentioned first in the list of prayers that every Catholic should know by heart? We say that *the Our Father is the best of all prayers because it is the Lord's Prayer, taught us by Jesus Christ Himself, and because it is a prayer of perfect and unselfish love.*

There is not a more holy and excellent prayer than the Our Father. It is the simplest of all prayers and yet it is suited to every age and condition of men. *The Our Father is a prayer of perfect and unselfish love because in saying it we offer ourselves entirely*

The Our Father is the best of all prayers because it is the Lord's Prayer, taught us by Jesus Christ Himself, and because it is a prayer of perfect and unselfish love.

*to God and ask from Him the best things, not only for ourselves but also for our neighbor.*

The Our Father consists of an opening salutation and seven petitions. The first three refer to the honor and glory due to God by all men. In the last four petitions we ask God for spiritual and temporal blessings not only for ourselves but also for others. Does this explain why it is called a prayer of perfect and unselfish love?

## Our Father Who Art in Heaven

Can you think of a reason why we address God as Father, and not as King, Lord, or by any similar title? The words, "Our Father," help us lift up our minds and hearts to God as a loving Father. They make us realize that we are His adopted children and that He will care for us and hear our petition. He created us. As a good Father, He guides and protects us.

The word "our" reminds us that we are all members of one great family. That word impresses on us the fact that each of us is a brother or sister to everyone in this world. Are we justified, then, in disliking people because of their race, or color, or creed? The Fatherhood of God means nothing without the brotherhood of man in Christ.

We say, "Who art in Heaven" because, although God is everywhere, it is only in heaven that we behold Him face to face. Heaven is our true home. He has destined us for it. We will enjoy it with other members of God's family, the angels and saints. It must be a wonderful place (1 Cor. 2:9). We will have only ourselves to blame if we do not reach it. Christ told us to pray to our "Father in heaven" that we might be continually reminded of our heavenly home. To summarize: *We address God as "Our Father who art in heaven," because we belong to Him, our loving Father, who created us and watches over us, who adopts us through sanctifying grace as His children, and who destines us to live forever with Him in heaven, our true home.*

## Seven Petitions

### Hallowed Be Thy Name

The catechism states: *When we say "hallowed be Thy name," we pray that God may be known and honored by all men.* "Hallowed" is an old English word meaning praised and honored. Have you heard a word like it before? What do we call the eve of All Saints' Day? Why?

In this first petition we acknowledge the purpose for which man was created to glorify God. This petition expresses a sincere wish that God be glorified and His name honored. God is great. We must honor and adore Him.

> "We can invoke God as 'Father' because he is revealed to us by his Son become man and because his Spirit makes him known to us. The personal relation of the Son to the Father is something that man cannot conceive of nor the angelic powers even dimly see: and yet, the Spirit of the Son grants a participation in that very relation to us who believe that Jesus is the Christ and that we are born of God."
>
> —Catechism of the Catholic Church, 2780

It was the sole ambition of the saints to promote God's greater honor and glory. How did saints such as St. John Bosco, St. Vincent de Paul, and others by their works show this desire to give glory and honor to God?

How can we hallow God's name? We can hallow the name of God by making Him known, loved, and served by all men everywhere. What are some ways we can make Him known, loved, and served?

### Thy Kingdom Come

In the second petition *when we say "Thy Kingdom come," we pray that the kingdom of God's grace may be spread throughout the world, that all men may come to know and to enter the true Church and to live as worthy members of it, and that, finally, we all may be admitted to the kingdom of God's glory.*

In this petition we ask for eternal salvation for ourselves and others. Christ Himself founded His Holy Church, the Kingdom of God on earth, in order to lead all men to the Kingdom of God in heaven. He has endowed the Church with endless treasures, with

Much more is accomplished by a single word of the Our Father said, now and then, from our heart, than by the whole prayer repeated many times in haste and without attention.

His holy doctrines and life-giving sacraments. Through them the infinite merits of His Passion are applied to us. Where do we find the chief doctrines of the Church? Do you remember the sacramental grace imparted by each of the seven sacraments? Christ Himself reigns in this kingdom, the Church. He remains with us in the adorable Sacrament of the Altar. From this throne of grace, He rules His Church, as it were, in an invisible manner. He has given us sacred laws. By observing them we are helped to be holy and consequently happy. Can you think of some ways in which we could help spread this kingdom on earth and thus promote the happiness of others?

We pray also that His kingdom may reign within us. If we avoid sin and strive to be charitable to all, He will establish His kingdom within us. Others will then discover Christ because of us. That is one of the best ways we can obtain heaven for ourselves and for others.

### Thy Will Be Done on Earth as It Is in Heaven

God's will should be our first aim and our final law. By what means does He make His will known to us? Let us refer to Matthew 19:18 and Luke 10:16. It is not God's way to tell us His divine will directly. He has appointed others as His representatives. They make His will known to us. Refer to the story of Dives and Lazarus—Luke 16:19–31.

The will of God is manifested in all the events of our life. Everything that happens to us is at least permitted if not actually willed by God. Joys as well as sorrows are meant for our good. The trials of life—sickness, calumny, failure, poverty, and death—are easier to bear, if we realize Who sent them and why. Christ Himself taught us resignation when He said, "Not My will but Thine be done" (Lk. 22:42).

We have very striking examples of how God's will was done both in the Old and New Testaments. Let us read the story of St. Joseph and the conversion of St. Paul and tell how this point is brought out. Do you know any other stories from the Bible stressing submission to God's will?

When we use the words, "as it is in heaven," we are reminded that in heaven the will of God is done promptly, exactly, cheerfully, and purely. That is how we want to do God's will on earth. Doing God's will, will win heaven for us. We all like to have our own way. There is one way in which we can always get it, and that is to want what God wants. So, in the difficulties of life, let us remember: *When we say "Thy will be done on earth as it is in heaven" we pray that all men may obey God on earth as willingly as the saints and angels obey Him in heaven.*

### Give Us This Day Our Daily Bread

It is God's will that we ask daily for our many needs. In this fourth petition of the Lord's prayer *when we say "Give us this day our daily bread," we pray that God will give us each day all that is necessary to support the material life of our bodies and the spiritual life of our souls.*

When we ask God to "give," we acknowledge our own dependence on Him and recognize Him as the giver of all good gifts. Jesus taught us to say "us" because He wants us to pray for all who are in need. If He gives us more than we need, it is because He wants us to share with others. Consider the following story once sent home by a missionary.

"Rice tickets! How precious they often have been to the many starving millions in China. First we see a feeble old lady limping on her cane. "Father, you are so good, please give me a ticket. I am seventy and have no one to care for me." The ticket obtained,

Prayer is the place of refuge for every worry, a foundation for cheerfulness, a source of constant happiness, a protection against sadness.

389

she hobbles to secure the little portion of rice that will keep her alive for another day. Next comes a young lady with a hungry, pinched face and the most tattered and patched clothing you would ever want to see. She receives a ticket.

"Next is a boy, a living skeleton, with a hacking cough. He does odd jobs for the mission every day, depending on how well he feels, and this wins for him a portion of rice. Another man follows, so crippled by arthritis that he is almost unable to walk. He holds out a shriveled hand for the ticket that will keep him alive. Last in line is an able-looking fellow who seems capable of work, but does none. The truth is, he cannot, for hidden beneath the rags that clothe his figure are the horrible marks of a leper. He, too, must be fed. On and on continues the seemingly endless line of those who are begging daily for food."

Thank God we do not have to stand in line to procure a bowl of rice that will keep body and soul together. God feeds us without obliging us to stand in line. Let us show our gratitude by generously aiding the less fortunate.

The Son of God has taught all of us, rich and poor, to pray for our daily bread. The word "bread" includes not only material, but spiritual bread, especially the Bread of Life, that is Holy Communion. What else might be included in this spiritual bread?

### And Forgive Us Our Trespasses As We Forgive Those Who Trespass Against Us

"Trespass" is an old English word that means an injury, an offense, an insult, a sin. A trespass signifies an offense against the goodness and justice of God. Offending God requires us to seek forgiveness.

We ask God to forgive "our" trespasses because all men have

**TERMS TO KNOW**

- destined
- trespass
- kingdom
- amen
- hallowed
- deliver
- petitions

*"Pray as though everything depended on God. Work as though everything depended on you."*

—*St. Augustine*

offended Him. Not only do we ask forgiveness for ourselves, but also for all sinners, especially those who do not ask for forgiveness.

Then we state a condition on the basis of which we ask God to forgive us, namely, "as we forgive those who trespass against us." This fits in with what the Scripture says about the pardon for sin. "Forgive, and you shall be forgiven" (Lk. 6:37). "So also my heavenly Father will do to you, if you do not each forgive your brothers from your hearts." Christ confirms this again in the parable of the Unmerciful Servant—Matthew 18:23–35.

*When we say "and forgive us our trespasses as we forgive those who trespass against us," we pray that God will pardon the sins by which we have offended Him, and we tell Him that we pardon our fellow men who have offended us.* The trespasses of others against us are often imaginary. In our pride and vanity, we imagine that another has offended us when no hurt was intended. Forgiveness of others should be practiced even if the offense is real and intentional. To forgive those who strike us, steal from us, or who lie about us is expected of a true follower of Christ, Who said: "Father, forgive them, for they know not what they do." Who has offended us as grievously as we have offended God? And God always forgives us if we are sorry!

The true spirit of forgiveness is well illustrated by the following incident. James Talbot was heartbroken when he learned the terrible news that his best friend, Tom Corrigan, a Franciscan missionary, had died for his faith in China. Passing through his home town, James decided to stop at the home of the Corrigans, pay his respects to the mother of a martyr, and learn more about the last days of his friend. Anger and pity filled his heart when he heard the details of the tortures inflicted upon Father Tom.

"What did you do when you heard the tragic news?" asked Jim. "I hardly knew what to do," replied the mother, "my heart was so heavy."

"I do not blame you," interrupted the caller. "If I could lay my hands on them I would kill them." His eyes flashed with anger.

"That is just how I felt at first, as I drenched the letter with my tears."

"You mean, you do not feel that way now, Mrs. Corrigan?" asked the young man in surprise.

With a peaceful glance, Mrs. Corrigan gazed into the still angry face of Jim and said, "I learned my lesson at the foot of the crucifix. There I gained strength to bear my cross. Now I spend my time collecting alms to send to the pagans who killed my son."

### And Lead Us Not Into Temptation

*When we say "and lead us not into temptation," we pray that God will always give us the grace to overcome the temptations to sin which come to us from the world, the flesh, and the devil.* When we pray the words, "And lead us not into temptation" we must realize that God cannot and will not tempt us to sin. "Let no man say that when he is tempted, that he is tempted by God" (James 1:13). What do you understand by that? Does our Lord permit temptations? Can you give some reasons why He does? In this part of the "Our Father" we ask for the power to overcome temptations from whatever source they come. God will never permit us to be tempted beyond our strength. Let this thought console us.

Temptations come from three different sources: the world, the flesh, and devil. Read and discuss the following references pertaining to temptations by the devil (Mt. 4:10; 1 Pet. 5:8). Our circumstances in life, such as poverty, sickness, and unhappy home life can be sources of temptation. In what way?

Finally temptations come to us from the flesh, that is from our own weaknesses and evil inclinations. What are some of the best methods to be used against temptations?

### But Deliver Us From Evil

*When we say "but deliver us from evil," we pray that God will always protect us from harm, and especially from harm to our souls.* This petition asks God to keep evil away from us as much as possible and keep us away from evil. It also means, if we come perilously near to committing sin, that we want God to protect us.

Again we use "us" because we want not only ourselves to be delivered but also others. Why? All men are brothers of Christ because they are children of God. We want Him to deliver everyone from trouble and affliction. It is the prayer of all God's children for all God's children. We are all in this together. Each one helps or harms his neighbor—that is, his fellow men.

The word "evil" refers to evils of both body and soul. Name some of the ways the body can be harmed. The soul. What are some of the physical and spir-

*Let us every day say the Our Father slowly and with great attention; let us meditate upon it, with love accompanying our faith.*

itual evils of today? How can we counteract them? Sometimes God permits physical evils to accomplish a greater spiritual good. Can you think of an example?

If we ever feel depressed because of numerous trials, let us recall how others acted under similar circumstances. How did the saints act?

## Conclusion

The Church ends the Our Father as she ends most prayers with "Amen." This means, "So be it." By it we express the ardent desire that our prayers be heard, and we show our confidence in God.

## Summary

The Our Father is the best of all prayers because it is the Lord's Prayer. It was taught us by Jesus Christ Himself. It is a prayer of perfect and unselfish love. In it we offer to God the truest love of our hearts, and we ask from Him the best things, not only for ourselves but also for our neighbor.

### ✓ FOR ME TO REVIEW

*Catechism Lesson*

3. **Q. Why is the "Our Father" the most excellent of all prayers?**

   A. The "Our Father" is the most excellent of all prayers because our Lord Himself made it and because its petitions ask for all we can need for soul or body.

4. **Q. How is the Lord's Prayer divided?**

   A. The Lord's Prayer is divided into seven requests or petitions. Three of these petitions refer to God's honor and glory, and the remaining four to our corporeal or spiritual wants.

5.   Q.  **Whom do we address as "Our Father" when we say the Lord's Prayer?**

   A.  When we say "Our Father" in the Lord's Prayer we address Almighty God, Father, Son and Holy Spirit united in the adorable Trinity.

6.   Q.  **Why do we say "our" and not "my" Father?**

   A.  We say "our" and not "my" Father to remind us that through our creation and redemption, we are all members of the great human family of which God is the Father; and that we should pray for and help one another.

9.   Q.  **What does "Hallowed be Thy Name" mean?**

   A.  Hallowed means set apart for a holy or sacred use, and thus comes to mean treated or praised as holy or sacred. "Thy name" means God Himself and all relating to Him, and by this petition we ask that God may be known, loved and served by all.

10.   Q.  **What do we ask for in the petition: "Thy kingdom come"?**

   A.  In the petition "Thy kingdom come" we ask: 1) that God may reign in the souls of all men by His grace, so that they may attain eternal salvation; 2) that the true Church—Christ's kingdom—may spread upon earth till all men embrace the true religion.

11.   Q.  **Who do God's will in heaven?**

   A.  In heaven the angels and saints do God's will perfectly. They never disobey or even wish to disobey Him. In the petition, "Thy will be done on earth as it is in heaven," we pray that all God's creatures may imitate the angels and saints in heaven by never offending Him.

12.   Q.  **What do we ask for by "our daily bread"?**

A.  In the petition for "our daily bread" we ask not merely for bread, but for all that we need for the good of our body or soul.

13.   Q.  **Why do we say "daily"?**

A.  We say "daily" to teach us that we are not to be avaricious but only prudent in providing for our wants; and that we are to have great confidence in the providence of God.

14.   Q.  **What do "trespasses" mean?**

A.  "Trespasses" mean here injuries done or offenses given to another, and when God is the person offended, "trespasses" mean sins.

15.   Q.  **What do you mean by "forgive us our trespasses as we forgive those who trespass against us"?**

A.  In this petition we declare to God that we have forgiven all who have injured or offended us, and ask Him to reward us by pardoning our sins.

16.   Q.  **When may we be said to forgive those who trespass against us?**

A.  We may be said to forgive our enemies when we act and, as far as possible, feel toward them as if they had never injured us.

24.   Q.  **From what evil do we ask to be delivered?**

A.  We ask to be delivered from every evil of body and mind, but particularly to be delivered from sin, which is the greatest of all evils.

*Questions and Exercises*

## Completion

1.  The Our Father is a prayer of___(a)___and___(b)___love.

2.  The Our Father was taught to us by___(a)___, after the ___(b)___petitioned for it.

3.  In the Our Father, we ask what is best for___(a)___and for our___(b)___.

4.  The first three petitions refer to the_____due God by all men.

5.  The last four petitions refer to all things needful for ___(a)___and___(b)___.

6.  The condition we state for our forgiveness in the Our Father is_____.

## ✓ FOR ME TO DO

1.  Write the "Our Father" from memory. Correct what you have written with a copy of this prayer in your book.

2.  Make a list of the things you ask of God in the Our Father for yourself and your neighbor.

# Achievement Test

*Write your answers on a separate sheet of paper*

 **I. Multiple Choice**

1. The best prayer is the:
   A. Hail Mary.
   B. Apostles' Creed.
   C. Our Father.
   D. Confiteor.

2. Christ said we should pray:
   A. sometimes.
   B. in sickness.
   C. always.
   D. on Sunday.

3. Christ taught the Our Father to:
   A. St. Joseph.
   B. the Pharisees.
   C. the holy women.
   D. the apostles.

4. The most necessary prayer is:
   A. the act of faith.
   B. the act of contrition.
   C. grace before meals.
   D. the Memorare.

5. The most necessary requirement for prayer is:
   A. attention.
   B. the position.
   C. the intention.
   D. name of prayer.

6. The prayer which was partly composed by an angel is the:
   A. Hail Holy Queen.
   B. Apostles' Creed.
   C. Memorare.
   D. Hail Mary.

7. Holy things or acts set apart and blessed by the Church are called:
   A. mysteries.
   B. sacramental.
   C. sacraments.

8. Sacramentals:
   A. give sanctifying grace.
   B. insure salvation.
   C. stir up devotion.
   D. perform miracles.

9. The following is a sacramental:
   A. Holy Eucharist.
   B. holy water.
   C. Holy Orders.

10. Candles are blessed on:
    A. Holy Saturday.
    B. Pentecost.
    C. Candlemas Day, February 2.
    D. Immaculate Conception, December 8.

## II. True or False

1. Prayer is not necessary for salvation.

2. Sacramentals obtain favors from God.

3. We must kneel to pray.

4. Sacramentals stir up devotion.

5. The blessing of the throat on the feast of St. Blaise is not a sacramental.

## III. Recognition Exercise

*After each, write "sacrament" or "sacramental"*

1. Anointing of the Sick

2. Blessed Palms

3. Candles

4. Confirmation

5. Rosary

6. Scapular

7. Matrimony

8. Baptism

9. Crucifix

10. Holy Orders

Our Father. Name of love and trust.
God wishes us to speak to Him with
filial confidence and familiarity.
God is the Father of all men: all are
equally his children; all, then, rich
and poor, are brothers, and ought
to love one another.

–Fr. F. X. Schouppe

APPENDIX:
# Why I Am a Catholic

**I.  How does our reason point out the truth of the Catholic religion?**

Our reason points out the truth of the Catholic religion by these principles:

*first*, there is a God;

*second*, the soul of man is immortal;

*third*, all men are obliged to practice religion;

*fourth*, the religion God has revealed through Christ is worthy of belief;

*fifth*, Christ established a Church with which all must be connected, at least in desire, in order to be saved;

*sixth*, the only true Church of Christ is the Catholic Church.

**II.  How can we prove that there is a God?**

We can prove that there is a God because this vast universe could not have come into existence, nor be so beautiful and orderly, except by the almighty power and the wisdom of an eternal and intelligent Being.

**III.  How can we prove that the soul of man is immortal?**

We can prove that the soul of man is immortal because man's acts of intelligence are spiritual; therefore, his soul must be a spiritual being, not dependent on matter, and hence not subject to decay or death.

**IV.  How can we prove that all men are obliged to practice religion?**

We can prove that all men are obliged to practice religion because all men are entirely dependent on God and must recognize that dependence by honoring Him and praying to Him.

**V.** **How can we prove that the religion God has revealed through Christ is worthy of belief?**

We can prove that the religion God has revealed through Christ is worthy of belief, because:

*first*, Jesus Christ, announcing Himself as the ambassador and the true Son of God, whose coming was foretold by the prophets, preached doctrines which He said all must believe;

*second*, Christ worked wonderful miracles, which show that the God of truth approved His teachings.

**VI.** **How can we prove that Christ established a Church with which all must be connected, at least in desire, in order to be saved?**

We can prove that Christ established a Church with which all must be connected, at least in desire, in order to be saved, because:

*first*, He gathered about Him a group of disciples, and called it His Church;

*second*, He promised that this Church would last until the end of time;

*third*, He declared that all men must believe and be baptized, that is, be connected with His Church in some way, in order to be saved.

**VII.** **How can we prove that the only true Church of Christ is the Catholic Church?**

We can prove that the only true Church of Christ is the Catholic Church because:

*first*, only the Catholic Church possesses the marks of the Church established by Christ, that is, unity, holiness, catholicity, and apostolicity;

*second*, the history of the Catholic Church gives evidence of miraculous strength, permanence, and unchangeableness, thus showing the world that it is under the special protection of God.

**VIII.** **Whence do we chiefly derive our historical knowledge of Jesus Christ, His life and teachings, and of the Church He established?**

We derive our historical knowledge of Jesus Christ, His life and teachings, and of the Church He established chiefly from the books of the Bible, which can be proved to be reliable historical records.

**IX.** **What else are the books of the Bible besides being reliable historical records?**

Besides being reliable historical records, the books of the Bible are the inspired word of God, that is, written by men with such direct assistance of the Holy Spirit as to make God their true Author.

**X.** **How is the Bible divided?**

The Bible is divided into the Old Testament and the New Testament; the Old Testament being the inspired books written before the time of Jesus Christ, and the New Testament the inspired books written after His coming.

**XI.** **Are all the truths revealed for us by God found in the Bible?**

Not all the truths revealed for us by God are found in the Bible; some are found only in Divine Tradition.

**XII.** **What is meant by Divine Tradition?**

By Divine Tradition is meant the revealed truths taught by Christ and His apostles, which were given to the Church only by word of mouth and not through the Bible, though they were put in writing, principally by the Fathers of the Church.

**XIII. Why must Divine Tradition be believed as firmly as the Bible?**

Divine Tradition must be believed as firmly as the Bible because it also contains the word of God.

**XIV. How can we know the true meaning of the doctrines contained in the Bible and in Divine Tradition?**

We can know the true meaning of the doctrines contained in the Bible and in Divine Tradition from the Catholic Church, which has been authorized by Jesus Christ to explain His doctrines, and which is preserved from error in its teachings by the special assistance of the Holy Spirit.

**XV. How can we best show our gratitude to God for making us members of the only true Church of Jesus Christ?**

We can best show our gratitude to God for making us members of the only true Church of Jesus Christ by often thanking God for this great favor, by leading edifying and holy Catholic lives, and by bringing the message of the Gospel to others.

# Prayers

### The Sign of the Cross
In the name of the Father, and of the Son, and of the Holy Spirit. Amen.

### The Lord's Prayer
Our Father who art in heaven, hallowed be Thy name; Thy kingdom come; Thy will be done on earth as it is in heaven. Give us this day our daily bread; and forgive us our trespasses as we forgive those who trespass against us; and lead us not into temptation, but deliver us from evil. Amen.

### The Hail Mary
Hail Mary, full of grace, the Lord is with thee; blessed art thou among women, and blessed is the fruit of thy womb, Jesus. Holy Mary, Mother of God, pray for us sinners, now and at the hour of our death. Amen.

### Glory Be to the Father
Glory be to the Father, and to the Son, and to the Holy Spirit. As it was in the beginning, is now, and ever shall be, world without end. Amen.

### The Apostles' Creed
I believe in God, the Father Almighty, Creator of heaven and earth; and in Jesus Christ, His only Son, Our Lord; who was conceived by the Holy Spirit, born of the Virgin Mary, suffered under Pontius Pilate, was crucified, died, and was buried. He descended into hell; the third day He arose again from the dead; He ascended into heaven, and sits at the right hand of God, the Father Almighty; from thence He shall come to judge the living and the dead. I believe in the Holy Spirit, the Holy Catholic Church, the communion of saints, the forgiveness of sins, the resurrection of the body, and life everlasting. Amen.

## The Confiteor

### Ordinary Form
I confess to almighty God
and to you, my brothers and sisters,
that I have greatly sinned
in my thoughts and in my words,
in what I have done,
and in what I have failed to do;
through my fault, through my fault,
through my most grievous fault;
therefore I ask blessed Mary ever-Virgin,
all the Angels and Saints,
and you, my brothers and sisters,
to pray for me to the Lord our God. Amen

## Extraordinary Form
I confess to Almighty God,
to blessed Mary ever Virgin,
blessed Michael the Archangel,
blessed John the Baptist,
the holy Apostles Peter and Paul,
and to all the saints
that I have sinned exceedingly
in thought, word, and deed,
through my fault,
through my fault,
through my most grievous fault.
Therefore, I beseech blessed Mary ever Virgin,
blessed Michael the Archangel,
blessed John the Baptist,
the holy Apostles Peter and Paul,
and all the saints,
to pray for me to the Lord our God. Amen.

## Morning Offering

O Jesus, through the Immaculate Heart of Mary, I offer Thee my prayers, works, joys and sufferings of this day for all the intentions of Thy Sacred Heart, in union with the Holy Sacrifice of the Mass throughout the world, in reparation for my sins, for the intentions of all our relatives and friends, and in particular for the intentions of the Hold Father. Amen.

## The Angelus

V. The angel of the Lord declared unto Mary.
R. And she conceived of the Holy Spirit.

Hail Mary, full of grace! the Lord is with thee; blessed art thou among women, and blessed is the fruit of thy womb, Jesus. Holy Mary, Mother of God, pray for us sinners, now and at the hour of our death. Amen.

V. Behold the handmaid of the Lord.
R. Be it done unto me according to thy word.

Hail Mary, etc.

V. And the Word was made flesh.
R. And dwelt among us.

Hail Mary, etc.

V. Pray for us, O holy Mother of God.
R. That we may be made worthy of the promises of Christ.

*Let Us Pray*
Pour forth, we beseech Thee, O Lord, Thy grace into our hearts, that we to whom the Incarnation of Christ, Thy Son, was made known by the message of an angel, may by His passion and cross be brought to the glory of His resurrection, through the same Christ Our Lord. Amen.

## Regina Coeli

*(Said during Eastertide, instead of the Angelus)*

Queen of heaven, rejoice, Alleluia.

For He whom thou didst deserve to bear, Alleluia.

Hath risen as He said, Alleluia.

Pray for us to God, Alleluia.

V. Rejoice and be glad, O Virgin Mary! Alleluia.

R. Because Our Lord is truly risen, Alleluia.

*Let Us Pray*

O God, who by the resurrection of Thy Son, Our Lord Jesus Christ, have vouchsafed to make glad the whole world, grant, we beseech Thee, that, through the intercession of the Virgin Mary, His Mother, we may attain the joys of eternal life. Through the same Christ Our Lord. Amen.

## Hail, Holy Queen

Hail, Holy Queen, Mother of Mercy; hail, our life, our sweetness, and our hope! To thee do we cry, poor banished children of Eve; to thee we do send up our sighs, mourning and weeping in this vale of tears. Turn, then, most gracious advocate, thine eyes of mercy toward us; and after this our exile, show unto us the blessed fruit of thy womb, Jesus. O clement, O loving, O sweet Virgin Mary!

## An Act of Faith

O my God, I firmly believe that Thou art one God in three Divine Persons, Father, Son, and Holy Spirit; I believe that Thy Divine Son became man, and died for our sins, and that He will come to judge the living and the dead. I believe these and all the truths which the Holy Catholic Church teaches, because Thou hast revealed them, who canst neither deceive nor be deceived.

## An Act of Hope

O my God, relying on Thy almighty power and infinite mercy and promises, I hope to obtain pardon of my sins, the help of Thy grace, and life everlasting, through the merits of Jesus Christ, my Lord and Redeemer.

## An Act of Love

O my God, I love Thee above all things, with my whole heart and soul, because Thou art all-good and worthy of all love. I love my neighbor as myself for the love of Thee. I forgive all who have injured me, and ask pardon of all whom I have injured.

## An Act of Contrition

O my God, I am heartily sorry for having offended Thee, and I detest all my sins, because of Thy just punishments, but most of all because they offend Thee, my God, who art all-good and deserving of all my love. I firmly resolve, with the help of Thy grace, to sin no more and to avoid the near occasions of sin.

## The Blessing Before Meals

Bless us, O Lord, and these Thy gifts, which we are about to receive from Thy bounty, through Christ Our Lord. Amen.

## Grace After Meals

We give Thee thanks for all Thy benefits, O Almighty God, who livest and reignest forever; and may the souls of the faithful departed, through the mercy of God, rest in peace. Amen.

## The Mysteries of the Rosary

### The Five Joyful Mysteries

1. The Annunciation
2. The Visitation
3. The Birth of Our Lord
4. The Presentation of Our Lord in the Temple
5. The Finding of Our Lord in the Temple

### The Five Luminous Mysteries

1. The Baptism of Our Lord in the Jordan
2. The Wedding Feast at Cana
3. Our Lord's Proclamation of the Kingdom of God
4. The Transfiguration of Our Lord
5. The Institution of the Eucharist

### The Five Sorrowful Mysteries

1. The Agony of Our Lord in the Garden
2. The Scourging at the Pillar
3. The Crowning With Thorns
4. The Carrying of the Cross
5. The Crucifixion and Death of Our Lord

### The Five Glorious Mysteries

1. The Resurrection of Our Lord
2. The Ascension of Our Lord into Heaven
3. The Descent of the Holy Spirit Upon the Apostles
4. The Assumption of Our Blessed Mother into Heaven
5. The Coronation of Our Blessed Mother in Heaven

The Immaculate Conception with the Fifteen Mysteries
of the Rosary

# Answer Key

# Unit 1

## CHAPTER 1

### LESSON 1

### Part 1

1. D
2. A
3. A
4. C
5. B
6. C
7. B
8. D
9. A

### Part 2

*Answers will vary.*

# CHAPTER 2

## LESSON 2

### Part 1

1. Yes
2. Yes
3. No
4. Yes
5. Yes
6. Yes
7. Yes
8. Yes
9. Yes
10. Yes

### Part 2

1. H
2. B
3. E
4. J
5. A
6. D
7. G
8. I
9. F
10. C

# CHAPTER 3

LESSON 3

## Part 1

1. that is not sinful.
2. God.
3. voting honestly and without selfish motives; paying just taxes; defending his country's rights when necessary.

## Part 2

1. B
2. B

## Part 3

1. No
2. Yes
3. No
4. No
5. No

**Part 4**

*Answers will vary.*

LESSON 4

**Part 1**

1. C
2. E
3. F
4. B
5. A
6. D

**Part 2**

1. Suicide
2. Murder
3. Anger
4. Life
5. Hatred
6. Scandal
7. Revenge

## Part 3

1. True
2. True
3. False
4. True
5. True
6. True
7. False
8. True

LESSON 5

## Part 1

1. C
2. A
3. B
4. E
5. F
6. D
7. I
8. J
9. G
10. H

## LESSON 6

### Part 1

1. No
2. Yes
3. Yes
4. No
5. Yes
6. No
7. Yes
8. Yes
9. Yes
10. Yes

## LESSON 7

### Part 1

1. C
2. D
3. B
4. A

# CHAPTER 4

LESSON 8

## Part 1

1.  Mortal

2.  (a) Christmas. Dec. 25; (b) Solemnity of Mary, Jan 1; (c) Ascension, 40 days after easter; (d) Assumption, Aug. 15; (e) All Saints, Nov. 1; (f) Immaculate Conception, Dec. 8.

3.  (a) fast; (b) abstinence

4.  (a) 1st Sunday; (b) Lent; (c) Trinity Sunday

## Part 2

1.  B

2.  D

3.  C

4.  E

5.  A

# ACHIEVEMENT TEST

## Part 1

1. D
2. A
3. C
4. C
5. D
6. C
7. A
8. D
9. B
10. A
11. C
12. B
13. B
14. A
15. D
16. B
17. A
18. A
19. D
20. A
21. A
22. C
23. B
24. C
25. D

## Part 2

1. True

2. True

3. True

4. True

5. True

6. False

7. False

8. True

9. True

10. False

11. True

12. False

13. True

14. True

15. True

16. True

17. False

18. True

19. True

## Part 3

1. J
2. E
3. F
4. G
5. A
6. B
7. D
8. C
9. I
10. H

## Additional Statements for the multiple choice test

1. D
2. B
3. B
4. A
5. B
6. A
7. D
8. B

# Unit 2

## CHAPTER 5

LESSON 9

### Part 1

1.  B
2.  D
3.  A
4.  D
5.  C
6.  A
7.  B
8.  B
9.  C
10. D
11. D
12. B
13. D
14. D
15. A

# CHAPTER 6

## LESSON 10

### Part 1

*Answers may vary*

1.  In case of necessity he may have to baptize.

2.  The person bearing the name should have someone to imitate.

3.  Christ said: "Unless a man be born again of water and the Holy Spirit, he cannot enter into the kingdom of God."

4.  They are children of God.

5.  It is the duty of godparents to know the true Faith, live up to the duties of their religion, and bring the children up as good Catholics.

6.  Without Baptism no one can enter heaven.

7.  He is in the state of sanctifying grace.

8.  Christ had not instituted the sacrament as yet.

9.  They are responsible for the upbringing of the children in the catholic religion if the child's parents die or fail to live up to their responsibilities.

10. Neither imprints the special character of the sacrament of the soul.

**Part 2**

1. Heaven
2. The priest
3. To be a practical Catholic
4. Baptism of blood

# CHAPTER 7

## LESSON 11

**Part 1**

1. Bishop
2. Holy Spirit
3. Chrism
4. Soldier
5. Living

# ACHIEVEMENT TEST

**Part 1**

1. Sanctifying grace
2. Right dispositions
3. Sacrament of the dead
4. Sacrament

5. Baptism

6. Bishop

7. Chrism

8. Holy Thursday

9. Sacramental grace

10. Character

11. Christ

12. Baptism of blood

13. Confirmation

14. Matter

15. Form

16. Godparents

17. Catholics

18. Religion

19. Baptism of desire

20. Anointing

21. Faith

22. Practice

23. Merits

24. Catholic Action

25. Sanctifying grace

## Part 2

1. Yes
2. Yes
3. No
4. No
5. Yes
6. No
7. Yes
8. Yes
9. No
10. Yes
11. Yes
12. No
13. No
14. Yes
15. No
16. No
17. Yes
18. No
19. Yes
20. Yes
21. Yes
22. No
23. Yes
24. No
25. No

# CHAPTER 8

LESSON 12

## Part 1

1. C
2. E
3. B
4. A
5. D

## Part 2

1. Last Supper
2. Holy Eucharist
3. Forgiveness of sin
4. The Apostles
5. His Apostles
6. Bread
7. Wine
8. Priests
9. Consecration
10. "This is My Body" "This is My Blood"

## Part 3

1. (a) bread, (b) eat, (c) body, (d) wine, (e) drink, (f) blood, (g) sins, (h) apostles, (i) Do

2. (a) sacrament, (b) sacrifice, (c) body, (d) blood, (e) soul, (f) divinity

3. (a) commemorating, (b) renewing, (c) Holy Communion, (d) altars

## LESSON 13

## Part 1

1. C
2. I
3. E
4. G
5. F
6. H
7. B
8. A
9. D

## Part 2

1. Yes
2. Yes
3. No
4. No

5. No

6. No

7. No

8. Yes

9. Yes

## Part 3

1. E

2. D

3. B

4. F

5. G

6. A

7. C

8. H

## LESSON 14

1. Easter time

2. Sacrilege

3. One hour

4. Mortal sin

5. Pius XII

6. Water

7. Charity

8. Sin

9. Holy Eucharist

# CHAPTER 9

## LESSON 15

### Part 1

1. Eternal

2. Temporal

3. Temporal

4. Jesus Christ

5. Priest

### Part 2

1. (a) know; (b) confess

2. Merits

3. Examination of conscience

4. Sanctifying grace

5. (a) forgive; (b) forgiven; (c) retain; (d) retained

# LESSON 16

## Part 1

1. True (perfect)
2. Sin
3. Perfect
4. Contrition
5. Imperfect
6. Heart
7. Make an act of contrition (perfect)
8. Contrition - examination of conscience
9. Universal
10. Sin

## Part 2

1. False
2. True
3. True
4. False
5. True
6. True
7. True
8. False
9. True
10. True

## LESSON 18

### Part 1

1. No
2. Yes
3. Yes
4. No
5. No
6. No
7. Yes
8. Yes
9. No
10. No
11. No
12. No
13. No
14. Yes
15. Yes
16. Yes
17. No
18. Yes
19. Yes
20. Yes
21. Yes
22. Yes
23. Yes
24. Yes

## Part 2

1. C
2. E
3. J
4. G
5. B
6. H
7. A
8. F
9. I
10. D

## Part 3

1. Ask God's help... (F)
2. Examine... (C)
3. Be sorry... (E)
4. Have firm purpose... (D)
5. Confess... (A)
6. Be willing... (B)

## LESSON 19

### Part 1

1. False
2. True
3. True
4. True
5. False
6. False
7. True
8. True
9. True
10. True

### Part 2

*Answers will vary.*

# CHAPTER 10

## LESSON 20

### Part 1

*1-3. Answers will vary.*

4. Baptism, Confirmation, Extreme Unction
5. Answers will vary.

## Part 2

1.  False
2.  False
3.  True
4.  True
5.  False
6.  True
7.  True

## Part 3

1.  F
2.  E
3.  H
4.  G
5.  C
6.  B
7.  A
8.  D

# ACHIEVEMENT TEST

## Part 1

1. D
2. C
3. C
4. D
5. B
6. C
7. D
8. A
9. C
10. A
11. D

## Part 2

1. Mass
2. (a) prayer (b) sacraments
3. Sacrilege
4. Confession
5. Contrition
6. Eternal
7. (a) world (b) purgatory
8. Seal
9. Last Supper

10. Health

11. Sin

12. Dispositions

13. Transubstantiation

14. Christ

15. Holy Communion

16. (a) restores (b) increases

17. Holy Viaticum

## Part 3

1. G

2. F

3. H

4. A

5. I

6. D

7. B

8. J

9. C

10. E

**Part 4**

1. A
2. D
3. F
4. B
5. I
6. E
7. H
8. J
9. G
10. C

# Unit 3:

## CHAPTER 11

### LESSON 21

1. B
2. A
3. A
4. A
5. A
6. B
7. A
8. A
9. B

## LESSON 22

### Part 1

1. Religious
2. (a) priest and (b) two witnesses
3. Matrimony
4. Nuptial Mass
5. Sacred
6. Marry
7. (a) parents; (b) God
8. Man and woman
9. (a) sacrament; (b) contract
10. (a) parents; (b) confessor

### Part 2

1. False
2. True
3. True
4. True
5. True
6. False
7. False
8. True
9. False
10. False

# Unit 4

## CHAPTER 12

LESSON 23

### Part 1

1. True
2. False
3. False
4. True
5. False
6. True
7. True
8. False

### Part 2

1. C
2. F
3. A
4. E
5. D
6. B

# CHAPTER 13

LESSON 24

## Part 1

1. Loyalty

2. Thank

3. Pardon

4. Ask

5. Willful

6. Words

7. (a) Blessed Trinity; (b) Redemption

8. (a) minds (b) hearts

## Part 2

1. True

2. False

3. False

4. True

5. False

6. True

7. True

## LESSON 25

### Part I

1. (a) perfect; (b) unselfish

2. (a) Christ; (b) Apostles

3. (a) soul; (b) body or physical and spiritual life

4. Honor

5. (a) body; (b) soul

6. As we forgive those who trespass against us

# ACHIEVEMENT TEST

### Part 1

1. C

2. C

3. D

4. B

5. C

6. D

7. B

8. C

9. B

10. C

## Part 2

1. False
2. True
3. False
4. True
5. False

## Part 3

1. Sacrament
2. Sacramental
3. Sacramental
4. Sacrament
5. Sacramental
6. Sacramental
7. Sacrament
8. Sacrament
9. Sacramental
10. Sacrament

# Image Credits

Front cover  Jesus with angels, 1900s (colour litho) / Russian School (20th century) / Russian / Bridgeman Images

pVIII-1  The resurrected Christ gives the good word to the disciples to go to preach. Miniature of Cristoforo De Predis from the History of the New Testament, 1476. Biblioteca Reale, Turin. 153-013168 / Tarker / Bridgeman Images

p2  Staff Serving Food In Homeless Shelter Kitchen © Monkey Business Images, Shutterstock.com

p2-3, 18-19, 38-39, 100-101, 132-133, 150-151, 168-169, 182-183, 240-241, 300-301, 324-325, 356-357, 368-369,   Christ and Saint John the Baptist in Hagia Sophia (mosaic) / Byzantine, (13th century) / Hagia Sophia, Istanbul, Turkey / Bridgeman Images

p5  The Good Samaritan / English School, 19th century (colour litho) / English / Bridgeman Images

p7  The healing of the leper / Copping, Harold (1863-1932) / English / Bridgeman Images

p11  Christ and the Rich Young Man (engraving) / English School, (19th century) / English / Bridgeman Images

p12  Girl helping senior woman cross street © CGN089, Shutterstock.com

p19  Christ to Capernaum takes his way… (coloured engraving) / English School, (19th century) / English / Bridgeman Images

p22-23  Boy sleeping in the hospital bed © PanPanWorld, Shutterstock.com

p25  A boy is praying in the church © No-Te Eksarunchai, Shutterstock.com

p39  Joseph and Mary with Jesus (colour litho) / English School, (19th century) / English / Bridgeman Images

p43  Teen girl in field holding American flag © Karkhut, Shutterstock.com

p44  Portrait de Saint Thomas More, mort à Tower Hill (Londres) en 1535, Transferred from fr.wikipedia to Commons by Bloody-libu using CommonsHelper, Gwengoat at French Wikipedia, Creative Commons (CC), via Wikimedia Commons

p48  Cain and Abel (colour litho) / Private Collection / Bridgeman Images

p51  The Good Samaritan (coloured engraving) / German School, (19th century) / German  / Bridgeman Images

p57  Our Patron Saint Francis de Sales, 16 March 2020, Rojosfscollege, Creative Commons (CC), via Wikimedia Commons

p60  Joseph Sold by His Brothers, as in Genesis 37:5-28; illustration from a Bible card published by the Providence Lithograph Company, Source: http://thebiblerevival.com/clipart/1907/gen37.jpg, Author: the Providence Lithograph Company, [Public domain], via Wikimedia Commons

p62  Christ in the Garden of Gethsemane by Heinrich Hofmann, 1930s (print) / Hofmann, Heinrich (1824-1911) / German / Bridgeman Images

p68   Jesus of Nazareth: His life and teachings; founded on the four Gospels, and illustrated by reference to the manners, customs, religious beliefs, and political institutions of His times, 1869, Source: https://www.flickr.com/photos/internetarchivebookimages/14781313924/, Author: Abbott, Lyman, 1835-1922, [Public domain], via Wikimedia Commons

p69  Pious image: portrait of Saint Maria Goretti (1890-1902) known as Marietta, virgin martyr (Portrait of Maria Goretti Italian virgin-martyr) - Chromolithography of the 20th century Private collection / Photographer: Luisa Ricciarini / Bridgeman Images

p72  O Mary, Mother of God. Extract of writing by Saint Ephrem (chromolitho) / French School, (19th century) / French / Bridgeman Images

p78  The Rich Man and Lazarus (colour lithograph) / French School, (19th century) / English School, (19th century) / English / Bridgeman Images

p80-81  Pail of thalers—ancient european silver coins © Anton Starikov, Shutterstock.com

p88  The Judgement of Solomon, oil on canvas, Peter Paul Rubens (1577 Siegen - 1640 Antwerpen) Source: WAHXmaCV-zSYig at Google Cultural Institute, [Public domain], via Wikimedia Commons

p91  Jesus Christ before Pontius Pilate, wooden statue © Vivida Photo PC, Shutterstock.com

p93  Christ and the Adulteress, oil on panel, Pieter Breughel the Younger (1564–1638), Philadelphia Museum of Art, [Public domain], via Wikimedia Commons

p94  Silhouette of woman kneeling and praying © asiandelight, Shutterstock.com

p99  Christ Blessing (oil on canvas) / Greco, El (Domenico Theotocopuli) (1541-1614) / Greek / Casa y Museo del Greco, Toledo, Spain / Bridgeman Images

p100  Moses breaking the two stone tablets on which were written the ten commandments. The Book of Exodus, Old Testament. From The Children's Bible, published c. 1883 / Photographer: Ken Welsh / Bridgeman Images